Improving Food and
Beverage Performance

I would like to thank the following colleagues for their support throughout the preparation of this text: Jane Shaw, Beverley Hopping, Sean Mooney and Mike Coyle. Peter Blair, a friend and colleague now sadly departed, deserves a special mention. To many of us Peter was a guiding light, a true caterer of the 'old school' whose knowledge and understanding was continuously adapted to the modern industry. The abiding message being that whilst there is always something new that we can learn from, we do not necessarily need to discard the lessons (good practice) of the past.

Keith Waller

Improving Food and Beverage Performance

Keith Waller

BUTTERWORTH
HEINEMANN

Butterworth-Heinemann
Linacre House, Jordan Hill, Oxford OX2 8DP
225 Wildwood Avenue, Woburn, MA 01801-2041
A division of Reed Educational and Professional Publishing Ltd

R A member of the Reed Elsevier plc group

OXFORD   AUCKLAND   BOSTON
JOHANNESBURG   MELBOURNE   NEW DELHI

First published 1996
Reprinted 1999
© Keith Waller 1996

British Library Cataloguing in Publication Data
A catalogue record for this book is available from the British Library

ISBN 0 7506 2812 X

Typesetting and artwork origination by
David Gregson Associates, Beccles, Suffolk
Printed and bound in Great Britain by
Antony Rowe Ltd, Chippenham, Wiltshire

Contents

Preface   vii

Introduction   ix

1 Customer-centred performance improvement   1

2 Developing operational policy   40

3 Marketing   73

4 Merchandising   122

5 Quality   150

6 Product and service development   192

7 Systems management   256

8 Efficient staffing   313

9 Summary   361

Bibliography   364

Index   367

Preface

There are many writers who have shared with us their knowledge and understanding of the hospitality industry. Many more have written on the wider, more general, principles of management. The opportunity to compare and contrast ideas that the written word provides should not be undervalued. Reading, both general and specific (research) should be encouraged in all walks of life, particularly in business. Some authors have managed to achieve 'cult' status and their writings are eagerly sought out as providing the 'secrets' of success. But, when looking for an author that produces the 'best' advice, I turn not to any of my contemporaries nor to any lengthy tome of technical jargon and detail.

Success in business, as in life, is all about finding solutions to problems. The 'key' to finding the right solution is to ask the right questions. Rudyard Kipling, in his *Just So* verses, provided us with the simplest and soundest advice in this regard.

Taken from 'The Elephant's Child':

I keep six honest serving-men.
(They taught me all I know);
Their names are What and Why and When
and How and Where and Who.

Rudyard Kipling

Kipling is telling us that good management is not a case of knowing all the right answers but rather the culture of an enquiring mind. Like a doctor, a good manager will attempt to identify and treat the cause of illness rather than over-medicate or mask the symptoms. The objective of good 'health care', in business as in life, is to avoid the need for major surgery by regular and effective screening. A programme of health care, for each operation, may be designed by effective managers using a series of 'screening' tests, based on the 'Kipling technique' in order to identify potential problems at the earliest opportunity thus enabling preventative treatment.

Keith Waller

Introduction

The hospitality industry serves to meet two main objectives:

1 Ensuring a return on investment for the owners.
2 Provision of products and services for the consumer.

Response to these objectives is based on the management of a number of resources, the possible permutations of which provide for almost infinite variety of activity. It has been common, in some circles, to try to make sense of the hospitality industry by categorizing provision under various sectors.

Thus there have been many attempts to classify the various sectors of the hospitality industry and the way in which operations respond in terms of service style. Unfortunately, operators steadfastly refuse to co-operate, constantly inventing unique and novel approaches which defy current rules of classification. Distinguishing characteristics are more diffuse and the lines separating one sector from another have become more blurred. While counter service would once have been the domain of the cafeteria, customer 'involvement' is now a significant part of the system in all forms of catering and at all levels. The choice of silver service as an appropriate system of delivery (style of service) is now much more a response to specific customer need than it is representative of one particular sector of the industry.

Traditionally there has been a tendency to differentiate between the welfare and commercial sectors of our industry, primarily on the basis that one was earning a profit and the other was not. With regard to hospitality in general and catering – the provision of food and drink – in particular, this differentiation is becoming less apparent and less valid. Generally the rules for planning, implementing and controlling food and beverage provision will apply to all sectors. The effects of cross-fertilization of ideas and practices can be clearly seen in the number of hospitals, works and school canteens that now rely heavily on commercial principles such as merchandising. Similarly the effects of standardization, budgeting and strict cost controls can be seen to have increasing influence in the so-called commercial sector.

In what was once called the welfare sector where the general public, through government, are the investors, there may not be a demand for profit. However, the operation will be expected to run efficiently and consumers will be looking for quality and value in products and services provided. Many managers in this sector now recognize the benefits of seeking profitable, commercial, activities that can supplement and enhance their main provision.

Rationale

The problem then, for all catering operations, is to meet the needs and expectations of the customer within the constraints of financial targets. Taking the 'Kipling' approach to problem solving, we need to know:

who are our potential customers

why people eat away from home

when they eat, at which times during the day and on which occasions

where they eat and where they look for information which influences their choice

what they eat and what influences their preference/choice

how we can utilize this information to improve our response/performance

Aim
The purpose of this text is to help caterers answer the above questions in respect of their own particular operations and, in doing so, identify potential solutions.

Choosing the tools and techniques for effectively managing a catering operation is analogous to dining at a self-service buffet. The range of dishes (options) is extensive, the temptation to try them all is great. But meal quality is based on effective selection in response to identified need (objectives), such as: balanced nutrition, a light diet, high protein, gourmet, etc.; each of which may be successfully achieved with a number of different dish combinations. Whilst each dish (option) is perfect in its own right and in combination with a selection of other dishes, inappropriate choice or just plain 'pigging out' is only likely to result in illness rather than satisfaction. Good food and beverage managers will identify the benefits of each option offered, recognize the potential benefits of combining options and implement these in small 'portions' and observe the reaction before dining in larger proportions.

This text is designed to help caterers identify and respond to opportunities for performance improvement in order that their customers may increasingly benefit, through improved quality, value and service, from operational efficiencies, greater effectiveness and economic use of resources.

Objectives:
Improved performance
Added benefits (customers/owners/managers/staff)
Total customer satisfaction (quality, value and service)
Increased profits

Approach

In all aspects of life, but particularly where there is a competitive element (e.g. sport), success is dependent on having a plan which translates clear aims into effective action through the development of strategic objectives and the application of tactical activity. Individuals and/or teams will identify and deploy their strengths, cover and protect their weaknesses, in order progressively to gain advantage.

Aim   to win the event.

Strategy   to initiate a series of actions planned to achieve objectives in support of the main aim.

Tactics   operational activity chosen as the most efficient/effective method of achieving strategic objectives.

Even in non-competitive activities (e.g. entertainment), planning strategy and tactics are an essential requirement. There are, of course, apparent exceptions – improvization on stage, jazz music – but even here there is a generally agreed aim, and often objectives. The participants may be involved in more immediate response as a consequence of which they may be working to an independent plan and tactics may well be reactive rather than proactive. Colleagues will 'read' the plan as it evolves and work towards helping it achieve the main aim – to hold the tune. It may not always appear so, but they will be working together for the common good, rather than to gain advantage over one another.

Catering combines elements of competitiveness and improvization. We may treat the presence of other caterers as sport, or perhaps even open warfare. For our customers, of course, we provide a form of entertainment. We must ensure effective delivery by identifying appropriate aims and objectives.

Planning, strategy and tactics frequently involve the taking of 'hard' decisions, often made apparent by clearly identified aims. Doing the 'right thing' may not necessarily be the best way to get the job done. We will need the consensus of everyone involved if we are to be successful. We gain such consensus by clearly identifying the benefits which may be derived from the effective implementation of plans. There is a difference between 'doing the right thing' and 'doing the thing right'!

Good management, effective use of objectives, strategy and tactics, is an advantage to the operation, its staff and customers and to society as a whole.

Strategy
The approach of this text is to emphasize the importance of clear aims and objectives together with a well balanced selection of options in an effort to ensure improved operational performance.

Strategy and tactics

Robert Johnston (1989) provides us with a very useful series of diagrams (Figure I.1) which demonstrate the development of service strategy based on the identification of key elements. Needs and influences are added and finally the circle is completed with the identification of management activity. This text seeks to go further by examining strategic catering objectives in more detail and suggesting possible tactics in support of strategy.

For the vast majority of catering operations, the main aim remains fixed, but needs and influences are constantly changing. Consequently strategic objectives and tactics will need to be reviewed and perhaps modified in light of potential changes. It may be seen that there are both internal and external influences on the operation. Marketing and operational activity must be carefully integrated with customer needs, corporate objectives and the development of the product/service concept.

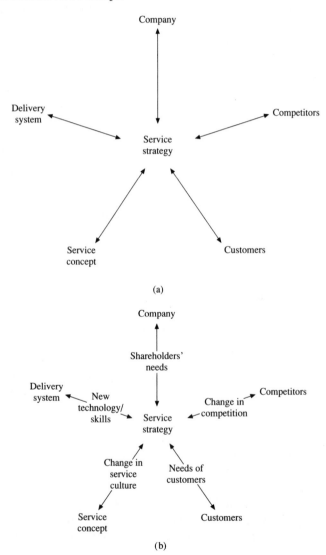

(a)

(b)

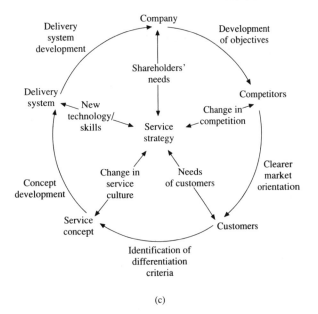

(c)

Figure I.1 (a) The elements of a service strategy. (b) Sources and types of needs for change. (c) The service strategy development framework. Source: Jones, 1989.

Tactics

It is hoped that the style and presentation of this text will encourage managers to examine their own operations in a similar way. It is recognized that all operations are different and that competitive advantage may be gained from identifying unique solutions (product/service differentiation) it is not anticipated that this text will provide 'off-the-peg' solutions, but the models and patterns used will allow managers to tailor their own 'made-to-measure' operational strategy. There will be considerable use of the 'Kipling' approach to problems. Comments and advice will be generalist in nature, specific examples will be provided where there is clear differentiation.

Table 1.2 The eating out market 1995–1999.

	Value (£b) 1995	1996	1997	1998	1999	*Change* 1995–99
Fast food*	5.79	5.87	6.01	6.18	6.42	+10.9%
Pub catering	4.30	4.33	4.37	4.39	4.44	+3.3%
Restaurants	2.15	2.13	2.11	2.12	2.15	—
Hotel catering	1.39	1.36	1.36	1.37	1.36	−2.2%
In-store	0.81	0.80	0.80	0.79	0.79	−2.5%
Roadside	0.57	0.58	0.59	0.61	0.63	+10.5%
Other#	1.49	1.48	1.58	1.63	1.69	+13.4%
Total	16.50	16.55	16.82	17.09	17.48	+5.9%

* includes take-away.
# includes clubs, camps, casinos, mobile catering.
Source: Mintel
Source: *Caterer and Hotelkeeper*, 28 September 1995, p. 14.

Choice of venue is likely to be influenced primarily by price supported by personal recommendation. The sort of 'attributes' most commonly looked for are cleanliness, well cooked food and efficient pleasant service. The most popular types of establishment are steak houses, pubs, Chinese and Indian restaurants. Food choices seem to vary very little but, when asked, customers frequently suggest that variety and novelty are desirable.

Table 1.3(a) Reasons given for eating out at least once every six months, 1986

Reason	Percentage
To celebrate a special occasion	34
To give self or spouse a treat	28
To meet with friends	21
To make a change from eating at home	21
To save having to cook	11
To treat friends or relatives	11
To enjoy a different type of meal from those cooked at home	10
Someone invited me	9
To give children a treat	5
Other reasons/don't know	4

Base: 868 adults

Source: BMRB/Mintel, 1986

Table 1.3(d) Most important attributes of eating establishments which customers frequent, 1985

Attributes	*Percentage*
Cleanliness and hygiene	70
Well-cooked/good food	58
Efficient and pleasant service	37
Atmosphere	25
Price range	24
Type of food	22
Clear prices/prices shown	13
No smoking areas	13
Convenient location	12
Facilities for children	9
Interesting/pleasant decor	4
None of these/don't know	4

Base: 1499 adults

Source: BMRB/Mintel, 1986.

Table 1.3(e) Adults claiming to visit most often when eating out for leisure purposes, 1986

Preference	*Percentage*
Steak house	41
Pub	26
Chinese restaurant	17
Indian restaurant	14
Hotel restaurant	11
Pizza restaurant	8
Wine bar	8
Italian/pasta restaurant	7
Hamburger restaurant	5
Fish and chip restaurant	4
French restaurant	3
Greek restaurant	2
Bistro	1
Chicken and chip restaurant	1
Other ethnic/foreign food restaurant	13
Other*	29
Don't know	3

Base: 868 adults

*Known to be mostly English restaurants which were omitted from this list of questions.
Source: BMRB/Mintel, 1986.

Table 1.3(f) Adults claiming to eat out in steak houses and pubs most often, 1986

Age and class	Steak houses (%)	Pubs (%)
All	41	26
15–24	41	15
25–34	49	19
35–54	48	25
55+	27	39
AB*	42	30
C1	40	27
C2	41	22
DE	40	25
North	36	24
Midlands	42	34
South	46	23

Base: 868 adults

*Notes
A = Upper middle class
B = Middle class
C1 = Lower middle class
C2 = Skilled working class
D = Working class
E = Lowest income levels
Source: BMRM/Mintel, 1986.

Why is customer-centred performance improvement important?

All too often operations target performance improvement in particular aspects of their operation without a clear appreciation of the relationship with other elements or the significance of improvement in regard to the ultimate aim. It is possible, for instance, continuously to refine and improve the production process and yet have no significant effect on sales (customer response) or cost savings.

Managers should focus attention on the customer and produce quality products (in response to identified need) at the right price. As a consequence of this, a more rational approach to performance improvement in staffing, systems, products and resource management will be apparent. Performance improvement within the operation can then be centred on (a) refining the process to produce the same product more efficiently/economically, or (b) adapting the process/product in response to changes in customer need.

Trading opportunities

In order to be successful operations must respond to consumer demand while being aware of current business environment pressures, which may include:

- polarizing markets, spending on meals which are either cheap or expensive (little mid-range)
- increasing competition
- growing importance of brand image and consequently brand integrity
- more professional response to environmental health and hygiene
- recognition of the effects of drink–drive campaigns, the anti-alcohol lobby and anti-smoking

- growth of retail parks and decline of town centres
- the increase in snack eating and all day trading
- Sunday trading
- the opportunities of being female/family/children friendly

	1971	1981	1991	2001	2011
Under 40	31.8	32.2	32	31.9	30.1
40 and over	24.1	24.2	25.6	27.3	29.9

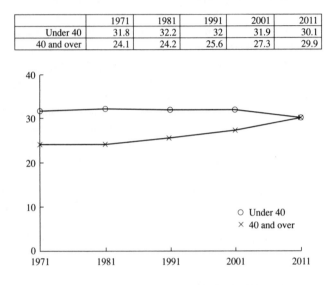

Figure 1.5 UK population 1971–2001 (millions). As can be seen, the gap between young and old consumers will have disappeared by the first decade of the new century and the balance is likely to be reversed thereafter.

Market forces relate to current socio-economic activity, particularly the amount of money in the economy. Social issues like the way we regard affluence and the flaunting of money, which often takes place within a hospitality context, will have a considerable effect on our industry regardless of the amount of money people have to spend. Some sectors of the industry, such as corporate entertaining, may be affected more than others. Other social factors like the drive for

Income per week (£)	under 100	100–199	200–299	300–399	400–499
Spent on alcohol	2.43	4.9	8.58	11.23	12.76
Spent on food	1.64	3.78	7.07	9.64	11.96

Income per week (£)	500–599	600–699	700–799	800+
Spent on alcohol	14.49	16.63	20.88	24.46
Spent on food	15.66	16.39	21.05	28.87

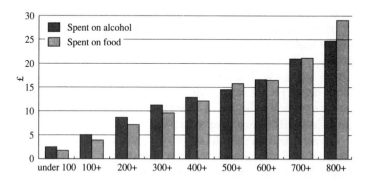

Figure 1.6 Average weekly spend on food and drink away from home (1990). Approximate figures based on available government statistics. Note that up until the £500 mark, spending on alcohol is greater than on food.

equality have seen a number of changes, pubs in particular are becoming increasingly 'female friendly'. There has been a polarization of the restaurant industry, the gap between moderately priced and expensive meals is increasing, with little on offer between the two. This may be because the benefits of the mid-range restaurant are unclear. Expensive meals offer extravagance, popularly priced meals offer value. What can we offer between? The relationship of catering with other industries is significant. The need for workers to be 'looked after' and for shoppers to be fed is providing increasing opportunities for the catering industry. The growth of retail parks which provide on-site caterers with 'captive customers' is a notable example. The nature of competition is also an important consideration. Competition tends to hold prices down and the need to remain competitive places extra demands on the manager. This is particularly true of the highly competitive, popularly priced, restaurant sector. By far the most important element of market forces is the consumer.

It has been suggested that the catering industry is not sufficiently innovative. It shows a tendency for following retailing in its response to new technology, new tastes/textures, new exotic and unusual foods. With the increased visibility, 'high profile' (TV, etc.), of some chefs this is changing, but slowly. There are some 'innovative' exceptions, particularly in the moderately priced sector where some companies have been quick to take up the use of 'customer loyalty' credit building cards as used by many supermarkets.

Owners, whether public or private, will primarily demand efficient and effective use of their investment. Managers, as stewards of the owners' assets, will be concerned with economy, reduction in waste and profitability. There will be varying levels of acceptable profitability, dependent on market conditions.

Government action and involvement may be both political and/or legal. Government decisions may affect the nature of the business environment, as with increasing Europeanization and privatization. In the 1980s, the Government's decision to force hospital and school meal caterers to tender for contracts did not result in widespread take-overs by the private sector but it did initiate considerable change within the welfare catering industry.

Additionally the Government is responsible for the rules and regulations which control business activity. Of those that relate to the catering industry the most important are consumer protection, health and safety. In particular the increasing involvement of Environmental Health Officers should be welcomed. It is what our customers want and it provides for more confidence.

Who is involved with customer-centred performance improvement?

In simple terms, everyone: customers, managers, staff (internal customers), suppliers, etc., each having a role or function. For the present, attention will be focused on the key players; the customers who provide the incentive and the managers who direct the roles and activities of the other participants.

Customers

An understanding of customers, their needs and expectations is clearly the key to performance improvement. A considerable amount of information is available about our customers, from a variety of sources. Chapter 3 on marketing will discuss in some detail the analysis of this 'market' information; suffice to say at this point that our customers are all individuals but the following generalized traits are identifiable:

- ageing population
- rising consumer expectations
- disposable income/inheritance
- rise of the middle classes (status)
- time/leisure paradox (see Figure 1.7)
- young free and single, tame and together, old trapped and single

Expendable income for retired people will be dependent on pre-planning, investments and pensions, together with the increasing likelihood of inheritance. The current generation are likely to be the first recipients, on a large scale, of their parents buying their own homes. The potential for increasing wealth of senior citizens is obviously influenced by economic environment and government activity (taxation). Currently

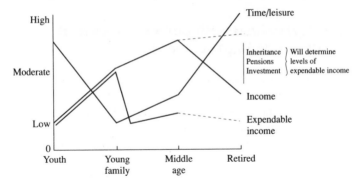

Figure 1.7 The income/time/leisure paradox. Frequently the time available for leisure (hospitality, food and drink) is not matched by available income. Caterers will need to adapt what they are offering to suit.

old people's savings are exhausted by paying for 'care' which they had expected to be 'free'. Current concern over decreasing house prices and negative equity may mean that the 'inheritance' generation may be a short-lived phenomenon.

Rising consumer expectations place ever increasing challenges before the manager. In particular, we need to be aware of the ageing population who will become fitter and potentially financially better off. They will have time on their hands and money to spend. Younger people may also become more wealthy but in order to do so will probably work longer and harder, leaving little time to spend their money. Finally there will be some, young and old, who for various reasons will be considerably less well off. Managers need to understand who their customers are, their background and their needs and expectations. Are they looking for leisure and value or a quick, extravagant, indulgence? We need to understand the significance of spending power, disposable income and opportunity cost. Although people may have money there may be 'opportunities' between which they are forced to choose. If I have £50 do I spend it on a single meal out or a week's food for the table at home. If I spend the £50 on food what else do I have to give up; clothes, electricity, other forms of entertainment? Finally we should not ignore the influence of trend and fashion. Things like anti-smoking and drink driving campaigns will influence both the provision we make for our customers and the way in which we manage our customers. There has been a noticeable growth in 'grazing': taking light, unplanned, snacks throughout the day. As a consequence 'foraging', the planned search for food to meet a particular need, (restaurants providing traditional lunch and dinner at set times) is on the decline.

Customer needs and expectations

Customer needs and expectations are based on the purpose or reason for eating out. Perceptions are influenced by the realization that a meal experience is, in most cases, more than just an opportunity to eat and drink.

The meal experience (influencing factors):
- social
- business
- convenience
- atmosphere and service
- price
- menu

Additional concerns include: location, accessibility, atmosphere and mood, interior design and decor.

While all of the above will contribute to customer satisfaction, obvious attention will be drawn to service and products (food and drink).

Attributes of food and drink:
- choice
- quality
- quantity (portion size)
- standards (consistency)
- range
- performance (competence – hot food is hot!)
- presentation
- price

} meeting consumer expectations

There has generally been an increase in healthy eating and preference for white meat and fish. There is some interest in organically produced foods but currently the cost of most caterers using such foods is not supported by consumer demand.

There appears to be increasingly more rapid change (trend/fashion) in products. In the case of beers and ales in particular, while we may have seen the last of the lime wedge in bottles of Mexican lager, we are seeing a renewed interest in traditional brews and a wider variety of fruit-flavoured beers. Some of the new products will disappear quite quickly, others will remain thus increasing the available variety and choice and providing opportunities for matching beers and ales (instead of wine) with food.

Customer choice

Dr Jon R. Bareham (1989) provides us with an interesting model of consumer choice (Figure 1.8) which highlights in particular; external environment, external stimuli and individual disposition.

Additionally we need to consider the psychology of choice (see Chapter 4, Merchandising, for more detailed discussion), specifically the relationship between liking, preference and

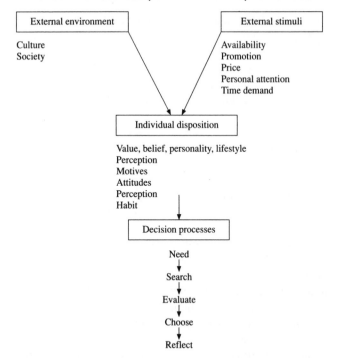

Figure 1.8 A model of consumer choice. Source: Jones, 1989.

choice. Liking may not correspond to choice: they are overlapping but not precisely equivalent.

> *'I like alcohol, I prefer gin, but I choose wine.'*

All result from experience (trial and error) and/or recommendation (other people's experience). Learning and acquiring preferences, evolves from experience supported by observation and reflection. Choice is determined by preference as influenced by situational variables, external environment, external stimuli and individual disposition.

Managers who understand choice, and manage their response accordingly will help to develop positive attitudes in customers towards the products and services provided. Managers will need to be more proactive, alter their perspective and take a new approach to new products and services, recognizing and selling the benefits.

The food and beverage manager

A variety of factors exist which determine or influence the way in which we manage. Some, like political and socio-economic development, are outside our operation and beyond our control. Other elements, like technological development, are also outside our direct control but we are able, by making demands or offering advice, to influence such factors as equipment manufacturers and food processors. Similarly, within the operation itself, some elements will be beyond the control of the manager and some will be subject to the manager's influence if not control. At unit level there are three main elements over which the food and beverage manager has direct control: raw materials, equipment/machinery and people/staff. The manipulation of these three main resources, balanced by use of time and money, provides the opportunities with which the manager is able to respond to demands of the operational environment and external and internal influences. In most cases there is a direct, usually inverse, relationship between each of these main resources. If a new vegetable rumbler is purchased then the additional cost should be reflected by a similar or greater reduction in labour cost as a result of less hand peeling of potatoes. If the number of skilled kitchen staff are increased then there should be a reduction in the amount of convenience foods purchased. Occasionally the cost of all three elements will rise as a result in a change to one. If fresh Dover sole were purchased in place of fish portions then there would need to be a subsequent investment in preparation and service equipment and skills. In which case an increase in selling price is bound to be required. Clearly such action should only result from demonstrable customer demand and willingness to pay.

The manager will manipulate resources in response to pressure on the operation. Such pressure may arise from five main sources:

- owners
- government
- labour
- market forces
- consumers

Roles and responsibilities of the food and beverage manager, catering manager or bursar

Managers plan, set objectives, organize, monitor performance, analyse results, communicate, train, motivate and control.

The responsibilities of the food and beverage manager:
- The provision of facilities for a defined market
- The provision of systems of delivery
- Total customer satisfaction
- Formulation, establishment and maintenance of systems of control to:
  - monitor costs, prices, sales and profitability
  - provide management information
  - ensure performance reconciliation
- Training, motivation and control of staff
- Co-ordination of resources and activities

A useful exercise for new managers or new teams is to get to know your role, the role of others and how they see your role (responsibilities) (see Figure 1.9).

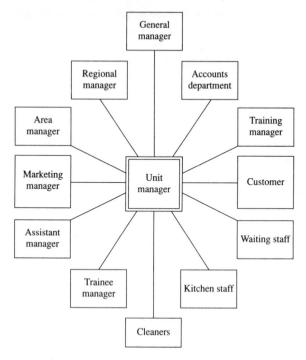

Figure 1.9 The role set of a unit manager.

This may be achieved by drawing a 'management wheel' (see Figure 1.10) which defines your role as you see it. Get someone else to draw a similar diagram of your role as they see it. Discuss the differences – there will be differences! Resolve the major differences and areas of potential misunderstanding/conflict.

The management wheel should be used to identify activities and responsibilities, the perceived importance of which is demonstrated by the length of the line drawn from the circumference to the centre. Ideally there should be little which extends into the centre (sole responsibility). There should be a high degree of shared responsibility (delegation/empowerment). The manager's time should be devoted to customer contact and a supportive role within the team.

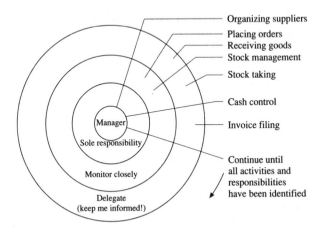

Figure 1.10 The management wheel is used to identify activities and responsibilities and demonstrate their perceived importance in relation to one another. Ideally there should be a reasonably even distribution. Wherever possible, reduce the number of 'sole responsibility' activities. That is not to say that the manager should have little to do, but that there is more to be gained from delegation and empowerment. Management time should be devoted to customers and support for team members.

Customer-centred performance strategy

How is customer-centred performance improvement developed?

Customer-centred performance strategy should be based on effective market analysis resulting in products and services which are developed to meet a clearly identified need at an appropriate price.

- Marketing–research–customer needs, which identifies
- Product/service development–response, followed by
- Marketing–promotion–offer

The marketing activities above will be supported by operational activity which highlights:

- Quality assurance
- Systems and staffing   } resulting customer satisfaction
- Merchandising   – delight

All of the above are discussed in detail in the chapters which follow.

When should customer-centred performance improvement be implemented?

Pressure to change

As we have seen there is continuing pressure on the food and beverage manager to modify or change the operation. There are three main elements of change within a food and beverage environment: food and drink, the menu and drinks lists and systems of production and service.

Changes in food and drink

We have already noted the competitive nature of the industry; this will demand that the manager search for low-cost, high-profit alternatives to the more traditional menu items. Health consciousness, leading to changes in eating and drinking habits, must be reflected in the nature of products offered for sale. As a result of increased foreign travel and wider publicity given to food and drink in the national press and on television, customers will be looking for innovation and variety as well as value and quality. Presentation styles for food and drink will change: sometimes as a result of fashion, drinking beer from the bottle; sometimes as a result of developments in technology. The influence of ethnic, regional and international cuisine is increasing.

Changes in the menu and drinks list

As a result of the drive for efficiency and economy menus and drinks lists have become shorter, reducing the stock holding and waste associated with menu items which do not sell. The importance of brand imagery has lead to a greater instance of themed menus. Descriptive details, which help the customer to identify the benefits of each dish and make assumptions about its value, are more widely used. There is an increasing tendency to present menu items and drinks in merchandised groupings rather than in traditionally accepted sequence.

Changes to systems

By far the greatest influence for change to systems is the cost and availability of traditionally skilled staff. There will be opportunities for change throughout the operational cycle and in particular there will be a change of emphasis from production and service to purchasing and sales. As a result of developments in food manufacture, production is increasingly seen as less important. Production no longer needs to take place on site; it is not essential that we produce our own dishes. There is a growing tendency for much of the industry to become more like retailing.

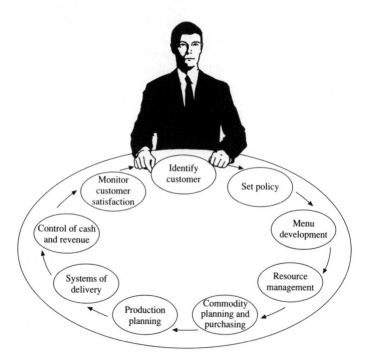

Figure 1.11 The catering cycle must be continuous and customer driven. Source: Fuller and Waller, 1991.

Micro-environment

Managers should look carefully at what is actually going on within their operation. How do effective operations respond?

Customer-centred performance improve,

Look at changes in:

- Food and drink
- The menu
- Systems of production
  and delivery

} response to
external influences

Changes in food and drink
- the search for low-cost, high-profit products
- healthy eating, low alcohol drinks
- market demand (price, quality and value)
- presentation
- fashion and trend – ethnic/regional/international

We may be able to charge the customer **more** for putting **less** fat/cream/protein into the product/dish because it is better for them!

Changes to menus and drinks lists
- shorter
- themed
- descriptive
- merchandised groupings rather than traditional
  sequence

Menu objectives include:

- selling
- making money
- communication (implicit/explicit)
- basis for planning (forecasting and costing)
- not just a piece of paper/card

There needs to be greater emphasis on communication, telling the customer about quality and selling the benefits of products and services.

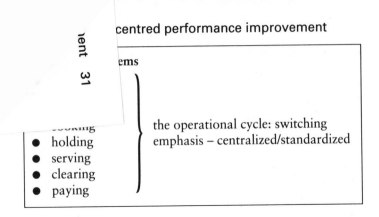

ems

cooking
- holding
- serving
- clearing
- paying

the operational cycle: switching
emphasis – centralized/standardized

Entire systems include:

- cook-freeze
- cook-chill
- sous-vide

Changes in customer expectations and the environment are reflected in new product development, production methods, product promotion, staffing and systems of delivery and service. Because the catering industry seeks to satisfy a multiplicity of differing needs, there are therefore an almost infinite variety of operational responses.

There are bound to be problems for managers developing service systems, based on the understanding that services are perishable, intangible, heterogeneous (different from one customer to the next), interactive/participative and the customer never 'owns' the service.

Employment

Changes to products, production methods and systems of service and delivery are bound to put pressure on staffing and employment strategy. Managers will need to understand the impact of:

- the core/periphery split (see Figure 1.12)
- the impact of technology
- the growing number of technicians
- the increasing use of prepared/convenience products

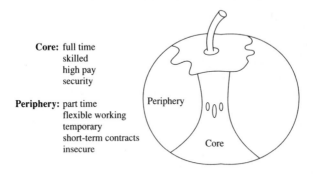

Core: full time
skilled
high pay
security

Periphery: part time
flexible working
temporary
short-term contracts
insecure

Periphery

Core

Figure 1.12 The core/periphery split. Many employers are decreasing their employment of core workers and placing greater reliance on peripheral employees. Although the increased flexibility can have obvious cost benefits there are evident dangers in the strategy, not least of which is that it may not always work out cheaper – especially if all the costs of running a peripheral work force are properly accounted for. (NB: Although job security is clearly a problem, the periphery worker is not necessarily financially worse off. There may be advantages – self-employment, variety of work, more freedom – that periphery workers can build on.)

Labour availability, or lack of it, will force the manager to consider a variety of alternatives, as fewer young people enter the labour market and the opportunities that exist in other industries appear more attractive. Managers will have to change their attitude to staff recruitment and development. This will normally result in a trade-off between available skills and convenience produce. For most of the industry there is a growing change in emphasis from preparation, production and technical service skills to social skills and interpersonal relationships. There will be an increasing move from demarcation of narrow traditional skills and shift work to multi-skilling and more socially acceptable working conditions.

There are positive career opportunities within the hospitality industry, although there is an increasing lack of security in all forms of employment, including hospitality. The nature of hospitality does provide the workforce with more potential for mobility between contracts. Good managers will help employees to adjust, by providing support and advice. Independent managers will initiate consortiums to provide managed (secure/reliable/dependable) employment opportunities for flexible staff with easily transferable skills.

Performance improvement tactics

Where can customer-centred performance improvement be used to gain competitive advantage?

Targets and objectives

The food and beverage manager will be expected to provide a range of successful products and services in an environment conducive to customer expectations. In doing so they will be concerned with:

- establishing and maintaining effective systems of purchasing, production and delivery
- setting standards which lead to consistent customer satisfaction
- formulating and maintaining systems of control to:
  – monitor costs, prices, sales and profitability

   – provide management information
   – ensure performance reconciliation
● directing, training, motivating and controlling staff activity and performance
● ensuring effective use of resources and reduction of waste

The manager will be constrained by a variety of external and internal forces. However, these can be managed if an effective operational policy is developed.

Constraints on the food and beverage manager:
External factors :
● Political   (legislation, taxation, licensing law, local regulations, planning law, etc.)
● Economic   (rising costs, changes in disposable income, credit facilities, interest rates)
● Social   (demographics, socio-economic groupings, ethnic influence, fads, fashion)
● Technical   (innovation, product development, energy conservation, IT, etc.)

Internal factors :
● Company policy (financial–market–operational)
● Resources   raw materials: transferability, perishability, etc.
               equipment/machinery: maintenance, replacement, system requirements
               people/staff: availability, skills, supervision, etc.
● Control   transactions, standards, variance, etc.

A programme of customer care critical control points (CCCCPs) is needed to identify all possible opportunities of weakness in the system leading to loss of customer satisfaction (see Figure 1.13).

36 Customer-centred performance improvement

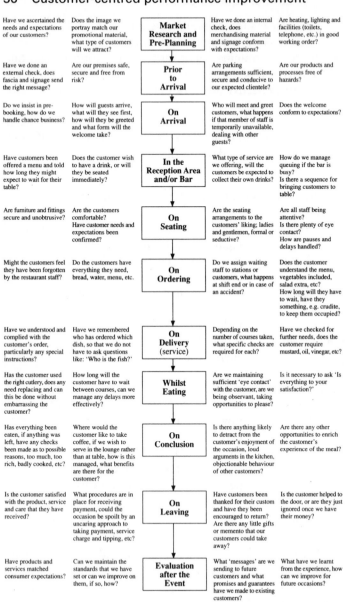

Have we ascertained the needs and expectations of our customers?	Does the image we portray match our promotional material, what type of customers will we attract?	**Market Research and Pre-Planning**	Have we done an internal check, does merchandising material and signage conform with expectations?	Are heating, lighting and facilities (toilets, telephone, etc.) in good working order?
Have we done an external check, does fascia and signage send the right message?	Are our premises safe, secure and free from risk?	**Prior to Arrival**	Are parking arrangements sufficient, secure and conducive to our expected clientele?	Are our products and processes free of hazards?
Do we insist in pre-booking, how do we handle chance business?	How will guests arrive, what will they see first, how will they be greeted and what form will the welcome take?	**On Arrival**	Who will meet and greet customers, what happens if that member of staff is temporarily unavailable, dealing with other guests?	Does the welcome conform to expectations?
Have customers been offered a menu and told how long they might expect to wait for their table?	Does the customer wish to have a drink, or will they be seated immediately?	**In the Reception Area and/or Bar**	What type of service are we offering, are the customers be expected to collect their own drinks?	How do we manage queuing if the bar is busy? Is there a sequence for bringing customers to table?
Are furniture and fittings secure and unobtrusive?	Are the customers comfortable? Have customer needs and expectations been confirmed?	**On Seating**	Are the seating arrangements to the customers' liking; ladies and gentlemen, formal or seductive?	Are all staff being attentive? Is there plenty of eye contact? How are pauses and delays handled?
Might the customers feel they have been forgotten by the restaurant staff?	Do the customers have everything they need, bread, water, menu, etc.	**On Ordering**	Do we assign waiting staff to stations or customers, what happens at shift end or in case of an accident?	Does the customer understand the menu, vegetables included, salad extra, etc? How long will they have to wait, have they something, e.g. crudite, to keep them occupied?
Have we understood and complied with the customer's order, particularly any special instructions?	Have we remembered who has ordered which dish, so that we do not have to ask questions like: 'Who is the fish?'	**On Delivery (service)**	Depending on the number of courses taken, what specific checks are required for each?	Have we checked for further needs, does the customer require mustard, oil, vinegar, etc?
Has the customer used the right cutlery, does any need replacing and can this be done without embarrassing the customer?	How long will the customer have to wait between courses, can we manage any delays more effectively?	**Whilst Eating**	Are we maintaining sufficient 'eye contact' with the customer, are we being observant, taking opportunities to please?	Is it necessary to ask 'Is everything to your satisfaction?'
Has everything been eaten, if anything was left, have any checks been made as to possible reasons, too much, too rich, badly cooked, etc?	Where would the customer like to take coffee, if we wish to serve in the lounge rather than at table, how is this managed, what benefits are there for the customer?	**On Conclusion**	Is there anything likely to detract from the customer's enjoyment of the occasion, loud arguments in the kitchen, objectionable behaviour of other customers?	Are there any other opportunities to enrich the customer's experience of the meal?
Is the customer satisfied with the product, service and care that they have received?	What procedures are in place for receiving payment, could the occasion be spoilt by an uncaring approach to taking payment, service charge and tipping, etc?	**On Leaving**	Have customers been thanked for their custom and have they been encouraged to return? Are there any little gifts or memento that our customers could take away?	Is the customer helped to the door, or are they just ignored once we have their money?
Have products and services matched consumer expectations?	Can we maintain the standards that we have set or can we improve on them, if so, how?	**Evaluation after the Event**	What 'messages' are we sending to future customers and what promises and guarantees have we made to existing customers?	What have we learnt from the experience, how can we improve for future occasions?

Companies who declare themselves to be concerned with total quality and customer care, will develop the notion of the internal customer. Everyone in the operation serves and is served by others and the quality of each transaction influences the success of the final customer contact. Such philosophy must be actively built into the operation through a planned series of CCCCPs and the manager must lead by example.

The person in contact with the customer is not always responsible for the problems or able to correct them but can, if given the authority, compensate for weaknesses in the system. Front line staff should be allowed to put things right, if they should go wrong. The resolution of problems should be efficient, effective, economic and speedy.

Measuring success

In general terms the indicators of successful, competent, food and beverage management might best be defined as efficiency, effectiveness and economy.

- Efficiency may be seen in optimum use of resources – minimum input for maximum return. Examine the ratio of staff to satisfied customers, stock levels and stock turnover, productive life, energy usage and volume output of equipment.
- Effectiveness is to be found in levels of customer satisfaction. Examine compliments and complaints, numbers of returning customers and market share.
- Economy is to be seen in return on investments. Were efficiency and effectiveness achieved for minimum outlay? Was all necessary expenditure incurred? Was all incurred expenditure necessary?

(left)
Figure 1.13 Customer care critical control points (CCCCPs)

Detailed indicators of achievement and success for specific aspects of the management function are to be found in each of the chapters that follow. Remember that the role of the food and beverage manager is to manage, not to react; to deal with the causes, not the symptoms.

Summary

The successful manager will be able to:

- Look at the environment
- Identify trading opportunities
- Concentrate on customer choice and benefits
- Plan for change
- Be proactive rather than reactive
- Manage resources in the most cost effective way
- Measure success

The food and beverage manager is responsible for the development and implementation of operational policy (strategy and tactics). This may be achieved though a questioning attitude and, specifically, the use of the Kipling technique: what, when, where, why, who, how!

To put things in perspective – what does it all mean?

We live and work in a changing political/social/economic environment. We deal with changing customers, changing needs and expectations. In order to be successful we will need strategies which are adaptable (not weak) so that we may be able to provide an effective response to continuously evolving trading opportunities.

Successful operations are those that are always able to provide products/services suited to customer needs.

Customer-centred performance improvement can be the one 'unchanging' factor. However, no matter how good we get, we will always be striving to do better.

Suggested additional reading

Croner's Catering. Croner Publications.

Davis, B. and Lockwood, A. (1994) *Food and Beverage Management: A selection of readings*. Butterworth–Heinemann.

Davis, B. and Stone, S. (1991) *Food and Beverage Management (2nd ed.)*. Butterworth–Heinemann.

Fearn, D.A. (1985) *Food and Beverage Management*. Butterworth–Heinemann.

Fuller, J. and Waller, K. (1991) *The Menu, Food and Profit*. Stanley Thornes.

Jones, P. (ed.) (1989) *Management in the Service Industries*. Pitman.

Jones, P. (ed.) (1996) *Introduction to Hospitality Operations*. Cassell.

2
Developing operational policy

Aims and objectives

The aim of this chapter is to demonstrate the relationship between the provision of effective operational policies and successful customer-centred performance.

In order to be effective, managers should understand the relevance of sound operational policies. Some knowledge of how policy is formulated, implemented and reviewed would be useful, particularly an understanding of the influence of financial, marketing and personnel policies.

The prime objectives of policy development are to enable managers to:

- Recognize the needs, expectations and rights of the consumer.
- Identify policies and establish the resources required to operate a range of catering systems.
- Distinguish between departmental functions, structures and responsibilities.
- Implement procedures and practices in regard to health, safety and hygiene.
- Establish criteria for setting and maintaining standards.
- Identify and adapt to opportunities and constraints relating to the provision of food and drink.
- Respond to the continuing effects of change: economical, social and technical.

Policy development activities
- Respond to customer needs and expectations.
- Set levels and standards of product and service quality.
- Manage costing and pricing in line with consumer expectations.
- Establish and maintain systems and procedures to obtain customer feedback.
- Maintain systems for providing customer information.
- Monitor customer compliments and complaints.
- Identify trends and develop improvement plans.
- Monitor customer behaviour to minimize disruption to the service.

What is policy?

A policy is a clearly defined statement of intent, normally defined before the commencement of a new operation, which may need to be re-defined (modified) in the event of change. Policies should be clear and well defined and not themselves subject to change, although they should be adaptable to minor modification, particularly changes in customer needs and expectations.

Whilst there may be one overall company aim, this will be supported by a range of subordinate policies. Policy development requires long-term planning which will identify both trends and limitations. For example, average income, food and drink trends, the availability of investment funds, labour and materials, and potential cost/price limits. This will enable policy to be determined for product/service development: refinement of standards for products and services offered, standardized recipes, methods and processes. In particular, issues of potential conflict between supporting policies; financial policy (profit) versus customer policy (quality and value), for example, will need to be addressed in order that a complementary and manageable package evolves.

A 'mission statement' is frequently used to encapsulate the main policy aims. A mission statement should be short and simple, preferably a single sentence. Wherever possible the mission statement should recognize or make reference to:

- the market
- the product/service
- quality
- the price (range)
- the competition

For example:

> *'Trucker's Treats aims to provide the working traveller with the finest hot pies at a price unmatched by any other truck-stop.'*

Policy is often supported by detailed documentation (manuals and handbooks). Such documentation would normally identify 'procedures' necessary for the implementation of policy, a 'bible' which can be interpreted for the purpose of decision making in line with company thinking. Procedures go hand-in-hand with policies.

Definitions

Policy   Guidelines to ensure that various managerial decisions are both consistent and complementary with the corporate objectives.

Procedure   A detailed set of instructions for activities that occur regularly and are found in every part of the organization. Procedures may be documented in Standard Operating Procedure (SOP) manuals.

For example, a company may have a policy of requiring payment within one month and procedures will be established to ensure that this is achieved.

There are four basic policies (see Figure 2.1):

- Financial
- Marketing
- Personnel
- Catering (operational)

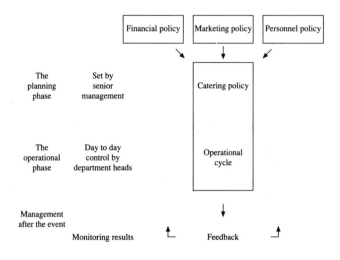

Figure 2.1 The influence of policy.

Financial policy

Financial policy determines levels of profitability and sets targets for the operation as a whole and individual units within the operation. Unit contribution can be divided into percentage contributions for each area of activity (sales mix), e.g. food and drink. Performance indicators such as Gross Profit and Net Profit will be set and monitored.

Financial policy will determine both limits and targets:

- Cost limits

- budgets (staffing, etc.)
- purchases (equipment, raw materials)
● Sales targets
- covers (occupancy, rate of restaurant turnaround (RRT))
- sales (average spend per customer (ASP))

Marketing policy

Marketing policy determines the intended market, market mix (present and future) and anticipated market share (sales volume and profitability, target percentage). In order to respond effectively, marketing policy will need to determine customer profile:

● socio-economic groups
● needs, wants and expectations
● measures for customer satisfaction

Brand image, identity and integrity, will be built around a product range in response to identified customer needs and prices will be set based on anticipated consumer spending power (see Chapter 3, Marketing, for a more detailed discussion on these points).

Personnel policy

Personnel policy determines management approach to recruitment, training and staff development. It will be influenced by current legislation: contract of employment (conditions and wage/salary structures) and discrimination. Personnel procedures – organization, supervision, authority and responsibility, grievance and discipline – should be particularly clear and adhered to rigidly.

Recruitment and selection:

- procedures – use of agencies versus internal functions
- job descriptions and personnel specifications
- Application forms, CVs, interviews and trade tests

Training and induction:

- time and availability
- essential induction (health, safety and hygiene)
- skill requirements (job description)
- spotting a training need

Career development:

- staff development/motivation/empowerment
- progression and succession
- retirement

(See Chapter 8, Efficient staffing, for a more detailed discussion on these points.)

Catering (operational) policy

As can be seen from Figure 2.1, operational policy is normally based on the requirements of marketing, financial and personnel policies. Catering policy determines the operational style, and provides guidelines for menu development, systems of production and service as well as methods of purchasing and control. Current legal requirements, specifically health, safety and hygiene, will be an integral part of operational policy.

Operational style (characteristics):

- systems, levels and standards
- customer profile (marketing)
- quality, price and value
- comfort and design
- hours of business

Menu and drinks lists:

● food and drink provision
● menu type, range, choice

Production/service systems:

● raw material usage, process methods, yield/waste, acceptable limits
● systems of delivery and customer management
● staffing (personnel)

Control:

● processes and procedures
● accounting for materials (stock), work in progress, cash, quality
● risk management, safety and hygiene, HACCP (Hazard Analysis and Critical Control Points)

Why is policy important?

Principally because it determines how customer needs – quality, price, value, etc. – will be met, thus ensuring customer satisfaction and return business.

Policies provide:
1 Statements of the main aims and objectives of the company.
2 Guidelines and codes of practice for mangers, supervisors, staff and customers.
3 The basis for decision making, responsibility and authority.
4 Precise 'quantifiable' (realistic) statements of performance expectations:

- turnover
- occupancy
- revenue
- volume (number of customers per hour/day/week/etc.)
- average spending power (ASP)
- ratios (food cost:revenue, labour:revenue, labour:food cost)
- GP, GP percentage, margin (after materials and labour), NP, NP percentage
- stock, materials usage (waste, loss, fraud)

5 Procedures which ensure a quality meal experience for all customers.

Quantifiable measures (statements of performance) for a product, and particularly for service quality, are difficult to identify and maintain. We frequently rely on customer comment, which although valid may not be consistent or reliable. We may use the principle of 'total meal experience' to assist in setting and measuring standards of product/service quality.

What contributes to customer enjoyment of a meal experience?

- the food itself – presentation (appearance/colour/portion size)
  - smell, taste, texture
- the service – matches the image
  - skills (where necessary)
  - timely
  - friendly
- hygiene – general appearance
  - staff
  - cutlery/crockery/linen/furniture and fittings
  - toilets
- staff – properly dressed (uniform)
  - personal hygiene
  - social skills

- ambience – facia, welcoming
            – decor and furnishing
            – lighting
            – air conditioning
            – acoustics
            – other customers
- price – clear and unambiguous
         – value for money

Managers should attempt to identify quantifiable measures for each of the elements above.

It is also important to determine policies for the management of customers. An interesting example is provided by queuing, an activity which most companies try to avoid by developing policies for customer management. Conversely, for the customer it provides a wonderful opportunity for observation and reflective thought.

I was recently a participant in the queuing activity at my local supermarket, which like most other similar operations tries to identify and differentiate between the needs of two specific types of shopper: those buying a lot and those buying a little. Various strategies have evolved, typically a nine or ten item restriction at a specified checkout, often supported by a 'cash only' restriction. Customers, of course do everything to defeat the system and then moan about it because it doesn't work.

On this particular occasion the supermarket in question had introduced a modification to the normal policy of 'nine items only', probably because customers were continuously abusing it. The new system was 'one basket only'. Within the space of a minute, two 'customer care' opportunities arose. First, a couple, who had only used a trolley to transport their young child, attempted to present their four items (others in our queue had managed to pack well over ten items into their single basket). The couple were summarily dismissed, company policy 'one basket only', no rational judgement, no initiative. Second, as my (five) items were processed, one item was found to have neither price nor barcode. The check-out assistant called into the microphone, 'Bakery, can I have a barcode for bagels.' I could feel hostility growing in fellow shoppers; queue-rage was developing and some of it would be directed at me. I imagined that it would take an age for the bakery assistant to wander around the bakery shelves checking prices before returning to the check-out to heap further embarrassment upon me. But, to my amazement, the response on the communication system was immediate, 'We must have slipped up, no charge to the customer, I will correct the error immediately.' Obvious initiative and equally obvious empowerment. I left the store, with my 'free' bagels, quite impressed with the service, but concerned for the young family who clearly were less than happy. This particular implementation of policy was observed by at least six other customers, in my queue alone, who were probably left with similar doubts about the company's objectives.

There are times when policies will need to be modified and frequently adjustments to one policy will require compensatory development in another policy. In this case, customer policy (customer/queue management) was not effective. A change to the system will be required and such change may require staffing policy to be modified.

It is worth noting at this point that at least two of the major supermarket chains are currently advertising on the basis of queue management, guaranteeing to provide additional check-out assistants should queues begin to form. This policy clearly requires an employment policy which includes contract flexibility and multi-skilling of all staff, such that any employee may be called (from the store-room, cashier's office, secretariat, etc.) at an instant's notice to operate a till. (See Chapter 8, Efficient staffing, for further discussion of flexibility, multi-skilling and empowerment.)

Customer care and the law

It is also essential to develop policies to ensure that the company continues to operate within the limits of current legislation:

- health
- safety
- security
- welfare

We have concentrated, so far, on the actions and responsibilities of managers and staff. Customer care has been presented very much in terms of a social if not moral expectation. In most circumstances customers should not have to resort to law to effect a reasonable service. However, should the need arise, customers do have the full protection of the law, not just in terms of trading standards and contractual obligations but also in respect of their health, safety, security and welfare. Managers must be aware of their responsibilities under the following Acts of Parliament:

Trades Description Act 1968
Deals with false or misleading statements.

Sale of Goods Act 1979
Deals with contractual obligations.

Price Marking (Food and Drink on Premises) Order 1979
Deals with pricing and display of prices.

Food and Drugs Act 1955
Food and Drugs (Control of Premises) Act 1976
Food Hygiene (General) Regulations 1970
The Food Safety Act 1990
All of the above deal with the quality, nature and fitness of food for human consumption.

Licensing Act 1964
Determines the permitted hours of opening, who may be served, and enables managers to deal with under-age drinking, drunkenness and undesirable behaviour which may impinge on customers' enjoyment of their meal.

Children's certificates for pubs enable children under 14 into the bar area. It has been suggested that this is not working; where police had turned a 'blind eye' under the existing legislation they are less likely to with the new. Landlords are required to satisfy the justices that the bar is 'suitable' for children. Interpretation of 'suitable' has varied in different parts of the country.

Clearly the decision to apply for a Children's Licence is a matter of policy. Are facilities already available (satisfactory) for children? What will have to be changed to comply with local justices' requirements (suitability)? Will increased revenue cover the cost of changes. Will children 'drive out' existing customers? Will parents be 'responsible'?

Under common law owners and occupiers of premises owe a duty of care to anyone – staff or customers – using their premises. This duty of care is further reinforced by the following:

Occupiers Liability Act 1957
Deals with fixtures and fittings and risk resulting from such as worn carpets.

Health and Safety at Work Act 1974
Deals with employees' and customers' exposure to risk.

Notification of Accidents and Dangerous Occurrences Regulations 1980
As with the Health and Safety at Work Act, while most managers will be aware of the implications for their employees few will appreciate that the law applies equally to customers.

Fire Precautions Act 1971
Deals with

- use of premises
- means of escape, width of doors and gangways
- fire resistant doors
- permitted surfaces, walls, ceilings and partitions
- fire alarm system
- emergency lighting, heat and smoke detectors
- number, type and location of fire fighting appliances
- provision of fire exit signs
- conduct of fire drills, testing and maintenance of alarms
- introduction and dissemination of fire evacuation procedures

Who is responsible for operational policy development?

Although operational policy can be designed and imposed from above it is much better when there is an element of design from within in order to meet effectively the broader company marketing, finance and personnel policies. Clearly leadership style will be a significant influence on the successful development and implementation of operational policy. Policy statements will include clear identification of responsibility and, where necessary, delegation and authority.

The food and beverage manager's role

The food and beverage manager will be responsible for planning, organizing, motivating and controlling according to policy requirements:

- Provision of facilities for a defined market.
- Systems of provision (modifying the operational cycle).
- Total customer satisfaction.

- Formulation, establishment and maintenance of control systems – to monitor costs, prices and sales – providing management information for performance reconciliation
  - budget targets
  - measuring performance
  - establishing causes of variance
  - rectifying discrepancies.
- Training, motivation and control of staff.
- Co-ordination of activities.

Policy development strategy

How is operational policy developed?

Policy will be developed in line with the current business environment and customer expectations. Decisions will be based on SWOT analysis (the identification of company strengths, weaknesses, opportunities and threats) and the clarification of company objectives. Once general strategy has been agreed then tactical detail may be refined, leading to the implementation of operational policies (see Figure 2.2).

Policy development
- Find the 'needs' of the external environment.
- Set up the operation in response to those needs.
- Needs mean change which creates pressure.
- Variability = variety = variance = potential for change (adaptability).
- Predictability means control.
- Limit undesirable variety – things not in your control.

The strategic planning process may be quite simple, or extremely complex, reflecting the size and scale of the business. However, whenever possible go for simplicity.

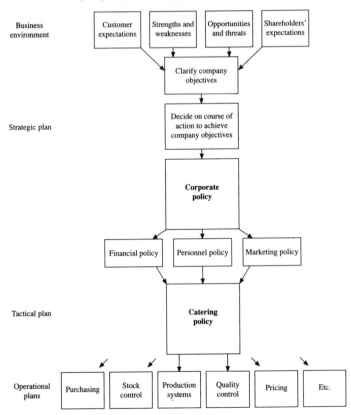

Figure 2.2 Developing operational policy: the difference between strategic, tactical and operational planning.

> **Example**
> A cafe owner's main aim may be to stay in business: a secondary aim will be to earn enough to provide a good living. This may be achieved by setting a few, simple targets such as GP percentage and sales revenue.
>
> For larger organizations the plan must be broken down under departmental and budgetary heads, but must still be understandable for all concerned.

For effective development and implementation of policy:

- know your market
- know your product and its strengths and weaknesses
- know your business patterns
- know your profit expectations
- know the opportunities and threats, particularly your competition

Developing the catering (operational) policy

First, produce a policy statement identifying the main aims and objectives of the operation. Such a statement may include:

- response to change (market/technology)
- increased efficiency/effectiveness
- reduced costs
- improved quality
- improved profitability
- improved market share

In addition there may well be some aims that are specific to an individual unit, e.g. 'to provide the best free entertainment in town'.

Second, define the procedure that will ensure the successful implementation of the policy. The following are important factors in ensuring success:

- more information (market/costs/profit)
- documentation
- more efficient purchasing
- standardization (products and procedures)
- staff development (delegation/responsibility/authority)
- job descriptions and personnel specifications
- more control

Finally set achievable targets for everyone in the organization; without targets we are unable to measure achievement, effectiveness or success.

As can be seen above, there is always a danger that when trying to identify and manage a system there is an over-concentration on those parts of the system that can be quantified and written down. Organisation charts, job titles and job descriptions do not improve organizations; encouraging communication and understanding does.

Policy and tradition – breaking the rules

Some of the more interesting operational policies have been introduced by people who have come to catering from other industries. The late Bob Payton developed several successful operations by breaking with 'British' tradition (American 'deep pan' pizza; Henry J. Bean's American Bars, and the Chicago Rib Shack with its bibs, finger bowls and American-style, round-tray service).

Julian Metcalfe and Sinclair Beecham knew nothing about catering but knew what they wanted as customers: the outcome was Prêt à Manger. Policies were developed from the customer back through the catering cycle. Attitudes, particularly those of suppliers, had to be changed. Product development was also a customer-centred activity: 'what materials do we need for this product?' rather than 'what products can we make from these materials?'. Because of the high standards and emphasis on production from fresh, there were high levels of wastage. Rather than modify product or process (quality) improved systems of forecasting were developed. Employment policy also broke with catering tradition, training and experience were considered unimportant, staff were selected on attitude and encouraged to become immediately involved in the company. Selection for both junior staff and managers involved working within the operation to gain the confidence and support of colleagues. Promotion is generally from within (again based very much on the support of colleagues) and staff benefit packages are designed not only to keep staff happy but also to develop the bond between employees and the company, targeting low staff turnover. Ownership and empowerment are seen to be the key to effective service.

When is operational policy implemented?

Policies are developed and implemented when we need to ensure consistency and reliability, in other words 'at every stage of the operational cycle'. Specific policies can be designed and implemented for particular elements within the system, e.g.:

● Health and safety policy
● Purchasing policy
● Employment policy

Or more general policies can be developed to ensure that particular concerns like company brand image/integrity, or the promotion of 'unique selling points' are re-enforced. Such activity might be prompted through marketing.

The main profit and cost centres

It was noted earlier that financial policy is one of three pillars on which catering and operational policy are built. All operations include within the catering cycle both cost and profit centres, e.g. procurement, preparation, processing, sales and service. The difference between operations lies in where each operation places its management emphasis. Which is the driving force of the operation, profit generation or cost control?

Policies may need to be modified in light of emerging economic conditions and socio-cultural change. Joining the EEC has caused some companies to modify policy both in line with European business ethics and in response to wider consumer opportunities.

Employment

It remains to be seen whether or not further changes will be imposed as a result of European legislation and, whether forced to or not, British companies respond to European (social) employment policies.

Operational policy tactics

Where can operational policy be used to gain competitive advantage?

First and foremost develop guidelines for training, motivation and commitment of staff. Because individual staff are involved at point of contact and because that point of contact is so critical to customer care, we have to be able to rely on staff skills and commitment to effect a successful transaction. The manager could not, nor indeed should not, be behind every interaction.

Second, the manager must be able to manage systems, procedures and products to support effectively point-of-sale staff. Therefore develop procedures in support of policy objectives.

Third, empower staff to make effective decisions concerning customer care. Empowerment is most effective when staff understand the constraints (policy) within which they are able to form their own decisions.

To deal effectively with staff training and motivation, systems, procedures and product management we must understand the full implications of the meal experience from the customers' viewpoint. Managers and staff using their own restaurant, and those of their competitors, need not be an extravagance. It probably costs little more than the more traditional 'back-of-house' feeding, but it is an essential and valuable aspect of customer understanding. Consider giving staff vouchers or allowances so that they may come in with family and friends and act, and be treated as, real customers. Encourage them, as customers, to observe and report on the quality of customer care provided by competitors.

With specific policies such as customer care policy, ensuring the quality of the meal experience is paramount.

Aims
- to understand why people eat away from home
- to understand influences on consumer meal preferences
- to consider the factors that contribute to a customer's enjoyment of a meal experience

The meal experience

Why do people eat away from home?
- convenience   (travellers/employees/students, etc.)
- variety   (need for change)
- labour   (someone else doing the work)
- status   (business lunch/impress friends)
- culture   (tradition – special occasions, weddings, etc.)
- impulse   (marketing – promotion – hunger)
- necessity   (hospital patients/prisoners/employees)

Eating away from home may be a matter of convenience – for travellers, workers and students – or it may be seen as a necessity. The implications for customer care are substantial. Catering for a captive audience – prisoners, hospital patients or workers on an oil rig – is often seen as being the least rewarding in terms of positive customer feedback.

Purchase of a meal may be on impulse or may be driven by the need for a change, leisure, convenience (someone else to cook and wash-up) or, when it comes to entertaining, status re-enforcement. In terms of the impulse purchase, consumer perception of the quality of experience and customer care will be influenced by our own promotional activity. If our operation is promoted as relaxed congenial atmosphere then this will be relatively easy to control, but control procedures must not impinge on the meal experience. Our customers may not respond to regimented service. When providing for consumers whose purchase is driven by status – business lunches or entertaining friends – then customer care is more difficult to manage. We now become part of our customers' image/alter ego, each must be treated differently.

An interesting example of customer care would be the example of the restaurant manager in a five star hotel who considered that recognition of the ladies who might accompany a certain 'noble gentleman' on his frequent visits to the establishment was critical of the quality of the meal experience. Where the lady was recognized as either a member of his Lordship's family or of suitable station in society then his Lordship was recognized with considerable flourish, he was seated in a prominent position and was addressed by his full title throughout the meal. However, should this particular Lord have chosen to dine with a female friend of dubious character then his lordship was recognized as Mr Smith and seated in a quiet corner with similarly unobtrusive service. Such tact could be commonly applied to a variety of public figures in all sorts of operations. For some customers it is, indeed, the essence of hospitality. Such operational activity may be impossible to write into policy documents!

Tradition and cultural background have a considerable influence on customer perceptions. Most hospitality operations are familiar with the nuances of the typical English wedding breakfast. Many managers have the necessary experience to handle a Bar Mitzvah well. Quite different perceptions of customer care might arise from a Greek or Moslem wedding. Ethnic and cultural concern should extend to seating and eating arrangements, such as the provision of finger bowls for symbolic hand washing, as well as to dietary requirements.

If we can predict consumer preferences we can more clearly define expectations and more effectively prepare consumer care programmes.

What influences consumer preferences?

Consumer preference can be influenced by a variety of factors including:

- choice available
- individual likes and dislikes

- influence of promotions and advertising
- recommendations of other customers
- customers' personal attributes: age, spending power, cultural/ethnic background

Not only will customers' expectations be influenced by age, spending power and cultural background but within such groupings they will be further influenced by time of day, reason for eating out and type of meal required. For instance, whereas Chinese and Indian meals are quite popular with typical Anglo-Saxons it would be unusual for either to be taken as a lunch, although particular dishes might be modified to make quite acceptable bar snacks, e.g. curry.

If it is difficult to define needs, expectations and preferences can we at least identify the principal factors that contribute to enjoyment or dissatisfaction with a meal experience?

What are the barriers to satisfaction?

- queuing
- ignorance
- rudeness
- indifference

Once again it is possible to see how social or cultural background can influence perceptions. It could be argued that queuing is a particularly British trait and therefore acceptable. Struggling to a packed bar at a discotheque may be quite acceptable, being ignored while bar staff chat to their friends is not. If queues are unavoidable, the problem may be alleviated to some extent by providing the customer with something to do.

For example
- provide menus to read
- circulate wine lists
- take orders
- provide promotional material
- have newspapers available
- provide entertainment, e.g. buskers
- get all staff to use social skills – talk to their customers

Whilst in most circumstances customers find staff's lack of knowledge about their products infuriating we often tend to accept ignorance in a fast food operation, where products are standardized and reasonably well known by the customers. There are no circumstances however where rudeness and indifference can be tolerated.

Quality of products and services

While all managers will be aware of the need for vigilant inspection of linen, cutlery, crockery and glassware in regard to cleanliness and hygiene, all too often egg-stained forks, torn serviettes, chipped plates and lipstick-stained glasses escape the notice of staff and managers to be discovered by the customer. This more than anything else is likely to develop in the customer's mind a notion of the level of care that they are receiving. The sort of attention to detail should extend beyond those small items of equipment that the customer might handle to the whole fabric of the building. The condition of curtains, wallpaper and paintwork will influence customer perceptions, as will lighting (bulbs not working or shades missing) and heating (or lack of it). Customers will not fail to note the state of toilets which can be as responsible for loss of business as the food or service. Many managers will recognize the need to provide toilets for the disabled and baby changing facilities. I have only ever seen one restaurant that felt the need to extend baby changing facilities to the male toilets. A meal out is often a treat for overworked mums, but how often are they left literally holding the baby because facilities, if provided at all, are restricted to the ladies' room.

Above all customers will perceive 'care' as being derived from the staff. Many a meal experience is made or lost on the actions of an individual member of the team. Customers return time and again to places where they are looked after. There are hotels where academic and technical knowledge and craft skills are almost non-existent. Yet the place is packed with customers because the manager knows them well, takes the trouble to talk to them and is prepared to 'bend the rules' to suit individual needs. Managers may be perceived as officious, particularly where nice helpful staff have to go to the manager to resolve a customer complaint and the manager deals with the problem in a mechanistic, rule-bound, impersonal way.

Dress, manner and personal hygiene of staff will contribute to customer perceptions. Uniforms not only set a standard but also help to define roles and responsibilities for the customer.

Finally it should not be forgotten that perceptions of quality and care are directly, although not proportionately, influenced by price. Whereas we expect extra care for paying more, we do not accept carelessness when paying less.

Policy for handling complaints

Customer complaints are often taken as a negative issue. Complaints should be treated positively – dealt with sympathetically and resolved quickly – even encouraged. Detail – cause, effect and response – should be accurately recorded. A complaints analysis database provides a valuable source of market information and consequently identifies opportunities for continuing improvement and greater customer satisfaction.

We have to ask why Marks & Spencer are retail market leaders. It must have something to do with high levels of consistent product quality, but also high levels of customer confidence based on the knowledge that recompense is quickly and simply achieved in the event of any product failing to satisfy.

Customer satisfaction

Looking more positively, what is it that contributes to customer enjoyment of the meal experience?

● the ambience
● the service
● the food
● facilities
● hygiene
● staff
    – friendly and responsive
    – competent and willing to serve
● novelty and ingenuity
● price, quality, value

In that customers' perceptions and anticipation of satisfaction will be formed prior to or on arrival at our establishment, the ambience, including promotional material, is critical to a successful event. Most people feel safest and most comfortable at home. We need to portray and provide a home from home environment, we need to be warm and welcoming. Overdoing the decor can, in certain circumstances be counter-productive. Too much affluence can put the consumer at a disadvantage. Similarly lighting; there is a difference between seductive lighting and trying to eat a meal in almost total darkness.

There was a time when air conditioning would have been considered an unnecessary extravagance in a temperate climate like ours. Now maintaining a steady temperature of 'clean' fresh air is considered desirable.

Furnishing, particularly seating, affects the meal experience. There is considerable evidence to suggest the style of seating affects the length of stay. Fast food restaurants often provide seats which slope forward, preventing customers from sitting back and relaxing. Deep chairs with arm rests are seen in few restaurants, typically only those whose prices reflect the fact that their customers are going to be encouraged to linger over their meal.

Acoustics and noise levels are another influence on enjoyment. Often music is used to define the theme, but sometimes it can be overdone and obtrusive. Inappropriate choice of music, volume and, in particular, sound systems that cannot cope can do considerable harm. It should be noted at this point that there is considerable growth in the 'rock-cafe' market where the entertainment, singing waiters and juggling bar staff, is the main part of the meal experience and the food plays a relatively minor role.

As a final point, but one of great concern, the last major influence on the ambience of an establishment is its customers. The decision to decline someone's custom may be based on the fact that either they will find our existing customers unacceptable or our present customers would be made uncomfortable by our new arrivals. For this reason many caterers have rules about pets, children or dress codes. It is not the purpose of this book to get into the political issues of race or sex, but it must be recognized that under certain circumstances, a gentlemen's club for instance, there is a particular design feature influencing customer care that the caterer should have little argument with. The caterer may be placed in great difficulty when so-called public areas become popular with a particular fraternity. It may be argued in these circumstances that customer care may best be achieved by advising someone of a different venue that may be more suited to their needs.

Customer care policy

Developing a customer care programme
- identify needs and expectations
- plan system of delivery (identify care controls)
- identify responsibility and authority
- define standards
- train and motivate staff
- test the system
- implement the system
- monitor performance – customer reaction
- obtain and react on customer feedback

Customer care programmes

It is apparent that although many companies have very clear guidelines about products, processes and procedures many of their customers remain unhappy with the service that they receive. Conversely, customers may speak very highly of some operations that have no identifiable quality control system. What is it that makes the difference between the local 'chippy' whose untrained staff manage to produce the 'the best cod and chips' in the area and the local four star hotel who, complete with job descriptions, product standards and training programmes, may be described as 'all right if you like that sort of thing'?

Of prime importance in understanding customer care is the realization that it is not the sole responsibility of the members of staff involved in the customer contact to ensure customer satisfaction. Customer care is the responsibility of everyone in the organization. Indeed we all have our customers; the waiter is the customer of the chef who is in turn a customer of the control clerk who relies on service from the store person and so on.

Developing understanding and total commitment to customer care is a management responsibility.

Customer care philosophy

Customer care is all about meeting customer expectations: staff attitudes and behaviour are critical. The point of sale impact relies on helpful friendly service, explaining products and service to the customer, making sure we understand their needs and expectations.

When a customer in a hotel lounge asks for a pot of coffee it should not matter whether the member of staff that responds to that request is a receptionist, hall porter or chambermaid. Nor should it matter who delivers the product. It would perhaps be preferable for the lounge waiter, who has the necessary skills, to serve the coffee. But for the customer, who may just have returned from sightseeing or shopping and who is probably cold and/or tired, they do not want the problems of the system explained to them: It's not my job; the lounge waiter is off 'til three; we only serve tea in the afternoon; the manager has the keys to the stillroom and he is busy; only the chef knows how to work the coffee machine.

To the customer, systems and procedures are irrelevant. If something goes wrong customers don't have to understand, nor are they interested in, the system – but they will want to know what is going on and what is being done to resolve the problem.

My family once dined in a popular pizza restaurant. The original welcome was superb and our order was taken in an efficient and friendly way. The main meal was delivered effectively and mid-way through we were asked, in the usual fashion, if everything was to our satisfaction. Everything fine so far, system working well, but then our waitress disappeared. We waited and waited for dessert, several other staff could see, and apparently understood our predicament, but we were not 'their' customers. Eventually one member of staff asked if they could help. We asked to speak to the manager and were told he would be with us shortly. I had observed what was obviously the manager – he appeared to be interviewing a prospective member of staff. We waited, and waited. By now all the staff in the restaurant were aware that something was wrong and several made a point of asking if they could help. We were adamant now, we would only speak to the manager. The wait continued, the prospective employee was shown around the kitchen, forms were filled in. Eventually the manager approached. His customer skills were very good, we were offered coffee, he crouched by the table to effect better eye contact, he discussed the problem in a caring and sympathetic way and apologized, explaining that our waitress had come to the end of her shift. Perhaps other customers would have got more angry, or left or argued about the bill. Perhaps my knowledge of the industry enabled me to 'see' a little more than the average customer. The moral of this story is simple. This restaurant had practically everything right, there were systems and control procedures, staff and managers were well trained and had good customer skills. It would appear that with a shift system in operation staff had reasonable working conditions but apparently nobody had planned for staff coming to the end of their shift and leaving customers mid-way through a meal.

Many people dislike and mistrust catch phrases. There can be little benefit in saying 'Have a nice day' if there is no genuine care. Yet catch phrases do have their place. One of the most useful must be 'How can I help you?'. Note the use of Kipling technique to elicit response; it needs an answer which identifies needs, in contrast with 'Can I help you?' which normally elicits a yes/no response, which is not helpful.

Customers must be communicated with in a manner that promotes goodwill and understanding. They should be encouraged to discuss their requirements. Requests falling outside our own area must be referred quickly and effectively. We must ensure that all relevant information is accurately recorded in a suitable format and made available to appropriate people. Essentially the rule is: treat others as you would wish to be treated.

The quality of care in communication is considerably influenced by the stake which individual members of staff have in the company. This does not have to be financial investment, but staff do have to feel that they play a significant part in the success of the company. That sense of belonging is naturally transferred to customer transactions. Staff should be encouraged to work as part of a family welcoming customers, like family friends, into their 'home'.

It is perhaps useful at this point to differentiate between customers and consumers. Often the two definitions are interchangeable and either expression may be used. But on some points it is necessary to be more specific about these terms. In order to provide customer care it is necessary to attend to the needs of the consumer (person receiving product or service) as well as the needs of the customer (person paying the bill). This can provide opportunities for conflict in certain circumstances. Persuading the groom's family that you do not serve triple measures of spirits while the bride's father is paying for the 'free' bar is bound to lead to some disappointment.

Summary

We have considered the importance of policy development. Whilst recognizing the importance of the foundations of policy – finance, personnel, marketing – we have concentrated primarily on the development of operational policy for obvious reasons. So far, much has been made of the problems and pitfalls of policy development. No prescriptive answers can be given because every operation will have a different customer mix requiring varying emphasis on different aspects of policy development. However, it is possible to provide a guide to the preparation and implementation of operational policies.

Policy is primarily the development of strategy which gives rise to tactical activities.

Some generalized examples have been provided and the importance of staff involvement has been recognized. For staff to be involved and, more importantly, committed, it is necessary for policies to be reflected in management philosophy. Senior management provide structure, policies provide the guidelines and unit managers will need to implement procedures in support of policies. Such procedural activity may be supported by documentation and manuals, but should not become mechanistic.

Policy is not an excuse, *'I'm sorry madam, but it's company policy!'*, e.g. not my fault!

Do not attempt to explain policy to customers; if it is designed on their behalf then it should be self-evident. If you have to explain your policy to your customers then it is almost certainly not meeting their needs, in which case either (a) your policy is wrong (motives wrong), or (b) you are in the wrong market (attracting the wrong customers, sending the wrong message).

It is no accident that most space was given to discussion of customer care policy. Ideally all other policies, even those that appear to result from the imposition of legislation, should be geared towards the management of customer satisfaction. Performance can not be improved in the absence of concern for our customers.

Think like customers, see your operation through your customers' eyes and develop policies which effectively deliver products and services which meet their needs.

Suggested additional reading

Cracknell, H.L., Kaufmann, R.J. and Nobis, G. (1987) *Practical Professional Catering.* Macmillan.

Davis, B. and Lockwood, A. (1994) *Food and Beverage Management: A selection of readings.* Butterworth–Heinemann.

Jones, P. (ed.) (1989) *Management in the Service Industries.* Pitman.

Venison, P. (1990) *Managing Hotels.* Butterworth–Heinemann.

3
Marketing

Aims and objectives

The marketing function is surrounded by a good deal of mystique and, not unnaturally, considerable confusion. Is it selling, advertising or research?

The following definition is provided by the Institute of Marketing:

> 'The management process responsible for identifying, anticipating and satisfying customer requirements profitably.'

Although this definition refers to 'profit', marketing activity is not restricted to commercial operations. While the simple solution might to remove the word 'profitably' from the definition above, it is important to recognize that marketing cannot be effective if it does not relate in some way to costs and revenue. An alternative definition might therefore be:

> 'The management process responsible for identifying, anticipating and satisfying customer requirements in the most cost effective manner.'

In effect the aims and objectives of marketing are quite simple. The function of marketing is to recognize the effects of the business environment, identify opportunities and communicate operational responses. It requires an understanding of economics, sociology and psychology as well as technical/industrial knowledge. In effect marketing is self and environmental examination, diagnosis, prescription and treatment for the continuing health of the operation. Successful operations will be skilled in adapting to circumstances, ever-changing market needs and customer expectations.

What is marketing?

The purpose of marketing

Simply put, the purpose of marketing is to recognize and meet consumer wants and needs. More specifically marketing activity will aim to:

- evaluate and select market segments to be served
- select product and service attributes, tailored to customer needs
- set prices (which may be influenced by cost, competition, market)
- determine availability of products and services on offer
- design internal and external communication systems, in order to:
  - encourage enquiries
  - create awareness
  - persuade
  - remind

The function of marketing then is to invest in time and personnel in order to identify target groups and determine their needs, expectations and spending power (see Figure 3.1). This then enables further investment (time/personnel) in the design of products, processes and procedures to meet customer needs. Having done all this we now need to tell all concerned – suppliers, employees and prospective customers

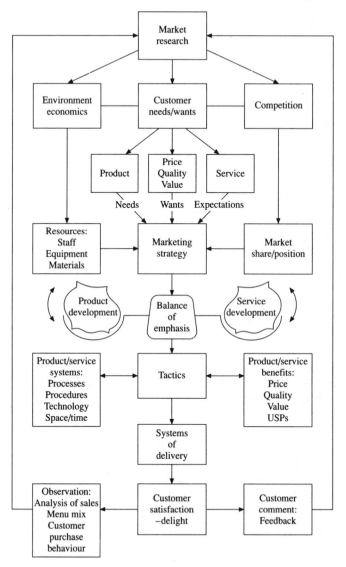

Figure 3.1 The marketing function.

– who we are, what we do, why we have developed the products and services in the way we have, where and when these products and services are available and how much they will cost.

Marketing is identifying customer
- needs, wants and expectations
- income and spending power
- frequency of use of catering establishments
- levels of demand for particular products and/or services and then developing and managing catering responses:
- products and services (design and attributes)
- communications, what is on offer, where, when, how much
- promotion, advertising and selling
- efficient, effective and economic use of resources
- adaptability, flexibility, response to change, without compromising policy or image

---

Some problems associated with marketing food and beverages

This process of identifying customer needs and catering responses tends to quickly highlight problems, particularly the potential conflict between different elements of production and service delivery: the need, for instance, to invest in quality versus the demand to keep prices low. Fortunately, an understanding of marketing may result in the recognition of potential solutions.

Potential problems/solutions
- product orientation (tradition) versus market orientation
- what are we selling, and why
- the impact of communications
- operational size

Product orientation (tradition) versus market orientation

Traditionally catering tends to be product focused. Management activity is centred on the control of costs and quality in the hope that if we maintain standards, customers – prepared to pay any price we set – will beat a path to our door. Unfortunately the world has moved on and customers will tend to pass the 'traditional' operation by. That is not to say that tradition is dead; it will be possible to identify segments of the market that still demand traditional service and may be prepared to pay a premium price. But production methods and service style must be a response to market demand, not an imposition on consumers.

Caterers must be more responsive to the market which will be increasingly more price conscious. Their needs will change and these 'trends' are usually identifiable. Operational managers must be more responsive to these developments, particularly as the pace of change seems to increase with each passing year.

What are we selling, and why?

Frequently we are confused in regard to what it is we are actually selling. We have become more conscious of what is generally referred to as the 'meal experience', the notion that we are not selling food and drink but an occasion, of which food and drink is just a part. In some respects we are selling an illusion. That is not to say that we are being deliberately deceptive but that what we are selling is an abstract idea capable of being seen differently by different individuals. Marketing has always recognized that every product carries a degree of illusion:

'Revlon sell hope, not cosmetics.'

Charles Revlon

But, at the end of the day, every product comprises something that is tangible which remains even if the illusion disappears. So we can employ standard marketing practice to the dishes, food and drink that we sell.

A more substantial problem arises with the marketing of services, which are considerably more illusive as a concept. Because service is entirely dependent on human activity and attitude, specifically the relationship (reaction) between two or more individuals, it will never be exactly the same on each occasion. We can try to standardize using 'roles and scripts' (discussed in more detail in Chapter 5, Quality), but even if we could 'clone' each member of staff we could not do the same for our customers. We are therefore limited in one aspect of marketing services, namely the 'description' of what is on offer. Even if we were able to describe the objectives of our service provision these are subject to the pressures of demand. There is good reason why service on a Saturday night is not the same as that for a Thursday lunch, and in all probability our customers would not wish it to be. Our customers suffer further limitations in that even if they understand what it is we are offering they never actually get to own it and have nothing left to show after the event, which makes pricing of the service element of the experience problematic.

Problems of service marketing
- tangibility
- ownership
- justification of price
- perishability
- standardization
- inseparability
- quality control
- managing demand

It has been argued that marketing services is not the same as marketing products, particularly in regard to tangibility and ownership. It would be nice to be able to market our products and services separately, but as we do not usually provide products and services separately there would seem little point. However, it would be useful to know whether customer motivation is product- or service-centred in order that we might focus our 'message' appropriately.

The impact of communications

For many producers marketing communication is always indirect, media advertising. The hospitality industry is unique in its direct customer/producer contact and this should be used as a positive marketing advantage. The benefits of direct communication should not be underestimated. The impact of social skills and attitudes may provide significant advantage. However, for every positive there is usually a negative, often equally significant, as is the case with direct communication. If the social skills or attitudes of our staff are in any way suspect, even if it is just an 'off day', this will quickly be communicated to our customers.

There are potentially four reasons why customers stop patronising a restaurant:

- they die, move away, or develop new interests and/or friends — approx. 10%
- the competition offers greater appeal — approx. 10%
- dissatisfaction with products or physical attributes — approx. 15%
- indifference or apathy by one or more employees — approx. 65%

Not only will these customers be lost, but if they are unhappy they are likely to tell at least ten friends. Had they been satisfied, statistics suggest that they might only tell three.

This has long been recognized as the 'Achilles heal' of the hospitality industry and yet we seem to do so little about it. No other modern industry would allow its greatest asset (people) to be its greatest weakness. We have to recognize that some of the hostility/inhospitality that our customers experience results from 'careless' employment and poor personnel management. Fostering a positive attitude in the service staff is the best form of marketing activity. The marketing budget should provide for investment in staffing, staff training and motivation. Explain the business aims and objectives, recognize staff contribution and encourage them to become more involved.

Staff involvement in marketing activities

- with your customers, seeking out needs and wants that can be fulfilled
- with the business, selling items that please consumers and make a profit
- with products and services, participating in design and development, testing, tasting and quality assurance

Operational size

The hospitality industry consists primarily of small (independent) units. It is frequently argued, that as a small independent operator, we really are unable to get involved with marketing. This attitude is normally based on the perception that research and particularly advertising are expensive. As was suggested at the beginning of this chapter, it is important to manage marketing costs in relation to revenue earned as a result of marketing activity. Marketing may require an initial 'pump priming' investment but once up and running marketing activity should, quite literally, be self-financing.

Good marketing does not mean national TV campaigns (see Figure 3.2). A small, single-unit operation will gather local statistics, communicate with local consumers and provide products and services most suited to the local community. Much of this activity will be 'word of mouth' and effectively free. It is worth noting at this point that some of the most successful 'brands' started out as small operations that were successfully marketed. The current trend appears to be for the larger organizations, particularly the breweries, to identify and buy up these smaller operations so that they may build on their marketing success and incorporate the 'brand' into their own operations on a national scale.

Why is marketing important?

The origins of hospitality as an industry can be traced at least as far back as the dawning of travel and transportation. Ever since the Romans refined the art of road building there has been a need for 'service areas' as may be evidenced by coaching inns. The provision of food and drink was developed in support of travelling and accommodation. For travellers the practice was that the coach would arrive at a particular hostelry, horses would be stabled and the

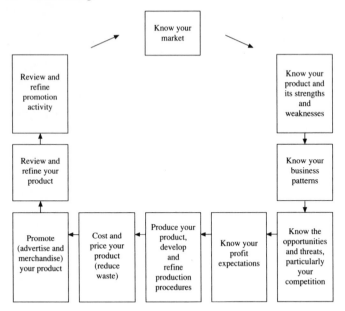

Figure 3.2 Basic marketing activity

passengers would be invited to eat from the host's table (table d'hôte). There was little choice, take it or leave it, and of course nowhere else to go so no competition and little need for marketing.

The industry is considerably different today; there are few caterers who deal with a truly 'captive' market and even they know only too well the influence of choice on customer satisfaction. Understanding our customers' needs, wants and expectations (and where applicable the strength of our competition) is a key to running a successful operation.

It has been said that an army marches on its stomach. Such an army is divided into various specialities that enable strategic objectives to be met. The engineers, for instance, construct bridges which enable the passage of troops and resources to the front. Marketing may be likened to the intelligence service, gathering and analysing detail (enemy strength, terrain, resources, etc.) and disseminating the resulting information to the relevant troop commanders (when, where and how to position their troops).

Marketing provides us with valuable information (intelligence). Typically, current statistics suggest that 20 per cent of customers account for 80 per cent of the business and that dining out in the evening is generally twice as popular as eating out during the day. For 'English' restaurants the ratio (evening to day) is closer to 4:3, for Chinese and Indian the ratio increases to 4:1 and 5:1 respectively. Hamburger restaurants are an exception where the relationship is reversed at 2:5. Managers will need to use market intelligence to develop business plans. Many will make use of a rolling plan (typically five years) which is adaptable; product/service planning may be modified in response to changes in the market, local/national economy and/or technology. Internal statistics such as menu mix and product life cycle should be compared to national and local standards. Business patterns, ideally based on charts and graphs, will demonstrate the current position of the business and its potential opportunities.

Charting business patterns
- volumes, of cash, products and customers
- food sales
- beverage sales
- 'special' business
- average spend per cover (ASP)
- percentages and ratios

Marketing – corporate culture, management activity or management tool?

The culture of the organization, its management style and employee involvement/empowerment will have a significant influence on the effectiveness of marketing activity. A market oriented culture will be customer centred, treating everyone involved in the operation – supply, production and service staff – as internal customers. (See Chapter 5, Quality, for further discussion on the principle of internal customers.)

Marketing activity will be devoted to the gathering and analysis of data. Management activity will provide an historical view of performance: where have we been and where are we now? This gives rise to the obvious question, where do we want to be and how are we going to get there?

The 4Ps:
- Product: Brand, quality, choice
- Price: Price, discounts, differentiation, terms
             Pricing methods (competitive, marginal, discounts, etc.)
             (see Chapter 6, Product development, for more detail)
- Place: Location, accessibility, transportation (geography)
             Retail marketing often makes reference to distribution channels; while these are not relevant to many caterers they do become more relevant with the application of centralized production.
- Promotion: Advertising, selling, publicity, PR
             Merchandising and personal selling
             Information, communication, persuasion

The marketing mix, commonly known as the 4Ps (product, price, place and promotion), is the basis of marketing activity. Its importance lies in the way in which it focuses attention on the core activities and in consequence provides opportunities for the use of marketing as a management tool.

Although the 4Ps are generally recognized as being the main components of the marketing mix we might, additionally, consider the importance of ESP. Not so much extra-sensory perception (although some would have us believe that is the way that marketing is really done), but the relevance of the environment, systems and people.

Environment: facilities, furniture, fittings, design
Systems: procedures, processes, technology, mechanisation, customer participation
People: staff (attitude, training, commitment), appearance, social skills

The operational environment provides tangible evidence of the organization's 'attitude' and represents an important influence on customer perceptions and judgement. System procedures and processes give rise to levels of efficiency and effectiveness and may well provide competitive marketing advantage. Staff are a major influence on the consumers' buying decision (perceptions of service quality), therefore marketing becomes involved in recruitment and staff development particularly through the principle of internal customers.

Who is involved in marketing?

It should be clear, from comments already made, that nobody can be excluded from marketing activity. While for some operations there may be a marketing department and/or a sales team, this should not be taken to mean that responsibility is isolated in those areas.

Marketing department

The benefits of having a marketing department are that it provides the opportunity to employ specialist knowledge and skills. It also assumes that time is set aside for marketing activity and that the process can be carried out in the absence of normal catering pressures. Although the provision of adequate time may be seen as desirable, taking the marketing function away from 'live' customer activity is less advantageous. Marketing is relatively new to the catering industry and consequently marketing departments are often staffed by people with a general hospitality background and little specific marketing expertise. It is right to criticize such practice, however there is much to be gained by adding practical experience to marketing expertise. The marketing team should spend some time, on a regular basis, on the shop floor. Conversely, appointments to marketing management should be made from the shop floor, but such appointments should be supported by the provision of further training, education and marketing qualifications.

Sales department

The presence of a sales department is also desirable, but much of the argument above can be directed also at sales teams. In particular many sales teams might be accused of placing too much emphasis on selling what we've got rather than finding out what our customers need.

Food and beverage manager

The food and beverage manager's role is to ensure that all activities, including marketing and selling, are co-ordinated, working towards clearly defined objectives and successful in their outcome. The food and beverage manager will need to ensure that customer details and sales records (marketing data) are effectively recorded. The manager will also need to direct marketing attention to specific areas or aspects of the operation. In particular the manager will need to direct, monitor and appraise all staff in the department.

Staff

It should be clear by now that staff may be seen as the key to marketing success. Good marketing does not happen without the co-operation of committed staff. Good marketing can still take place in the absence of both a marketing department and a sales team so long as shop floor staff are well advised and fully involved in marketing activity. The special strength of the ordinary member of staff is their direct contact with 'live' customers. The essence of good marketing practice is listening. Marketing is inevitably associated with quality (meeting customer needs); marketing and quality both provide a genuine opportunity for employee participation. The principle of 'quality circles' or what Holiday Inns refer to as 'service chains' is ideally suited to the development of marketing activity.

Customers

Marketing is ultimately concerned with listening and responding to customers. A variety of methods and procedures for 'listening' will be discussed, under the heading of research.

Marketing strategy

How is marketing activity developed and implemented?

Market research – SWOT analysis

In order to provide products and services that meet the needs and expectations of our customers we need to understand something about the marketplace in which we are competing. We need to know the number and type of customers to expect, the amount they are likely to spend and what sort of products and services they are looking for. We also need to know something of the competition we might expect. The SWOT analysis can be used to summarize the results of our research and consequently help us to compete more effectively. SWOT stands for strengths, weaknesses, opportunities and threats, the aim being to work to our strengths in those areas that offer greatest opportunity. However, we should not be foolish enough to overlook our weaknesses or ignore possible threats.

Strengths:
- popular products
- good service, fast service
- good price, good value
- nice staff, skilled staff
- good reputation
- well known brand
- unique selling points (USPs)

Weaknesses:
- poor product range, choice
- slow service
- poor parking
- high price, low value
- unskilled staff, bad attitude

Opportunities:
- growth potential
- open market
- improvements in efficiency
- technology

Threats:
- limited growth
- narrow, competive market
- increasing costs, resources
- inflexible systems

- competitive pricing
- niche markets
- limited supply of resources
- limited supply of funds

Market research may be used in both problem solving and planning activities.

The function of market research is to identify:
- type, size, location of market
- pattern of current demand
- size and segmentation of market
- customer profile, needs and wants
- strengths and weaknesses of products and services
- opportunities and threats, trends and competition
- effectiveness of marketing, advertising/promotional activity
- identification of gaps, potential for creating new demand

Research (market study)

Market study research may be defined as the collection and analysis of data, published or unpublished material and/or the observation and recording of our own data.

Customer profile may be based on age, sex, occupation and/or socio-economic grouping. We will also be interested in consumer purchase behaviour, their willingness to spend, their home and lifestyle and in particular their familiarity with the industry, attitude toward other guests and reasons for eating out. Understanding the size of the market and position in relation to competition (leader or follower) will be important in determining market strategy. Research should identify advertising opportunities and suggest techniques for exposure. One of the more important aspects of market research is the identification of 'gaps' in the market (see

Figure 3.3). Plotting product attributes (customer needs, wants and expectations) on a chart such as this can be useful in identifying new opportunities, although care must be taken with the assumptions.

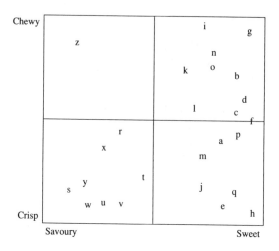

Figure 3.3 Identifying gaps in the market. a, KitKat; b, Mars Bar; c, Twix; d, Snickers, e, Maltesers; f, Creme Eggs; g, caramel toffee; h, nut brittle; i, Wrigleys Gum; j, Polos; k, Fruit Pastilles; l, Trebor Soft Mints; m, Extra Strong Mints; n, Wine Gums; o, Opal fruits; p, Werther's Originals; q, Dime Bar; r, Quavers; s, salted peanuts; t, assorted fruit and nuts; u, potato crisps (flavoured); v, potato crisps (Salt'n'shake); w, Pringles; x, Cheese Wotsits; y, Hula Hoops; z, Peperami. Although analysis suggests a particular gap (savoury chews), it is unlikely that 'pizza flavoured toffees' would meet with much success.

Sources of market information

Market study resource information may be primary or secondary. Secondary sources may be further divided into internal and external data.

Field research (primary) original source data
- observation
- consumer interview (personal, phone)
- guest questionnaires, comment cards

Desk research (secondary) available data/statistics
Internal:
- occupancy
- average spend per customer (ASP)
- preferences (menu mix/sales history)
- sources of business (bookings/accounts)
- departmental performance/effectiveness
- personnel (individual) performance/effectiveness

External:

• press (local/national/trade	statistics, innovation
• national/local government	government departments, town hall (planning and development) road building, car parks, shopping malls, etc.
• trade/professional associations	industry/sector knowledge, pay scales, etc.
• consultants, researchers and tourist authorities	trend, demand
• maps and surveys	geography (catchment areas), demographics
• guide books	competition

Is it possible to link actual business with marketing activity?

Recently, when looking to purchase some computer software through mail order, I was intrigued to discover what I thought was a mistake in the address of the company I was using. The address that I had originally copied from one magazine was quoted differently in another magazine. It differed in only one respect, that of the post box (PO) reference. The conclusion is that this is a very simple but certainly very effective form of measuring marketing effectiveness. Not only does it distinguish immediately between different magazines, but subtle adjustments may be made to style and positioning of advertising in one magazine and the effectiveness can then be isolated and measured. This is clearly very effective for mail order operations: can anything be learned for the catering industry?

Hotels generally have a large market area and are therefore inclined to rely on marketing at a distance utilizing a variety of strategies. If a hotel were to use a different PO box number, especially for direct mail (brochures, etc.) as opposed to more general advertising in publications, it would quickly be able to differentiate between the effectiveness of each. Restaurants, on the other hand, generally deal with a smaller, more localized, market. However, several newspapers may be used and it might be beneficial to differentiate between responses from each. Similarly it may be useful to collect guest 'postal' data. When taking bookings it is common to ask for a phone number, why not also ask for the guest's postcode? Analysis of such data would enable the restaurateur to pinpoint the source of most custom. Marketing could then be more effectively targeted.

Market research then is the collection, recording and analysis of financial/statistical data assessing:

(a) customer needs and wants
(b) market source
(c) competition

Study of customer needs and wants

● discussion (nominal group)	invited group, representative of target market
● questionnaire (new customers) and post purchase (existing customers)	clear questions, free of bias, opinion, motive yes/no, multi-choice, filter questions
● research interviews	clear objectives, structured, probing
● telephone research	simple, short answer questions, select group
● desk research and observation	analysis of available information

---

Analysis of market source

● catchment area	driving distance (20–30 minutes), public transport
● natural or man made barriers	island or coastal resort, city parking problems
● competition	positive benefits
● other activities	theatres, shopping, leisure pursuits, etc.
● assessment of traffic flow	potential trade
● evaluation of spending power	disposable income

Analysis of competition
- market share/position
- leader/follower
- type (similarity)
- location (access)
- innovation (differentiation)

Most marketing activity is directed at customer analysis, differentiating customers by category:

- business customers
- conference delegates
- tourists (national/international)
- local residents

Further, more detailed analysis may provide more specific information.

Analysis of customers by
- user type (products/services)
- time (morning/evening)
- frequency
- value (ASP)
- attitude (relationship with you, e.g. first choice)

Use is frequently made of specialist consumer research. Although this information is available to all, its analysis (interpretation) requires care in regard to its relative significance to a particular operational context. Most people are familiar with the 'traditional' standard market classification, although many question its validity in modern society. Alternatives, such as ACORN, are also available but need to be used with equal caution.

Standard market classification

A	upper middle	higher managerial and administration
B	middle	intermediate professional
C1	lower middle	supervisory
C2	skilled worker	manual
D	working	semi-skilled or unskilled
E	lowest level of subsistence	casual, unemployed, pensioner, etc.

ACORN (a classification of residential neighbourhoods)
Draws a relationship between where people live, their possible lifestyle and likely purchase behaviour.

A	agricultural area
B	modern, high-income, family housing
C	older housing of intermediate status
D	poor-quality terraced housing
E	better-off council estates
F	less well-off council estates
G	poorest council estates
H	multi-racial area
I	high-status, non-family area
J	affluent suburban housing
K	better off retirement area

In order to be effective market research needs to be structured. Typical procedure might take the following form:

- identify problem/objective
- determine information needed
- decide on process/method (quality/accuracy of data/results)
- design customer profile, sample size
- pilot test and evaluate

- modify process
- implement research programme
- analyse data
- complete report recommendations

As a rule we would expect a certain outcome from market research. Whilst we may not be able to predict the specific content until results have been published, we would expect the answers to some more general (Kipling) questions.

The anticipated outcome of market research
- Who are our guests?
- Where do our guests come from?
- Why did they choose to eat here?
- How did they find out about us? How did they travel (get here)?
- What is their average spend? What are their preferences?
- When did they make their booking? When will they return?

The answers to such questions will provide the basis for planning activity.

Marketing plans

The development of a marketing plan involves the management process of organizing people, time and resources in order to enable effective research, product/service development and availability (distribution/advertising).

> **Marketing plan**
> ● set objectives
> ● research market
> ● develop products/services
> ● calculate costs, set price
> ● communicate offer

The marketing plan will determine objectives and either set policy or itself be developed within a wider policy framework. Plans for products, prices, promotions and profit should be precise, specific, quantifiable, relevant, realistic, achievable and measurable (e.g. to increase ASP for weekend evening meals by 10 per cent). A marketing plan should be based on the most cost effective means of generating business in light of customer profile and motivation, buyer behaviour, and social/environmental conditions.

It might be useful to have a marketing calendar identifying not only objectives and target dates, to avoid clashes (time and resources), but also 'ownership' and responsibility (see Figure 3.4).

Kipling's marketing calendar

Day/date	What *Marketing activity*	How *Marketing strategy*	Who *Ownership authority and staff responsibility*	Where *Which departments are involved*	When *Start and finish dates*	Why *Justification operational objectives*	Review/comment
January 1st							
2nd							
3rd							
4th							
5th							
etc.							

Figure 3.4 Marketing (plan) calendar.

Marketing plans should also identify controls (are we achieving our original objectives?) and procedures for monitoring customer satisfaction and financial results.

When is marketing implemented?

Marketing should be applied constantly and consistently at every stage of the operation. Marketing activity may not always be obviously visible; the most easily identifiable elements would be:

1   Measuring current performance.
2   Product/service development.
3   Promotion and advertising.
4   Predicting and managing future demand.

Assessing current operational performance (levels of customer satisfaction)

The use of guest questionnaires is the subject of some debate. Most doubt about the effectiveness of guest questionnaires is related to their construction. Generally accepted content includes:

● guest details – optional (useful for further marketing activity but may dissuade the consumer from replying)
● research questions
● control questions

Questions should ideally be logical and sequential, easy to understand and free of calculations. Forms should be simple to complete and enable a precise answer. Questions should be free of bias; avoid leading questions. Tick boxes fulfil many of the above requirements and also simplify the analysis, but over-simplification can dilute the validity of the data. Scales are often used; they can be good but are frequently ambiguous. The other main problems with satisfaction questionnaires are that they are either too short (and say nothing) or they are too long (and become a burden on customer).

A novel approach might be to encourage customers to leave business cards (offer free prize draw or a meal for two). Provide a choice of boxes in which they may be left, e.g. meal experience was good/indifferent/bad. If further information is required, particularly from dissatisfied customers, question-naires may be sent or a phone call made.

Keep records; historical data is the prime source of effective market research.

New product/service development

Market research may identify customer resistance to new products. Dealing with customer preconceptions and trying to explain new concepts may be a major problem. For instance, not having a menu detailing specific dishes and prices may be a difficult concept for consumers to come to terms with. The Carrington Arms in Buckinghamshire provides meats and fish from a butcher's/fishmonger's counter. Customers select items and pay by weight, products are then cooked in their view. The outcome is, by all accounts, highly successful but the owners do admit that explaining the concept is their biggest problem. Marketing activity should assist in the promotion of new products and services by emphasizing:

- product/service benefits
- added value
- unique selling points

Further advantage may be gained from the promotion of brands:

● known brands	(McDonald's, Pizza Hut, Kentucky Fried Chicken)
● own 'internal' brands	(Gardner Merchant; Strollers Deli, Pizza Gusta, Oriental Express)
● own 'high street' brands	(Sutcliffe; Brioche Doree (developed on P&O Ferries))

Promotion and advertising

Good advertising is dependent on 'message, media and timing'.

- The message – quality of copy and artwork
- The media – targeting the audience
- The timing – choose a time when customers are 'listening'

The message

The message should stress the benefits to the consumer, e.g. nutritional details. The purpose of the message is to influence consumer attitude and behaviour, to create desire and brand loyalty. Messages should be designed to maximize awareness and to impart knowledge and understanding of our products and services. Ultimately, in the case of successful products, the message may merely be a reminder; few of us need to be told about Coca-Cola but clearly we need reminding, frequently.

Many managers will already be familiar with the AIDA principle:

- attract   **A** ttention
- arouse   **I** nterest
- create   **D** esire
- stimulate   **A** ction

There may be dangers in choosing the message, its content and emphasis, and the media used. Customers may be given the impression of 'expensiveness' or they may feel out of place. It may be appropriate to consider the use of professional services for both design and printing.

The media

The term 'media' is generally used in reference to newspapers, radio and television. In terms of   marketing there are a number of additional media which we might use:

- Selling (merchandising)
- Direct mail
- Public relations (PR)
- Press advertising
- TV and radio
- Food guides/tour guides
- Signposts and hoardings

Selling (merchandising)
(see Chapter 4, Merchandising, for more details)
- personal sales
- telephone sales
- special materials
- reinforcement of theme or project
- consumer incentives (try something new)
- pricing strategy

Selling (merchandising) will require staff training and internal advertising and printed materials.

Direct mail

Before embarking on a direct mail campaign we will need to decide who we are trying to reach, what we are trying to achieve, how recipients are likely to be persuaded and when it is best to communicate. Consider carefully the real (total) costs, including administration time and resources. We should also consider the validity of the database used for addressing the mailshots: is the information up to date and relevant?

The effectiveness of direct mail is reliant on efficient targeting of customers'
- personal details – birthday cards/invitations, etc.
- credit card details – average spend frequency of use
- postal address/post code
- geographical area

Consider the benefits of associating your mailshot with other businesses, local events, theatres etc. and enclose reply cards, Freefone number and an e-mail address, if possible. Used properly, direct mail is reasonably cost effective and response is usually fairly quick, although the percentage response is generally fairly small (15 per cent would probably be considered good).

Public relations

Most companies invest some time and money in promoting and maintaining a favourable image, both locally and nationally. Maintaining goodwill, reputation and standing in the community is important for successful operations.

The objectives, strategy and tactics of PR can be quite diverse

- problem solving and troubleshooting (errors, accidents, incidents)
- sponsorship, competitions
- sales promotion
  - immediate or delayed discount (free offer)
  - self-liquidating promotions (cover costs)

Effective PR – speaking, being interviewed, preparation of press releases – needs specialist advice and/or training, consider advantages and disadvantages of using consultants.

Press advertising

Advertising in newspapers and magazines, local and national, is relatively simple. Because advertisements usually appear alongside competitors, customers know where to look. However the target market may be difficult to identify (geography, consumer profile, interests). One way of measuring the success of an advertising campaign is to link it with a special offer, available on presentation of the advertisement (cut from newspaper or magazine). Alternatively, try to recognize faces and new customers and make a point of welcoming them. Tell them briefly about the operation and then ask them about themselves, where they are from, how they learnt about your establishment. Whilst not everyone will co-operate, most will welcome your 'genuine' interest.

TV and radio

Television advertising is beyond all but the largest of operations. Local radio, however, can be quite cost effective. Most local radio stations know their market quite well and should be able to advise on appropriate times to reach your potential customers. As with press advertising, you will need to 'follow though' in order to test the effectiveness of a local radio campaign.

Food guides/tour guides

The benefits of guide books are difficult to determine. An entry into one or more of the guides in support of PR activity would be highly desirable. A restaurant that relies entirely on passing/tourist trade may well benefit. But for a restaurant reliant on entirely 'local' customers the benefits must be few. Local customers are more likely to look in *Thompson's Directory* or the *Yellow Pages*.

Signposts and hoardings

The main purpose of signposts is to help people identify a place they are already looking for, their effectiveness in collecting 'passing trade' must be questioned. In particular consider the travelling distance – the space between the sign, the time it takes to read and absorb the message, and the restaurant entrance – too late we've missed it! Additionally we should consider the message we wish to send and the fact that it may be difficult to display (in a limited space). The obvious 'Food 200 metres on the left' does not say a lot about what we are offering and yet to write more might make the sign impossible to read (for the motorist).

Predicting and managing future demand

The financial success of most businesses depends on their ability to anticipate future changes and successfully adapt to them. Further, a successful operation will match production to demand and loss (waste) will be reduced by avoiding over-production. Accurate forecasting, the provision of predictions about the future are essential in ensuring such goals are achieved.

Aims of forecasting

The aims of forecasting vary: in particular we can differentiate between long-, medium- and short-term planning. Long-term planning/forecasting is primarily concerned with policy development, 'what shall we produce and who shall we sell it to'. Medium-term planning is concerned with annual forecasts as a basis for setting budgets. Short-term planning and forecasting is generally the responsibility of the departmental manager who will be aware of the long- and medium-term plans and will have to apply these in the day-to-day running of the department. Short-term planning/forecasting is concerned with work scheduling, raw material and equipment management.

The aims of forecasting are:

● to predict the number of customers
● to predict the number of each item chosen (sales mix)
● to enable comparison to be made between potential and actual sales

---

The objectives at operational level are:
● to assist food cost control
● to assist purchasing
● to maintain optimum stock levels
● to reduce customer dissatisfaction
● to reduce the problems of re-using leftovers
● to ensure that production = demand

There are a number of constraints on accurate forecasting. In attempting to achieve the above objectives the manager will be constrained by the nature of the product, consumer and market.

The nature of the product:
- the range of foods and dishes
- the range of prices
- the variety of service styles

The nature of the consumer:
- context of the operation
- individuality
- motives and needs
- disposable income
- available time

The nature of the market:
- impact of advertising
- fashion/trends
- competition
- seasonality
- the weather

All of these options and variables need to be built into the forecasting model if it is to be reliable.

Predicting precisely what will take place in the future is impossible. The best we can do is determine the most likely outcome based on available information. Good information and applied knowledge is the key to accuracy. In this way we receive reasonably accurate weather forecasts. The more accurate and the greater the amount of information (data) and the more skilled the meteorologist, the more reliable the forecast. Yet people still rely on other methods: are the cows in the field sitting or standing?; are the crows at the tops of the trees?; ne'er cast a clout 'til May's out; if it rains on St Swithin's, etc. Some methods have no sound basis in science or proven fact. Others, the study of cloud patterns for instance, may be justified, but even here there are methods which are proven to be more reliable.

If I were to ask how many ducks were on my local pond of

a Sunday lunch time, you could hazard a guess. Results would probably range from zero to hundreds. If, however, I were to provide more information – shape, size and location of the pond, number and type of other waterfowl present, available food source (natural or provided by tourists), time of year, weather conditions and the feeding habits of ducks – the range of answers would be considerably reduced and most would be reasonably accurate. The same principles may be applied to predicting customer activity.

Forecasting is about:

- optimizing information exchange
- generating models for prediction
- analysing results
- assessing different perspectives
- applying values

There are three main methods of forecasting:

- extrapolative
- causal
- judgemental

Extrapolative

Such methods of forecasting rely on complex mathematical models and are best left to the expert. Where managers have access to computers, software is available to handle the necessary calculations, but it is still advisable that the principles of the calculation are understood before relying too heavily on the results produced. In addition, computers only manipulate figures based on given formula and statistical input. It is up to the manager to ensure that (a) the quality of input is controlled and (b) the output is interpreted correctly.

Causal

A far simpler principle to understand is cause and effect. If it is cold, wet and windy we sell more soup! The weakness in this system is that although it is only a single equation, a one-to-one relationship, it is almost impossible to introduce figures. How cold does it need to be for soup sales to increase? Do sales of soup continue to increase as it gets colder, if so in what proportion?

Judgemental

Although difficult to justify on the grounds of proven accuracy or mathematical certainty, we should not undervalue the benefits of good judgement, particularly when such judgement is based on years of experience.

Whilst it would appear that none of the above methods can be relied on entirely, using the three in partnership may be effective. Predictions may achieve greater reliability if the system of forecasting, whatever it may be, is used consistently.

It is essential to compare like with like, for example the historical presentation of data:

- Calendar months   Compare, for instance, March with March (year by year). There is no point in comparing August with February; not only are there a different number of trading days but also different seasons and different customer activity.
- Thirteen months   Divide the year into thirteen 'months' of four weeks, each of equal trading days. This still takes no account of seasonal variation.

- Four quarters — Divide the year into four equal quarters, of thirteen weeks each, with an equal number of trading days. In this way it is easier to account for seasonality.

Good forecasting requires the routine collection of information that may be obtained from:

- statistics (local/national) — population
  income and spending power
- trade press — current events
  current trends
- internal records — past activity (sales history)
  advance bookings
  current promotional activity
  (merchandising)

The value of accurate historical data cannot be ignored

A restaurant booking diary could include details about the number of guests but also:

- geographic source of those customers — (names and addresses, telephone numbers)
- where they first heard about you — (marketing, causal information)
- comments (good and bad) from customers — (causal)
- staff on duty
- weather conditions at the time
- prevailing economic conditions
- numbers of each menu item sold
- ratio of drinks to food sales

... all of which may contribute to more accurate prediction of future business.

Both internal and external influences will need to be identified and accommodated in the forecasting model. External influences could result in changes to predicted costs (labour, materials, equipment) or expected revenue (customer spending power, taxation, rate of interest on savings). Internal influences (specifications, procedures, techniques) will initially affect costs. Revenue will be affected if the customer's perception of the product or service is altered as a result of changes made.

Good forecasting needs accurate and reliable data to be analysed and interpreted correctly. The quality of analysis and interpretation will be influenced by the level of understanding of two main factors:

- Can what actually causes the demand be identified?
- Can quantified data be obtained?

It may seem obvious to associate the sale of ice cream with the weather. More ice cream is sold during the summer months, statistics are clear on that, but is it really a direct response to the weather? It may be argued that, for many customers, the purchase of ice cream is associated with a particular activity, a trip to the zoo or seaside, and on these occasions ice cream is purchased regardless of the weather. So we should be careful when making assumptions about origins of demand. For example, the government statistics regarding visitors to the UK should not be translated directly to tourism. Many visitors will be business people and others will be staying with relatives. Of those that are genuine tourists many will be on a very limited budget, hikers and campers, and may make only minimal use of our facilities.

Month-by-month statistics tell us what not why purchases are made. Customers, not calendars, make buying decisions. In order to determine levels of demand we need to understand the customer/causal relationships.

The customers' decision to purchase may be influenced by:
- politics
- economic climate
- price competitiveness
- opportunity cost
- season/climate

For forecasting to be effective:

- There must be clear objectives.
- Plans must be comprehensive.
- Plans must be based on sound research.
- Plans must use measurable standards.
- Plans should contain sufficient detail to enable effective control.
- There should be a level of flexibility in order to respond to unforeseen changes.
- Plans should be made as simple as possible

Forecasting is a continuous process, planning for the future and working to objectives. Plans will necessarily change as more information becomes available. Forecasts usually get more accurate as the deadline/objective gets closer. Forecasting future demand is one thing, coping with it is another.

Demand management

Having researched the market and forecast potential volume we must now consider the management of demand in order to ensure that all the business we have attracted is concluded successfully. More specifically we must ensure that supply equals demand and, unfortunately, there are a large number of variables that need to be managed. In order to balance demand and supply we may increase one and/or decrease the other. Alternatively, and perhaps more effectively, we might redistribute both.

	Increase	Decrease	Re-distribute
Demand	Product modification	Increase prices	Encourage bar meals
	Search out new markets	Raise quality	Room service
	Alter distribution channels	Reduce seating capacity	Garden barbecues
	Conferences and tours	Insist on pre-booking	Develop 'slow' days with
	Discount price		special promotions
	Promotion		Meals tailored to client needs
	Advertising		Differential pricing
	Selling		Happy hour
	PR		Two-for-one deals
Supply	Employ more staff	Product modification	Open up new service areas
	Buy more equipment	Limit availability	Manage advance bookings
	Increase use of technology	Control supply	Manage the queues
	Modify the system	• raw materials	Simplify service procedures
	Replicate the system (franchise)	• part-time staff	Employ staff with flexible skills
	Buy up competitors (and install your system)	• flexible staff	

Figure 3.5 Demand and supply matrix

Decreasing demand must be considered irrational, unless of course fewer customers can generate increased revenue and lower costs. Similarly a reduction in supply must be questioned; it may be applicable to unique, patented products, limited editions, special functions or exclusivity.

Managing demand
- have specific objectives
- monitor performance
- create interest in specific products
- gain and retain competitive advantage
- build employee involvement
- utilize market research more effectively
- predict (forecast) more accurately

Marketing tactics

Where can marketing activity be used to gain competitive advantage?

Marketing tactics are based on consumer orientation. Consumers have more choice and more information, knowledge and understanding of products and services on offer. As a consequence of this, our response must reflect cultural, economic and social factors that influence consumer choice. We must try to understand:

● buying behaviour
● preference, choice and decision (see Chapter 4 Merchandising, for further discussion)
● post-purchase evaluation

Stages in the buying decision are obviously influenced by marketing activity – particularly pre-purchase behaviour, the search for information and the consideration of alternatives.

The search for information is based on:
● past experience
● opinion(s) recommendation (the experience of others)
● promotional messages (advertising)
● location
● price
and the consideration of alternatives (a balance of benefits and disadvantages).

Purchase decisions are frequently based on the consumer's evaluation, previous experience and/or personal recommendation. Often the decision to use a particular restaurant will result from a group or family discussion. The use of values, likes and dislikes may be conscious or subconscious. A 'bland' operation may have the advantage in that whilst it offers few outstanding benefits it is acceptable to everyone. In order to be chosen, a restaurant must first be included in the selection list. On this basis the provision of a 'reminder' or discussion point – such as desk/car air fresheners, note-pads, etc., with company logo/message – may be a worthwhile investment.

Consumer buyer behaviour
- problem recognition
- information search
- evaluation of alternatives
  (Key quality issues, Chapter 5)
- purchase decision
- post-purchase behaviour

Customer choice is normally based on two factors: what and where:

- **What** type of restaurant, based on
  - finance, consumer spending power
  - justification/occasion/purpose

Here marketing activity is useful only in encouraging more people to eat out more frequently, increasing the size of the market as a whole and, possibly, our share.

- **Where** which particular venue, based on
  - type of restaurant
  - quality and value of products and services
  - the competition

In this case marketing offers greater potential for direct benefits for individual restaurants. Such marketing activity may be supported by 'brand' recognition.

Branding

Build a strong brand name which communicates a clear concept to customers, enhanced by good promotion/advertising and supported by quality merchandising activity. Branding supports customer preference of our products and services over those of our competitors, in which case our products must be distinctive. Product/service differentiation will be influenced by both image and reality:

- image positioning   customer 'perceptions' of reality (abstract)
- real positioning   objective, measurable attributes

Image and real positioning can work in tandem; they are mutually supportive. Products tend to be 'real' while service tends to be 'image' related. Operations may choose to customize or systematize their system of delivery:

- customize, e.g. Burger King offers customer choice – customers determine what they get
- systematize, e.g. most other burger outlets, limited choice – customers know what to expect

Brand objectives must be clear, accurate, consistent and reliable or else they are self-defeating. This is not difficult for products, but service is not easy to brand. Branding is most frequently associated with multi-site operations and it has particular advantages for national advertising. But it can be applied to small, single-unit operations. The use of a 'signature' dish is the commonest example (see Chapter 6). The growing importance of branding particularly in the low-spend (highly competitive) sector is becoming increasingly apparent. Breweries have invested heavily in acquiring and/or developing 'brands' like Brewers Fayre, Millers Kitchen, Harvester and Toby Restaurants. New trends, such as 'Irish' pubs, are continuously emerging. It is not uncommon for the larger operations to identify and purchase single-unit operations in order to capitalize by replicating the 'brand'. Multisite brands with standardized products and services offering assured meal experience allow for transferred loyalty. Additionally there are gains to be made from efficiency and economies which may be built into a branded operation.

Market segmentation

The principle of segmentation is based on the opportunities arising from more cost effective marketing which results from the identification of smaller groups. Segmentation calls for more detailed study of the customer:

1 Customer characteristics (profile).
   ● Socio-economic orientation   Sex, age, education, occupation, income, membership of organizations such as the Automobile Association and of professional associations
2 Customer behaviour (purchasing, etc.).
   ● Product orientation   Associated purchases: newspapers, services
   ● User orientation   Business person/ conference delegate, tourist/day tripper, local resident/traveller

When examining the market it is useful to group customers who demonstrate similar needs and expectations into smaller, more discrete segments. This process of market segmentation ensures that we do not send confusing messages to our prospective customers. Thus we can identify particular groups: business people, vegetarians, young people. The process is quite complex and can lead to some confusion: 'What do we do with the young vegetarian business person?'. The important rule is to look carefully at the needs expressed by customers. For example, we might identify a market segment that expresses a need for fast service of reasonably priced dishes delivered in an informal 'fun' environment. If the strengths of our operation are modern facilities, young lively staff with good social skills and a system of production based on use of convenience products we have the opportunity to appeal to this segment. If, however, our operation was based in a lavishly furnished Victorian hotel using traditional methods of production and highly skilled silver service staff, then trying to appeal to such a group would be a mistake.

Although it used to be common to divide people by what was referred to as socio-economic groups based on occupation and income, most people now recognize that market segments are more disparate. Individuals may belong to a wide range of market segments many of which derive from specific activities such as business, leisure, tourism and social occasions. Restaurants may find that different market segments emerge at different times and are able to organize themselves to respond effectively to business lunches, social evenings and week-end visitors. However, diversifying in this way may require different restaurant layouts, menu variety, pricing structure and levels of service. Pizza restaurants seem to be able to cope with differing markets – day-time shoppers and evening revellers – without significantly reorganizing any of their resources although evidence suggests that average spend and the type of menu items chosen may differ and the style of service, speed and use of social skills, may be modified slightly.

Segmentation presupposes the need for market differentiation which appeals to the smaller groups – segments – which have now been identified.

Market differentiation

Market differentiation may change, products may not (although packaging might), e.g. a town centre restaurant may provide for each of these different market segments:

- business lunches
- early evening family meals
- late night revellers
- and, in some cases, take-away meals

Such mixed market activity can provide problems for policy development and particularly marketing promotion (messages). If the emphasis of any advertising campaign is directed too strongly towards late night revellers then family business may be 'threatened'.

Differentiation criteria
- availability/accessibility
- standing out from the competition
- product/service range (choice)
- unique selling points
- quality
- price

Summary

To improve performance we must become more responsive to customers. We have direct channels of communication with our customers, we just need to listen more. As part of the 'listening' activity we should be measuring demand (forecast) more accurately which will enable us to reduce cost (eliminate waste), as a consequence of which we will be able to invest more in marketing. We should be 'selling' ourselves and our products more, we should have a strong message (brand image) to communicate and we should encourage everyone involved in the operation to become 'believers' in the company. Marketing should not be identified as a separate, independent, department; we should expand the 'sales force' to include everybody.

We will need to manage marketing in order to improve both profit and customer satisfaction – customer-centred performance improvement is the main objective of marketing. Opportunities for performance improvement may arise from a greater understanding of the 'pattern' of business. Using market research data we may develop graphs and charts in order that patterns (sales volume, menu mix, average spend, etc.) are easier to detect. We may identify profit and profit potential – the number of covers served, peaks and troughs, effects of promotions and discounting. We may additionally calculate marketing efficiency, cost effectiveness and the best way of generating business.

- How much did a campaign cost?
- How much revenue did it generate (short-term/long-term)?
- Were objectives (volume, new business, etc.) achieved?

Success will be based on continuous application of the marketing process.

Managers will develop systems, processes and procedures to identify market opportunities. It is important to keep marketing activity simple, easy for all to understand, share objectives and strategy with staff, gain their full commitment. The nature and direction of the business, its marketing objectives, target audience and house style should all be clarified. Keep messages clear and simple.

Marketing strategies

- Identify customer needs, wants, expectations and disposable income (profile).
- Develop products, services and environment to match customer profile.
- Set prices based on demand, manage costs.
- Promote quality assurance, be flexible with pricing but not standards.
- Plan customer-responsive production and service systems.
- Encourage and manage customer participation.
- Employ, develop and retain committed staff, with good social skills.
- Train staff in the marketing elements of service skills (listening, promoting and selling).
- Involve everyone in promotional activity.
- Perform regular SWOT analysis.
- Identify tangible and intangible benefits (particularly in regard to services).
- Promote the benefits of both product and service.
- Stimulate word of mouth promotion/recommendation.
- Emphasize personal communication, internal customer/marketing, empathy.
- Promote long-term customer relationships, manage fluctuating demand.

Remember that keeping existing customers is more cost effective (profitable) than chasing new ones.

Suggested additional reading

Fewell, A. and Wills, N. (1995) *Marketing*. Butterworth–Heinemann.

Kotler, P. (1984) *Marketing Management*. Prentice Hall.

Miller, J.E. (1987) *Menu Pricing and Strategy*. Van Nostrand Rheinhold.

4
Merchandising

Aims and objectives

There is usually one main aim associated with merchandising, that is to increase sales (revenue/turnover). There are basically three ways of achieving this objective:

1 Attract more customers.
2 Charge existing customers more.
3 Encourage existing customers to spend more.

In order to sell products and services customers must first be attracted to our premises. However, attracting customers to our restaurants is only half the battle. We must also encourage them to spend their money.

Merchandising aims
- Identify a range of opportunities to promote sales.
- Recognize and promote customer benefits.
- Maximize volume (covers) and revenue (covers plus ASP).

The impact of successful merchandising effort is reliant upon appealing to the customer, persuading the customer to participate, influencing the customer's evaluation of the menu and its product content and encouraging the customer to return.

This process is assisted by reference to standard management activity:

- **Marketing**: identifies demand.
- **Advertising**: brings the customer in.
- **Selling**: takes money for products/services offered.
- **Profitability**: makes it all worthwhile.
- **Customer satisfaction**: ensures the continuation of the process.

The role of marketing has already been noted in the previous chapter. The best form of advertising is word of mouth recommendation. This is most easily achieved by ensuring that our reputation is spread by existing customers whose needs and expectations have been effectively met.

The objective of merchandising is to make sure that all goods are displayed, priced, promoted and positioned in such a way as to maximize the profitability of every inch of sales space, whilst ensuring customer satisfaction. Merchandising activity is assisted by our knowledge of our customers through the service contact, knowing who they are, what they buy and where and when they buy it.

Merchandising objectives
- Maximize the profit potential of food and beverage service areas.
- Provide quality products.
- Maximize selling effort at the point of sale.
- Instruct, train and motivate staff to take advantage of selling opportunities.
- Increase margin (profit per item sold).
- Ensure total customer satisfaction.

What is merchandising?

The broadest definition of merchandising would be:

> '*All activities related to the buying and selling of goods (merchandise).*'

More specifically we may associate merchandising with responding to customer need at the point of sale:

- presentation of goods and services for sale
- non-personal promotion
- cross selling, 'in house selling'
- influencing customers' purchasing behaviour

Point-of-sale promotion
- what is happening
- what could happen

Point of sale promotion (merchandising) is primarily associated with product presentation; emphasis may be on temporal, product or display based activity.

Temporal promotion (assumes thought process, e.g. calculation of cost/value)

- drinks at reduced prices during quieter periods

Product promotion (impulse purchases)

- new product launch
- traditional products highlighted
- daily 'specials'

Display promotion (reminders)

- tent cards
- posters, wall decoration, blackboards
- displays

What purpose does it serve?
- to maximize sales
- 'in house' marketing
- 'brand image' re-enforcement

Promotional information – the use of description to make the dish sound good/tempting – may be explicit or implied, but products and services will have to live up to expectations. Promotional activity may involve dressing a dish to imply that it has more value or the use of menu design or posters to suggest that customers are getting more for their money. There are risks in the use of promotional methods which may cause the customer to expect more than we are prepared to give. However, we can use menu design effectively by placing those items that we wish to promote in prime positions and encouraging customers to link products (and purchases) by placing appropriate products in adjacent positions.

Sales development – promotional – activity should be planned in relation to the wider – marketing – activities of the company.

Managing the service encounter

Understanding of the service contact is an essential ingredient of sales development activity. Managing the service encounter involves setting standards for:

- **Arrival**: first impressions.

- **Welcome:** friendly and helpful, gaining customer confidence.
- **Enquiry:** caring and attentive, suggestions and recommendations, helping customers to make the right choice.
- **Description:** professional, product knowledge, encouraging the purchase of additional items.
- **Selling:** passive selling – using presentation and display material.
  Positive selling – open the conversation, point out promotions, identify product benefits thus adding value.

Why is merchandising important?

Research (see Table 4.1) suggests that there are eight critical stages in consumer purchase behaviour.

Table 4.1 Stages in the purchase decision

1	Indifference	the customer is unaware of any need
2	Interest	the customer is aware of need but unaware of products
3	Knowledge	the customer is aware of products but has no knowlege of their characteristics
4	Understanding	comprehension of characteristics and range of products
5	Preference	the customer develops a preference for a particular product
6	Intention	the customer confirms their intention to buy
7	Purchase	customer makes a purchase and evaluates the product
8	Return	if product meets needs and expectations customer returns for more

Source: Jenkins.

Whilst this information is clearly related to marketing activity the significance of merchandising should also be apparent, particularly during Stages 3 to 8. Stage 8, the opportunity to return, is relevant even if no initial purchase is made. Good merchandising, explaining the benefits of a product, will help to confirm a product's ability to meet needs and expectations in the customer's mind, encouraging them to return in the future.

The psychological aspects of liking, preference and choice

While eating and drinking are physical functions essential to life, choice is dependent on mind rather than body. It will require some physical participation, use of the senses; sight, hearing, touch, smell and taste (organoleptics).

The roots of modern psychology may be found in the seventeenth century, in the work of the French philosopher René Descartes and British philosophers Thomas Hobbes and John Locke. Descartes argued that minds have certain inborn or innate ideas. Hobbes and Locke stressed the role of experience through sensory perception.

More modern developments are based on the work of German physiologists Muller, Fechner and Wundt who were involved in the study of the function of the various human organs. Far better known, however is the work of Sigmund Freud, who devised the system of investigation and treatment known as psychoanalysis – the study of instinctual drives and unconscious motivational processes.

Conditioning and learning

A central area of study in psychology is how organisms change as a result of experience. Much research has been performed using animals such as rats. Two major kinds of learning are usually distinguished:

- Classical conditioning
- Instrumental learning

Classical conditioning is also known as Pavlovian conditioning after the Russian physiologist Ivan Pavlov who demonstrated that animal salivation is a conditioned response associated with the ringing of a bell as a signal to the imminent arrival of food. In instrumental learning the emphasis is placed on what the animal does and what kind of outcomes follow its actions. Associating response and reward, the consequence and benefits of certain actions.

Such developments in psychology are useful in understanding human choice, preference and liking.

Liking: the result of *nature*, we are omnivores. The innate liking for sweetness probably stems from our ancestors' fruit eating days and their resistance to bitterness (associated with poisons) and subsequent fear of certain fruits, berries and plants. Similarly the essential need for salt is fulfilled through a developed liking for salty foods.

Preference: the result of *nurture*, and the ability to apply discretion. The pleasurable flavours (thoughts) in food result in a greater flow of saliva which aids digestion. The end result is more positive and the experience is repeated.

Choice: problem solving and the opportunity to make a *decision*. Choice may not correspond to preference or liking. They are overlapping but not precisely equivalent. Customers will weigh the opportunity costs (measure what they have to go without) and assess other related criteria, effort, expectancy and potential outcome (benefits).

All result from experience (trial and error) and/or recommendation (other people's experience). Learning (preference) evolves from experience plus observation and reflection, the formation of concepts. Choice results from preference influenced by constructs (see Figure 4.1) and situational variables.

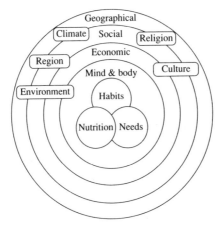

The influence of constructs on liking, preference and **choice**

Climate is	Geographical.
Religion may be	Geographical and social.
Region is both	Geographical and economic.
Culture is	Geographical, economic and social.
Environment	includes all of the above, but may also be influenced by mind and body.

Figure 4.1 Customer constructs.

Situational variables
- occasion
- company
- weather
- time
- funds available
- opportunity cost

Given an understanding of choice (preference and liking), obvious relationships can be drawn between consumer behaviour, need satisfaction, response to cue, fashion, trend, advertising and merchandising.

Choosing

The customer must exert some effort in order to make a decision, that effort must be rewarded.

- Positive/negative reinforcement.
- Degree to which expectations are met.
- Is selection instrumental in meeting other outcomes?
- Value/attractiveness of each of the outcomes.
- Equity between effort and results.

What are the implications for customer perspectives of quality and satisfaction?

Who is involved in merchandising?

The food and beverage manager

Managers will be responsible for the planning and provision of sales development activity:

- available resources (funds and materials)
- staffing (skills, training and instruction)
- identification of roles and responsibilities
- scheduling activities
- recording and documentation
- accurate measurement of effectiveness and feedback

Company policy, in particular the brand image the company is trying to promote and the consumer market it has identified, will significantly affect the style and nature of sales development activities that the manager can participate in. The amount of promotional activity will be influenced by market conditions such as the level of competition, the number of consumers and customer spending power. A buoyant competitive market, like fast food, will normally attract a comparatively high level of investment specifically allocated to promotional activity. In smaller independent units there may not be a promotions budget but a greater degree of autonomy will be given to the food and beverage manager who will decide how much of the current gross profit earned by the unit to invest in future sales development activity in order to maintain or improve the gross profit position.

The manager must be able to rely on all members of staff to participate in the service contact effectively. Providing effective training and instruction is the first step. In order for customers to believe in the product it is necessary to believe in the sales person; dress, manner, manners and mannerisms will all contribute to the customer's perception and influence their level of trust.

The staff

Selling may be a novel experience for some staff and managers will need to create awareness and understanding, helping staff to highlight the benefits, especially the importance of closing the sale.

When customers are 'browsing' the menu staff may assist with recommendations and explanations. Use of the phrase 'which means that' is a useful sales technique. 'Vegetables and fries are included in the price of the steak, *which means that* you can afford a starter!'. Obviously for such activity to be successful there is a need for sound product knowledge: portion size, weight, ingredients, origin (fresh/frozen). If products are frozen then staff should explain why (what are the benefits): frozen peas are better than fresh because they are processed immediately after picking whereas fresh peas may be several days old. Service staff knowledge should also extend to style and method of cooking, dish accompaniments and garnish. In particular merchandising is concerned with the sale of additional items which complement the customer's original choice. Staff should be competent in their recommendations for wines, beers and beverage sales. Effective merchandising requires a positive attitude which may be reflected in personal habits and body language. It will be necessary for managers to take account of factors such as this when designing staff development programmes.

Staff activity	Customer activity/response
Watch, listen, question	Consumer needs identified
Explain	Benefits
Compare/contrast	'Which means that'
Offer choice	Identify/select options
Reinforce choice	Confidence (customer has done the right thing)
Confirm	Needs satisfied

External influences

Merchandising, by definition, is a point-of-sale activity and therefore influence from outside will be limited. Unit managers may receive advice, perhaps even financial assistance from head office. Suppliers may suggest suitable products for promotion and in addition provide some of the promotional materials. Unit managers should decide whose interest is best served by supplier-led promotions. Merchandising will only be effective if it results in total satisfaction and return custom.

Customers

Clearly customers are directly involved in merchandising activity and the importance of understanding buyer behaviour and consumer choice has already been discussed.

Merchandising strategy

How is merchandising strategy developed?

There are three main factors which influence effective merchandising:

- accessibility
- sensory domination
- appeal

A product which is accessible sells better than one which is not (i.e. a rack of newspapers, self-selection from a wine display).

Four main senses are always available to merchandising stimulation: sight, hearing, smell and touch. If the product/promotion appeals to one or more then it is likely to be purchased (e.g. the smell of roasting coffee, the sound of bacon sizzling, the sight of fresh cream cascading over ripe red strawberries, the feel/touch of a well chilled lager). The hospitality industry has the added option of appealing to the fifth sense, taste, in order to attract sales (would you like to try our new pâté? take a sip of the Beaujolais nouveau? etc.).

If a product appeals to a customer, the customer feels motivated to buy it. Naturally the reverse is also true. Unsightly staff, uncomfortable furniture, warm lager, sour cream in the coffee will all lose sales, now and in the future.

Managers should examine the effectiveness of the service system design. Particular attention should be paid to the service encounter. What are the customers' first impressions, how effective was the welcome? Are guests provided with positive descriptions of products and services on offer? Do staff fully exploit selling opportunities, are they encouraged to use initiative? Service systems and staff should be responsive to the promotional opportunities associated with differing forms of customer purchase behaviour.

One-stop customers: Will stop once, they usually know what they want. You only have one chance to influence these customers and encourage them to buy high contribution products and extra items.

Cautious customers: Think before they act. These customers buy from more than one location so you have greater opportunity to influence their decision. Providing a range of choices and opportunities may be sufficient to prevent them going to your competitors.

Impulse customers: Are more open minded, what they see can influence them to buy. For the catering industry there are two identifiable stages to the impulse purchase:

- choosing a course
- choosing a dish for each course

Leave the dessert menu until after the main course, impulse customers might be tempted to extra vegetables or a starter if they are not concerned with dessert. Impulsive customers might have difficulty making up their mind if there are several tempting items on the dessert menu. If choosing a dessert is difficult for some customers offer a 'trio' – a combination of small portions of three appropriately combined desserts – at a premium price.

Customers will not always be 'one-stop', 'cautious' or 'impulsive'. Their purchase behaviour will change due to their circumstances, their frame of mind, the situation/environment and the quality of your merchandising. For example, if we provide a relaxed atmosphere and customers feel secure (they are not going to be 'ripped off') they may be more inclined to be impulsive. We need to be sure that all impulsive purchases result in high levels of satisfaction.

The decision to purchase is assisted by:
- quality
- atmosphere
- presentation
- staff attitude
- acceptable conditions
- previous experience

Merchandising and profit improvement

Charging existing customers more for products and services can be a two-edged sword. It may indeed achieve the initial objective of increasing revenue but it is a short-term, high-risk, manoeuvre. Just increasing the price is likely to cause customers to question the value of our products and services and may lead to dissatisfaction, loss of current customers and the wrong message being sent to potential new customers. However, we may be able to increase the price if at the same time the customer can be persuaded that we are also increasing benefits (value). Merchandising plays an important role in persuading customers about the likely benefits.

For example, the price of our standard breakfast (egg, bacon and sausage) can be increased if we add fried bread and grilled tomato and actively promote the new breakfast as 'special'. The additional cost plus an increase in margin is passed on to the customer who perceives the breakfast with the additional items to be better value.

A similar effect may be achieved by simply renaming the product using value associated words like giant, jumbo, house speciality, gourmet. In one case at least it may be possible to reduce the content, take out the cream, butter and eggs and sell a product such as chicken in white wine sauce at a premium price by identifying it as 'the healthy option'.

The true role of merchandising is to be found in its potential to encourage existing customers to spend more. This can be achieved in three ways:

- by encouraging customers to 'buy up'
- by encouraging customers to buy more
- by encouraging customers to come more often

The term 'buying up' is used, in this context, to mean encouraging the customer to purchase an item that is slightly more expensive than that which they might normally be expected to buy. This is normally achieved by persuading the customer that the increase in benefits outweighs the additional cost. For example, traditional gueridon service did not, in effect, provide the customer with more food – in many cases the ingredients were no more expensive than other menu items. But the customer felt special because food was being cooked at the table and they were the centre of attention. American-style bars achieve similar effect by ringing a large bell behind the bar when speciality drinks are ordered. Note that if the price difference is too big customers are discouraged from buying up.

Merchandising through the menu and drinks lists

The function of the menu is to inform and appeal to customers. Menu design provides for merchandising opportunities which may result in improving profitability. Emphasis will be placed on positioning, to encourage associated sales, and descriptions which enhance the perceived value of items and combinations on offer.

Adding value

Real value	*Implied value*
• portion size	• descriptions
• additional items	• presentations
• individual portions	• trendy items
• linking	• menu design

There are some constraints within which menu writers need to work. Whilst being concerned with the need to sell it may also be necessary, in some cases at least, to conform to the traditional menu requirements of sequence and balance. The use of description implies the effective use of language, not only English, French or Italian, but also form and, in most cases, grammar must be appropriate to operational style and merchandising message. Finally, but most importantly, descriptions must be written within the constraints of the law – specifically the Trades Descriptions Act, which in essence means that they must be honest and where specific terms have been used they must be adhered to.

When is merchandising implemented?

The manager should attempt to maximize sales opportunities by maximizing sales space. Initially concentrate on the overall effect, the use of complementary and contrasting colours, highlights and centrepieces. Only those items that we intend to sell should be given display space, but we should not feel restricted to just displaying menu items. Many restaurants use ancillary materials, such as flowers, lace and china, to enhance the display of menu items and these extra products may also be priced for sale.

A local hospital, in addition to its more traditional staff-feeding activities also sells snacks, domestic items, home medicines, books, cards and stationery. Not only is this a profitable exercise for catering management, it is also seen by customers to be a welcome and valuable service.

Display materials should be used to enhance product displays. They should complement restaurant design and furnishing as well as guide and advise customers. Display materials include: floor stands, bulletin boards, posters and wall displays (which are useful for areas where customers congregate or queue), menus, wine lists, speciality menus, children's menus, dessert menus, clip-on and tent cards for use where customers are sitting. Forthcoming attractions should be displayed at the exit or where people are paying.

Consider the use of 'give away' materials: book matches, children's menus which fold into pencil boxes, badges, calendars, desk jotters or 'note-its' which include the message 'let's meet for lunch!' and the restaurant telephone number as well as the company logo.

Positioning of menus is a critical feature. A bar in the southern counties pins bold copies of its menu on the beams above the heads of the customers. In a crowded bar on a busy lunch time everyone can see the menu. Having a sufficient number of clean, well presented menus is seen as important by managers, but all too often this is ignored in reality.

Specialities should be identified in such a way that customers become very quickly aware of their presence on the menu by appropriate use of promotion through colour, boxes, arrows, tent cards, publicity and advertising, and of course, personal selling. Directing attention towards preferred items allows the customer to make a decision, it will not ensure sales but such activities allow the customer no excuse for being unaware of those preferred products. The selling power of a menu may be enhanced by inclusion of what can only be described as 'trendy' items, i.e. items which are currently in vogue or in particular demand, for example, the 'healthy option'.

As we have seen, the product is not the only element of merchandising but it is the most prominent. A wide variety of options exist for product management within the merchandising context.

Product display

The most obvious form of display is the product itself. The retail industry makes effective use of its shop windows to display products to advantage. This is an opportunity frequently missed by caterers. In Japan restaurants would often display the dishes that they were selling in their shop window. Although initially attracting customer interest, as time passed and the dish naturally deteriorated in appearance, it became counter productive. True to their style the Japanese have overcome this problem by producing the most wonderfully accurate, lifelike and very realistic replications of their products: ice cream sundaes that never melt, fried chicken that still appears to be sizzling from the pan. In western society photographs tend to serve the same purpose, however the benefits of three dimensional models that give a clear indication of shape and size should not be overlooked. Naturally when produced, dishes must match promotional displays. Photographs can sometimes (intentionally or not) give the wrong impression of size, leading to disappointment. Whether the model is created to match the dish or the dish presented in the style of the model is less important. Putting an idea, anticipation, into the mind of the customer is the aim, which naturally we must then seek to satisfy.

Products may be displayed on counters, salad bars, trolleys and gueridon. We can display in product groupings – meats, fish, salads, pastries, for example – or by courses – starters, main and dessert. However, we can also promote sales by ignoring some of the more traditional aspects of food display in favour of meal groupings which anticipate consumer needs. For example we might assume that customers selecting from the salad bar are either weight or health conscious. By placing fruit juices, wholemeal breads, dessert yoghurts and mineral waters in close proximity to the salad bar we are more likely to generate a sale of these additional items.

Care needs to be taken with the use of display counters. Displays which are too long may be counter-productive, customer attention will tend to be focused on the centre resulting in lost opportunities at the peripheral edges. Similarly those that are arranging the display should be cautioned against 'visual overload'. The issue of temperature control and food safety needs to be addressed. All three problems – size of display, visual overload and food safety – may be resolved by the use of smaller displays and more frequent replenishment. Mirrors can be used to increase the attractiveness of the display and its apparent size. Mirrors also provide for increased visual access, appropriately placed mirrors will ensure products can be seen even when the service area is crowded. Counters can improve communication, customers will see and talk about what is on display.

Variety of choice and in particular range of sizes should be considered; if customers are not offered a choice of sizes we cannot be sure that we are completely satisfying their needs. This is most often seen, and most easily managed, in the provision of beverages, hot and cold drinks where portion size is determined by the size of the glass or cup. With the use of suitable portion control equipment and procedures the principle can be applied to other menu items. The Chinese were traditionally the greatest exponents of the half portion which did not often result in a reduction in sales. Usually customers were encouraged to try a greater range of menu items and consequently purchase more than intended. The customer can derive added value from individual portions, single portion pots of speciality tea, cafetière or filter coffee.

The manager can identify 'hot' and 'cold' spots in the display/service areas and on menus. These can be used to advantage with by moving more profitable items to the hot spots. The cold spots can be 'warmed up' with special attractions. In operations using counter service, gross profit can be improved merely by repositioning items on the counter. Putting an item with a high GP at the beginning of the line can increase the take-up of that item and subsequently improve the operation's overall profitability. The same lessons can be applied to the repositioning of items on the menu.

Linking food and drink may be achieved directly by the inclusion of, for instance, Guinness in steak and kidney pie, beer with beef stew, white wine with fish and chicken. Alternatively linking may be achieved by association, that is by packaging obviously associated items, e.g. 'Curry and ice cold lager', 'Ploughman's lunch and beer', 'Pasta and plonk', 'Wurst and Pils', although care must be taken not to match wrong items. Further linking could be by promoting association with regional difference, e.g. 'Lancashire nights', 'Scottish breakfasts', 'Devonshire cream teas'.

Sales may be encouraged by efforts in the presentation of food. No-one would doubt that the nouvelle cuisine of the mid-1980s was not valued by both customer and the industry in general. It was symptomatic of a renewed interest in food and cookery which has benefited us all. However, there comes a point where the 'novelty' wears off. Three slices of duck breast and four juniper berries in a blackcurrant sauce may well have attracted a very high price in any West End hotel but customers may demand something in the way of substance in addition to aesthetic value.

In addition to the display of products we should not ignore the merchandising value of displaying the skills of chefs, waiters and sommeliers.

The benefits of presenting a liqueur trolley can be further enhanced by a professional display of skills such as warming the brandy glass or flaming the Sambuca. Part of the meal experience for the customer is the opportunity to see professional staff doing a job well. This does not only apply to difficult or technical skills, even simple tasks performed well can be a joy to watch and add tremendously to the experience, a waiter making salad dressing at the table, or even just polishing glasses behind the bar. Many landlords keep an excellent pint of beer, giving care and attention to the cellar and pumps, but spoil it all with a slovenly approach to the care of the bar area, the counter and their customers.

We should not neglect the additional merchandising benefits of sight and smell which apply particularly to the cooking activity, grilling and flambé work that can be done in the restaurant area, nor should we neglect the role of customer participation in these sort of activities.

Sight sales present endless opportunity. The inclusion of highly flamboyant dishes on the menu and the showmanship abilities of the waiter at the gueridon or the barman with the cocktail shaker are all legitimate means of bringing to the attention of the customer those items which are preferred to be sold.

While bar and waiting staff are taking orders from customers they could be selling 'preferred items'. More than one restaurateur works on the principle of having no (printed) menu at all, relying instead on the obvious advantages of their most valuable asset, staff. Meals are described in delightful terms by good looking people who are obviously interested in their customers and enthusiastic about their food and service. Staff in a number of companies are trained to encourage additional items to be sold, most notably Gardner Merchant, TGI-Friday and McDonald's. Staff and management should take every opportunity to make sales without being intrusive.

Merchandising tactics

Where can merchandising be used to gain competitive advantage?

Maximum benefit may be obtained from merchandising through the careful selection of products that we wish to promote (see Figure 4.2). Obviously there is little point in promoting those items with a low GP percentage, but we must be sure that in promoting those products with a high margin customers will also benefit.

Maximizing profit potential and appealing to customers
- size and range offered
- additional and extra items
- added value
- launching new products
- presentation – impact, linking and grouping
- hot and cold spots

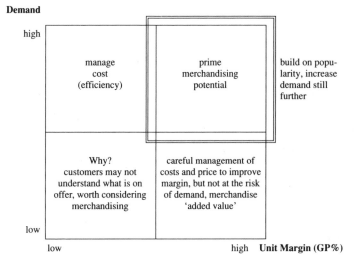

Figure 4.2 Selecting products for merchandising. Be aware of the effects of impulse demand which may be short lived. Also, try to identify seasonal fluctuations.

Adding value

Adding value from the customer's perception is important since the manager's perceptions of value may differ from those of customers. This can be achieved in three ways:

1 By adding 'real' value, i.e. by giving good sized portions, by additional items such as croutons or cream offered with soups and by offering individual portions.
2 By adding 'implied' value, i.e. by describing menu items in a way which is makes the item sound attractive, although the following may be seen to be slightly overdone: 'And now for your delectation, a dish from the depths of the east, Marco Polo brought some to the court of Catherine de Medici, ... etc.'

3   By enhancement of individual dishes in order to increase their attractiveness. Describing items in simple terms as 'Home-made' or 'the Healthy option' may be sufficient. The more sophisticated diner may also respond to more cryptic descriptions which use terms and words which bear little relationship with the dish or its component parts. A restaurant with a garden theme in Manchester referred to a T-bone steak as a 'Spade Handle Special', other examples include the 'Buffalo Wings' found in a number of American themed restaurants. A Blackpool restaurant features 'Fat Man's Misery' and so on. In each case the item is also described in more attractive terms.

We are unlikely to be able to persuade customers to buy twice the number of meals they require, but effective merchandising can encourage them to buy more in the way of additional items, which they may not have originally considered. For example, is the customer having steak? Would they like grilled mushrooms or french fried onions with it? When we serve coffee do we also ask if liqueurs are required? The benefit of presenting a liqueur trolley should not be underestimated. Customers who might normally refuse the offer of a liqueur are often tempted when presented with an array of colourful and exotic bottles. Such tempting activity, besides encouraging customers to buy additional items, might also encourage customers to visit more often.

The expression 'There are so many wonderful things on the menu that I don't know which to choose, we will have to come again,' is often heard.

Impact of the selling effort for the consumer
- appeal
- participation
- evaluation
- willingness to return

Summary

As we have seen the role of marketing is to ensure that customers are identified and clear messages about our products and services are broadcast. Marketing brings the customers to us. The role of merchandising is to encourage customers to purchase by clearly promoting the benefits of the product or service offered. In developing merchandising opportunities the manager will be concerned with point-of-sale promotion: what is actually happening and what could be done to improve both sales and customer satisfaction.

Look closely at the operation and consider the influence of:

- operational policy – ethos/concept/brand
- unit position/location/access
- operational and departmental budgets

Examine the role of:

- staff, selection, training and motivation
- product range and choice
- standards of quality and reliability
- promotional activity, display(s) and menu(s)

Establish a procedure for the implementation of sales development activity. It will be difficult to compare the relative merits of different activities if each is approached in a different manner.

Suggested sales development procedure
- establish potential opportunities
- calculate expected revenue
- identify staffing requirements
- set promotional objectives for teams and individuals
- monitor performance
- judge success

LOOKing for opportunities to increase sales:

LOOK at internal and external markets.

LOOK at point of sale signage.

LOOK at what you sell, or don't sell, and ask why.

LOOK at customers: do you know who they are and what they want?

LOOK at prices, purchasing and selling.

LOOK at the message you send.

LOOK at employee performance, set and communicate standards.

LOOK at assuring quality rather than controlling it.

Look in particular at sales points and analyse the activity
- appearance, attractiveness, welcome
- information, signs, advice
- temptation, colour, sensory domination
- temperature, hot food hot, cold food and drink chilled
- staff appearance and attitude, body language
- guests, queuing, motivation, reaction, buying behaviour
- tills, sales mix, GP percentage, margin on individual items

---

Customer observation

Observe the time spent in entering, purchasing and leaving the unit. Observe the time spent standing still, look for areas which are passed quickly and those which are passed slowly. Look at bottlenecks: do customers take a second alternative rather than waiting, do they go away disappointed?

How to influence the customer flow
- re-position products
- relocate purchase points (tills)
- relocate service points and displays

Customers expect to be enticed by new ideas, to see what they are buying and for those products to be served attractively. Customers will buy more if you make it easy for them.

To sell those products which yield a higher contribution, ensure that they are:
- quality products
- displayed and presented professionally
- located in the mainstream
- positioned within easy reach

Manage your space effectively, make sure paying is easy and, even where self-service is encouraged, ensure that there are sufficient staff to close the sale.

Remember that the customer's decision to return is assisted by the quality (fitness for purpose, consistency and reliability) of products and services, the perceived value (cost in relation to benefits) and the general atmosphere. Presentation and staff attitude will further contribute to the customer's enjoyment of the meal experience.

Merchandising is very cost effective, it requires little by way of additional resources, but the benefits can be considerable:

- performance improvement
- customer satisfaction

The benefits of successful sales development and merchandising activities accrue to all concerned. Customers appreciate value and service, return more often, stay longer and spend more. Staff feel good, enjoy working with happy and satisfied customers, and gain a sense of achievement. The company will be more successful.

Legal aspects and implications of merchandising

The general conditions of contract law (offer and acceptance) apply to sales promotion and merchandising activity. Sales promotion, in describing the goods and setting a price, constitutes an offer which is accepted by the customer when they place an order. At this point a contract exists between the two parties. The caterer is bound to supply products and services as described. The customer is protected from misrepresentation or misleading information. If there are any additional terms and conditions to the contract, such as service charge or half price drinks which are only sold between the hours of 6 and 8p.m., then these must be clearly stated on the promotional material.

As has been mentioned in previous chapters, careful attention is required in the wording of sales material. This is particularly true for merchandising where there can be a temptation to exceed the bounds of truth. Terms like large are not easy to define; what seems large to an office worker may not be so apparent to a labourer. In this, as in other cases where there is no precise definition, the rule of law relies on what a typical customer or the average member of the general public might believe.

Additionally the following legislation will have some bearing on sales development and merchandising activity.

Trade Descriptions Act 1968 Sale of Goods Act	Deal with contractual conditions.
Food and Drugs Act 1955 Food Hygiene Regulations Food Safety Act 1991 Weights and Measures Act 1979	Deal with product descriptions, the nature and quality of the product, its fitness for purpose and portion sizes

Continuing performance improvement as a result of effective merchandising

Merchandising is frequently associated with the promotion of new products. Once the novelty wears off the product becomes an established menu item and gets forgotten by managers and staff and, more importantly, by customers. Merchandising is an ongoing activity applied to all products and services, needing the total support and commitment of everyone involved.

People are essential to merchandising activity. All other action is pointless if managers or staff present themselves poorly or have the wrong attitude towards sales development. Managing the service encounter is critical to the successful development of the operation.

Suggested additional reading

Fewell, A. and Wills, N. (1995) *Marketing*. Butterworth–Heinemann.

Miller, J.E. (1987) *Menu Pricing and Strategy*. Van Nostrand Rheinhold.

Seaberg, A.G. (1991) *Menu Design, Merchandising and Marketing*. Van Nostrand Rheinhold.

5
Quality

Aims and objectives

The main aim of quality management is to identify those elements of a system which, if managed well, can significantly influence the customers' perception of the quality of service and product that they receive. Understanding the principles involved will enable the development of quality customer care programmes ensuring consistent delivery of sought-after products and services.

Quality management aims
To arrive at a workable (manageable) approach to consistent quality improvement.
To develop procedures, processes and practices which consistently match customer expectations.
To define standards of performance which conform to customer expectations.

Quality management cannot be a whim or fad; it must be a long-term, planned, monitored and measured activity which has the support of all connected with the operation – managers, supervisors, employees, suppliers and most important of all, customers.

As has already been noted in previous chapters, a successful operation is dependent on repeat business.

Reputation and return custom are dependent on consistent quality. Consistency is dependent on standards and standardization supported by an effective system. This chapter seeks to identify elements within the operation that contribute to good quality. Ultimately proposals for 'best practice' will be outlined.

Quality management objectives

To develop knowledge and understanding of the determinants of quality.

To identify suitable methods and processes of monitoring and evaluating quality provision.

To prepare documentation and recording procedures to support quality standards.

To instruct, train and motivate staff to achieve desired levels of performance.

To demonstrate the use and value of quality management as a problem solving technique.

To show how quality management can influence profitability.

What is quality?

The starting point for quality management is to arrive at a working definition for quality which is valid, relevant, reliable and understood by all concerned in the operation, particularly customers.

A number of definitions are available to us. A simple dictionary definition might refer to 'A degree or standard of excellence'. This tends to lead to comparison of products and often such comparison will be based on biased or influenced by monetary value. Quality is not necessarily the 'best' or the 'most expensive' product.

If asked to name a good quality watch people will often

identify Rolex. It may be argued that Rolex, as a method of telling the time, is not good quality, in fact good quality may best be found in the 'cheap' pages of the Argos catalogue. Why? Because the watches on those pages are easily accessible and designed for a specific purpose. They will tell the time to a fair degree of accuracy, be hard wearing and frequently water resistant, with the added benefit that if you tire of them, or they break, they are cheap enough to throw away and replace, without too much regret or recrimination. Rolex, on the other hand serves an entirely different purpose. In many respects it is not a timepiece at all. It is purchased and worn as a fashion accessory, a statement of wealth and position. Most of us would be frightened to use a Rolex as a timepiece for normal daily use. Its care, repair and security would become a hindrance. It may thus be argued that a Rolex is not suited to the purpose for which most of us would purchase a watch, therefore it is not good quality.

So, if quality has little to do with cost, what are the key issues or reference points? One very pragmatic interpretation might be 'Customers that do come back for products that don't'. Common to this definition and many others is the issue of product performance and reliability, such that quality may best be defined as 'fitness for purpose'. A quality product will fully and effectively meet the need for which it was designed, produced and sold. Quality is, therefore, that level or standard of product or service which best meets the needs and expectation of the consumer. Indeed quality is customer responsive and error free.

The British Standards Institute definition supports this 'customer responsive' perspective.

Quality – BSI definition
'The totality of features and characteristics of the product or service that bear on its ability to meet a given need.'

Because customer needs and expectations may be unique to each operation it follows that an operation's particular interpretation of quality will be unique.

Having arrived at a suitable definition, that definition must be 'sold' to all participants in the operation. It must become the watchword of every activity. It will be synonymous with the operation as a whole and may be built into the company 'mission statement'. It will certainly be a core element of the development of company and operational policy.

What are the features and characteristics of quality?

The characteristics of quality can be broadly divided into two main categories, physical and psychological. The physical may be defined as those objective elements which we can see, feel, touch and taste. The psychological include those subjective elements which are subject to more personal perceptions.

Quality characteristics

Physical	*Psychological*
● Component parts	● Design and presentation
● Material content	● Functional performance
● Delivery/service	● Brand image and reputation
● Price	● Reliability

Additionally other characteristics derive from quality.

● Value
● Satisfaction
● Delight

Value – definition
A function of quality and price, a balance of monetary
expectation and usefulness. The least cost for an essential
function or service at the desired time and place with the
required quality and reliability.

Delight might be described as satisfaction of needs, good
value, a product or service that offers that little something
extra. Delight is an important element of product differentiation. As we have seen, product differentiation plays a key role
in marketing and customer choice. Consequently, management emphasis on good quality offers the potential of continuous improvement for both customer and investor.

What is quality management?

The term TQM or total quality management has been used,
and misused, a great deal in the last few years. Based on the
apparent weakness in the earlier systems of control and assurance which were arguably narrow in their perspective, it
attempts to take a more holistic approach to the problem.
Whilst not referring specifically to TQM too often in this
text, it is recognized that the greatest advantage to be gained
from managing quality is when it is directed at the operation
as a whole rather than narrow elements being dealt with
individually. However, in order to aid understanding of the
holistic approach we will need to examine individual
elements separately.

Quality management is concerned with the systematic
planning and management of all operational activities, techniques, processes and procedures. The principal benefits of
quality management will be the development of product and
service guarantees, and commitment to customers. The attention of all employees, supervisors and managers will be
focused on customers and key service requirements,
providing a competitive advantage in the marketplace.

One of the key quality objectives is the aspiration toward 'zero defects'. Whilst it is easy to suggest that this may be an impossible dream, those companies that continue to strive toward this goal are seen to be more successful in attracting customers. The Japanese, renowned for their quality consciousness, refer to this aspect of quality management as the 'Poka-Yoke' concept. Loosely translated this means a 'fail safe' system, identifying and managing the stages in production where things could go wrong. Here in the UK, we are more familiar with the concept of HACCP (Hazard Analysis and Critical Control Points) which has been shown to be extremely effective in the management of hygiene and food safety. Although both concepts were originally designed for production processes the principles can be easily transferred to service systems.

Understanding the industry, its products and services

The nature of hospitality and the meal experience is unique. Products are designed, manufactured and sold under one roof. The customer is allowed, even encouraged, to interfere with the process. Unlike manufacturing and retailing, hospitality production and service cannot easily be divorced, yet they are different. Hospitality may be defined as a combination of the physical and the convivial.

Physical	*versus*	**Convivial**
Hard		*Soft*
Products		Service
Materials		Attitudes
(Method)		(Body language)
Process		*Procedure*

Television and the press continue to encourage the growth of 'personalities' in the hospitality industry, but creativity and technical excellence do not necessarily guarantee quality. Confusion arises between levels and styles of delivery making identification of common quality standards difficult. Whilst service quality continues to vary widely across the industry there is a growing application of 'standardization' in food production and an increasing reliance on convenience products as a basis for maintaining consistency and reliability.

Separating the customer and service from production makes quality control (of products) easier. Products designed to meet a particular need can be carefully controlled to be consistent and reliable. However, dishes designed and manufactured for the hospitality industry can easily be repackaged for the retail industry. As a consequence if you are looking for quality food, as opposed to a quality meal, you may be best served by your local supermarket. For the hospitality industry to survive it needs to concentrate on the quality of the meal experience as a whole.

Managing food and beverage systems

A typical food and beverage operation would normally involve at least three sub-systems, each having further sub-systems, as shown in Figure 5.1.

Whatever the method/system of production, the customer is the most important part of the production line. It is interesting to note that much of the growth in the hospitality industry is through developments of existing systems and new ideas, Benihana (sushi, teriyaki, etc.), Mongolian barbecue, the pub grill/barbecue, where levels of service (numbers of service staff) are reduced but there is greater customer focus (guests become actively involved in production/cooking).

Customers are concerned with consistency and reliability. Customers will enjoy participating, if that is the clear intention of the system. They will be less than pleased if they are

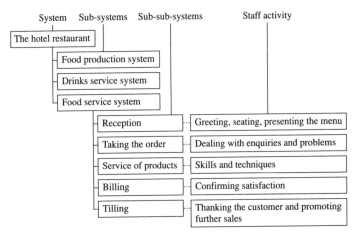

Figure 5.1 Food and beverage systems.

led to expect a level of service which is not supported by the system. Without doubt what irritates customers most is poor or inadequate service. Systems must be designed effectively to meet customer expectations.

Quality of service must be a response to the defined image of the operation. Customers will have preconceived expectations. The manager's job is to ensure that these are identified and provided for. In principle two elements are essential and relatively easy to provide for. Service should be both timely and friendly. Responsive but unrushed service delivered in an unobtrusive fashion is generally the key, although haste and exuberance can add a little colour if the meal experience demands it, as in a typical Italian meal for instance. A third element, skills, requires further consideration as a variety of options and styles of delivery may be available which could provide, from the customer perspective, the same level of service. Because traditional silver service is no longer seen as the norm, customers would not perceive lack of silver service skills as lack of care. Social skills take on more importance.

The manager is able to choose from a variety of methods of delivering food: plated, carvery and family service, for example.

Quality of the food is determined by features like presentation, portion size, smell, taste and texture. Many operations have moved to food production divorced from service – based on cook-freeze, cook-chill or sous-vide – in order to be more cost effective. Some caterers successfully utilize pre-prepared dishes. What should be considered is that many classic dishes, prepared under similar circumstances, can now be found on supermarket shelves. Customers may be looking for something different or unusual. In these circumstances the manager will have to determine methods of combining and presenting foods and dishes that demonstrate originality and generate genuine interest and anticipation in the mind of the customer.

Why is quality important?

Quality is important in every aspect of business. The marketing message normally has a quality 'hook', purchasing is based on specifications, defining the quality of input. Production activities are heavily influenced by standards (process and output), selling and ultimately customer evaluation are dependent on identifiable benefits. Operations are effective (profitable) if they manage quality. Quality is defined by customer perspective, therefore customers exert a great deal of control/influence over operations and operational management.

Quality management is primarily concerned with the control of '**input–process–output**'. To borrow computer phraseology: '*Garbage in equals garbage out!*'

Quality is a direct response to consumer pressure, as may be evidenced by the increasing importance of quality beers as a result of the activities of CAMRA (the Campaign for Real Ale). Providing a good choice of quality ale shows that we care about our customers.

Business needs
Quality management contributes to maintaining the competitive edge.
- Market share
- Competition
- Product differentiation
- Brand loyalty
- More customers
- Customer loyalty
- Staff loyalty

Consumers are increasingly open to new ideas, they travel more, are subjected to new ideas and new standards. Consequently needs are continuously changing and customers have become more demanding. Quality management is a continuous process of maintaining pace with change. Improvements in technology – and as a consequence, raw materials – make higher standards easier to achieve. However, there are risks. Avoid change for change's sake. For instance, when Coca-Cola created their 'new formula', it was 'better' but no-one liked it.

It is clear that the customer, and not the provider, determines the parameters of quality for any given product or service transaction. Customer perceptions will normally be based on five specific factors:

- price
- fitness for purpose
- performance

- reliability
- reputation (truth)

There is no significance in the sequence as presented above. While price might be the ultimate factor in deciding whether to make a purchase or not it becomes less meaningful when calculating the value (quality) of the transaction. In customer judgement of products and services 'performance' and particularly 'fitness for purpose' become much more critical. Reliability and reputation are prominent in the decision to return. Reputation, particularly in relation to the recommendations of others, is not necessarily 'truth' in its purest sense, but it does represent what is commonly 'believed' and consequently its significance cannot be underestimated.

If the senior manager of a company like Ratners, the jewellers, publicly announces that his products are 'crap', the truth (if that is what his analysis can be taken to be) is immaterial if customers continue to 'believe' in the quality of the products. We should not forget that the judgement of both parties is influenced by price (value) and if you are in a position to afford the most expensive then your judgement of cheaper products may be more critical. It is arguable that the real 'crime' was the insult, intended or not, to customers that the announcement gave. Altruistically, does this suggest that the real test of quality is the degree to which you can insult your customers without it affecting sales? I hope not. Whilst customers might ignore the insult when it is delivered far from the point of sale, it would not be condoned, even by Ratners, if it became part of the service activity.

More positive lessons may be learnt from other retailers, particularly Marks & Spencer, which demonstrate the significance of both reputation and performance. Most people believe that Marks & Spencers' quality cannot be equalled. Only the finest raw materials are used, the production processes are closely monitored, controls and assurance procedures exist from design through to sale. Should a product not satisfy it will be exchanged, without question.

This all costs money of course, but generally people are prepared to pay the additional price. Even where funds are not sufficient for a Marks & Spencers' purchase, M&S are still an influence as seen in the growth of 'seconds' shops selling M&S rejects.

Retailing examples might be useful, but what of the hospitality industry? Unfortunately good examples are rare. While some hospitality companies may have been operating for as long as Marks & Spencer, they have not had the mass appeal of M&S. At the top end of the market there is undoubted consistent and reliable quality, but at a price that very few of us can afford. The rest of the industry has a very chequered history, either failing to provide any real sustained quality, pricing themselves out of the market or falling victim to fashion or trend (failure to respond/change). Up until the early 1960s, Lyons' Tea Houses might have been sited as the catering equivalent of M&S. From the 1960s to the present day it has been the burger chains which have led the way in providing quality products to the masses, but they have only been able to achieve this by reducing choice and/or modifying production processes and procedures. Even so their consistency and reliability cannot be challenged.

With the advent of improved food processing and storage techniques (cook-freeze, cook-chill and sous-vide) has come the ability to provide high-quality products in a wide range of choice at a very reasonable price. But it has been the retail trade and the brewing industry not the hospitality industry that have responded most quickly to these opportunities. While we 'believe' that traditional methods of fresh production are best, customers are flocking to pubs and moderately priced chain-operated restaurants whose reputation is based on the high performance of reliable products which are fit for the purpose at a very reasonable price, even though they may well have been 'manufactured' in a central production unit 200 miles away.

The caterer must continually assess quality from the perspective of the customer, develop products and services which respond to customer needs which may be continually changing.

The cost of quality

It is important not to underestimate the cost of quality. However, in measuring the cost we must also identify the benefits.

- **Quality costs**: resources, procedures, documentation, training.
- **Quality benefits**: improved product, more motivated staff, increased turnover, increased market share.

The cost of quality must be measured against the cost of failure. The real cost of quality failure is frequently undervalued. Typically wastage is often valued at raw material cost whereas the real value is in lost sales and therefore waste should be costed at sales value.

Internal failure costs:
- time
- effort/skills
- materials

Appraisal costs:
- inspection
- documentation
- materials (destructive testing)

External failure costs:
- replacement
- repair
- reputation

Prevention costs:
- design
- training
- consultation

It may be argued that quality is 'free'. In the long term, waste reduction, elimination of mistake correction and the removal of non-value-added activities will reduce costs beyond the investment required. There will necessarily be short-term investment on consultancy, equipment, training, systems and procedures.

Quality management can be identified as a cost centre, this is desirable for control (measuring performance). However, operations should avoid 'cost dumping' from other departments/activities which will cause quality management to appear overly expensive.

Quality and profit

Profit may derived from a variety of quality responses:

● Customer loyalty: repeat purchases
● Security and market share: competition on quality not price
● Reduced marketing costs: improved reputation and growth

Are quality and profit linked? Yes, there is considerable evidence to show investment quality results in positive rewards. It is particularly important to recognize that, as management systems are perfected, quality cost may diminish whilst revenue and profit margins are growing.

The relationship with marketing

The following elements of marketing are essential to quality management.

Market research

● What features are most important to customers?
● What are their expectation levels?
● What do customers expect when problems occur?

> **Consumer expectation may be based on:**
> - verbal communication   (recommendations)
> - non-verbal communication   (Patients' Charter,
>   guarantees, advertising)
> - merchandising
> - personal needs   (Maslow, 1987)
> - past experience

As was discussed in Chapter 3, identifying customer needs is a function of marketing activity. Customers in a food and beverage operation do not necessarily need food and drink. Our ability to identify accurately customer needs and respond effectively will obviously influence customer perceptions of the quality offered.

Market analysis establishes organizational goals, enabling policy to be developed and targets and standards set. Quality once defined and achieved then becomes an important part of the marketing message.

Company policy

Company policy often results in guaranteed standards of performance (note in particular the examples of the recently privatized utilities: British Gas, British Telecom, and the electricity companies who support their guarantees with a money back commitment).

It would be possible for a restaurateur boldly to proclaim 'we guarantee total satisfaction'. It would not require a 'perfect', fault-free system although, if it were possible, it would be nice. What is required is that:

(a) customers are encouraged to identify problems at the earliest opportunity, and
(b) all staff are empowered to solve problems in the quickest and most effective manner, best suited to the particular occasion and without recourse to management.

As a consequence every customer, regardless of whatever problem may have arisen, should leave the restaurant totally satisfied.

Many believe that customers whose problems have been resolved actually become more committed 'believers' in the operation (system). They have tested it and not found it wanting; they feel more secure.

Setting and adhering to strict policy guidelines has other marketing/quality advantages. Prominent among these is the importance of 'brand image'. Little Chef, Happy Eater, Brewers Fayre and many others positively promote their 'brands' in the knowledge that customers who know the system and feel secure are inclined to return.

Look at TV advertising. How many companies sell (overtly) on quality, e.g. Center Parcs can 'guarantee' the weather.

Who is involved with quality?

Senior managers

Senior managers will be responsible for developing company policy and the 'mission statement' which are linked directly to quality management.

Unit managers

Unit managers will be responsible for ensuring that resources, systems and procedures are in place in order to deliver the 'standards' identified in company policy and the 'promises' made in the mission statement. Specifically unit managers will be controlling the operational cycle in order that quality assurance is applied at each stage of the system. While unit managers will be concerned to communicate with customers they will also manage quality-related communication throughout the operation. As a basis for effective quality management, unit managers may encourage empowerment of staff through the provision of quality circles or quality chains. In particular unit managers may consider the benefits to be derived from applying the principles of the 'internal customer'.

Communication and feedback:
- job descriptions
- personnel specifications
- staff training manuals
- equipment design specifications
- equipment instructions, use and cleaning
- maintenance schedules and records
- work schedules
- raw material specifications
- standardized recipes, methods and yield
- service manuals
- customer care policy and manuals
- sales history
- wastage records
- customer comments

... all of which have quality implications, either influencing design, monitoring/controlling performance or measuring success.

Staff

The notion of internal customers is based on the idea that, regardless of who actually serves the paying guest, everyone in the operation is a customer to someone else. The waiter is a customer to the chef, the chef is a customer to the storeman, the storeman is a customer to the control clerk, and so on. If each internal transaction is treated in this way the paying guest is likely to receive more effective and efficient service.

Quality circles, albeit of a fairly unsophisticated form, have existed in the hospitality industry for a long time. Chefs work together on product-centred quality development while waiters would concentrate on service quality. But, unfortunately, they have tended to be protectionist (self/departmental interest) rather than for the good of the whole operation and greater benefit of the customer. Circles that draw on mixed responsibilities and experience should be encouraged. This may well mean waiters telling chefs how to improve the product (based on received customer comments). We should create a culture where this becomes a desirable, rewarding, activity rather than the cause of a fist fight.

Customers

Customers will evaluate quality based on varying needs and expectations at a particular point in time. However, there are some key attributes which the food and beverage operator can be responsive to.

Quality attributes
- Access
- Responsiveness
- Communication
- Credibility
- Rapport
- Reliability
- Competence
- Courtesy
- Security

What other factors are important?

- spending power
- opportunity cost
- variety of choice

Customers and caterers alike are subject to changes in the

environment in which they operate. Obviously customer spending is influenced by earnings, taxation and current value of the pound. In order that a meal out may be enjoyed our customer must weigh the 'opportunity cost'. If a meal costs £20, then that means £20 of our customer's money cannot be spent on other interests or needs and the 'opportunity' of an alternative benefit will be lost. The quality of the meal must not only measure up to expectations, it must also confirm that the opportunity cost was not wasted. If our customer leaves the restaurant thinking that, on reflection, they would rather have bought a couple of CDs, their perception of our product/service quality will be affected.

> We frequently forget what our customers have to give up in order to enjoy our products and services.

For the customer, variety of choice is also an integral part of quality evaluation. Whilst reducing variety might enable the operator to maintain higher levels of quality control it may cause the customer to be more critical. As a society we generally find it easier to criticize decisions forced on us rather than those in which we have played a part. One approach to this problem is to reduce the range of raw materials (control problems) but allow customers to mix and match their own product. This tactic may commonly be seen in pizza restaurants, but it can be modified to suit a wide variety of operations. Even where menu items are well defined, the potential for customers to 'modify' the dish should not be ignored.

> Burger King challenged McDonald's quality image with their 'you wannit, you gottit' campaign.

Quality culture

Companies who emphasize service excellence may be seen to gain competitive advantage. It has been suggested that the best way to look after your customers is to look after your staff. Management attention to internal customers and chains of excellence at every stage of the catering cycle are to be encouraged. Service excellence through the empowerment of all staff should be a key feature.

In the final analysis quality assurance comes down to organizational culture:
- internal customers
- quality circles
- empowerment
- supportive management

Quality strategy

How is quality developed?

The starting point for quality is the mission statement, of which there are six elements:

- the market, customers
- the product/service
- people (employees)
- organization (structure)
- the price (range)
- the competition

based on total commitment to quality

Identifying and responding to customer needs

We need to ensure that we fully understand consumer needs. The man purchasing a drill does not actually want a drill, what he really wants is a hole! As soon as the solar powered, pocket laser hole maker is developed we will no longer be able to sell drills. The consumer is concerned with the 'benefits', not the product or process.

The same applies to food, particularly when fashion and tastes can change so quickly. What are the needs, how are they best satisfied, at what risk to the operation? In marketing terms, there is no difference between products and services. The difficulty arises when the caterer is not exactly sure which consumer 'benefit' is being delivered. Is service a bi-product of food and drink or vice versa?

Quality then is a direct correlation of 'customer satisfaction', ensuring and measuring customer satisfaction is a key quality activity. A customer complaint is a cause for concern, a product or service has failed to meet expectations. But customers don't always complain, so how do we know how well we are doing? Part of the marketing function is to identify customer needs which should be analysed carefully in order to assess how they may be satisfied. It is possible to identify various elements within the product or service which will assist in determining high levels of customer satisfaction.

Constituents of satisfaction
- psychological/physiological (wants, needs, expectations, motives)
- social (association, companionship, security)
- economics (disposable income, method of payment)
- situational (time of day and time available)

It is necessary at this point to differentiate between customer and consumer as both will have needs which may, to the great consternation of the provider, differ. The classic situation is parent and child. The parent (customer) will pay the bill and partake of some of the product or service. The child (consumer) will evaluate the quality of product/service provided. Unfortunately the wants, needs and expectations held by parents and children may be at odds. While parents may understand the benefits of clean, wholesome and nutritious food, such advantages will be completely incomprehensible to the child. Food is supposed to be colourful, sickly and preferably as messy as possible.

Treets – melt in your mouth not in your hand.
(cleanliness not taste)
The quality 'hook' is directed at the customer
not the consumer.

Traditionally the hospitality industry has either ignored the needs of one part of the parent/child package with a resulting slow decline in trade, or excluded both parties in order to compete in a smaller but more well-defined market. Such solutions would be relatively neat if families were a minority or if parent/child were the only area of customer confusion. Unfortunately the caterer is continuously faced with customer/consumer confusion.

Sometimes, if not frequently, in trying to best meet the needs of the customer (e.g. controlling price) the caterer risks antagonizing the consumer. The host and their guests (weddings), controlling conference delegates ('free' wine). It is tempting when offered functions or conferences to dilute the price in order to capture the business. Price negotiations for these sorts of functions must be a function of economies of scale not quality erosion. Indeed the maintenance of high levels of quality must be seen as a positive competitive advantage.

Differentiating between production and service

Quality management is an attempt to guarantee 'repeatability' of provision, through systems and procedures of control or assurance.

Recap on BSI definition of quality
'The totality of features and characteristics of a *product* or *service* that bear on its ability to satisfy a given need.'

Hospitality is a combination of so-called hard and soft elements. There is a strong temptation to control the hard *products* and assure the soft *service*.

The difference between control and assurance

BSI (British Standards Institute) define:

Quality control: A system for programming and co-ordinating the effect of various groups within an organization to maintain and improve quality at an economic level that allows for customer satisfaction. Quality control is generally associated with checking end product against design and fault correction. It is mechanistic in nature, normally identifying authority and responsibility.

Quality assurance: All activities concerned with the attainment of desired quality standards. Quality assurance means designing quality into the system, error prevention and ensuring that no problems occur. It needs organic organization, systems, philosophy and teamwork.

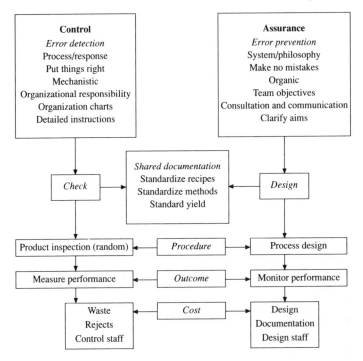

Figure 5.2 Control and assurance.

When is quality implemented?

Product (control)

Product and production quality (control) often gets most attention, because it is easier. Traditional control places the emphasis on error detection through the catering cycle and, ultimately, of the end product – specifically by the identification of critical control points (CCPs), illustrated in Figure 5.3.

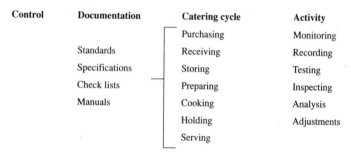

Control	Documentation	Catering cycle	Activity
		Purchasing	Monitoring
Standards		Receiving	Recording
Specifications		Storing	Testing
Check lists		Preparing	Inspecting
Manuals		Cooking	Analysis
		Holding	Adjustments
		Serving	

Figure 5.3 The catering cycle (CCPs).

Some critical control points in the catering cycle and possible means of reducing errors are given below:

- **purchase:** detailed specifications and standard order forms
- **receipt:** inspection (sample/test) on delivery
- **storage:** specific storage conditions, stock rotation procedures, date stamp products, sample stored items
- **preparation:** standardized recipes
- **cooking:** standardized recipes, methods and yield, product presentation specifications
- **holding:** temperature control, stock rotation, hygiene
- **serving:** dish/table setting specification, standard service procedures, portion control equipment
- **paying:** customer feedback, sales analysis

Levels of control (reliability) are dependent on:

- range of dishes
- dish complexity
- frequency of change

An up-market restaurant with imaginative/creative dishes on a daily changing menu might be impossible to control. It might even be argued that control, other than at the hotplate, is not necessary. Based on the price the customer is paying, we can afford to dispose of any product which is not perfect. The weakness in such an argument is that whilst waste might be affordable, such a system will not easily identify where things are going wrong and so mistakes will continue to be made. Such an approach would be inherently inefficient. There is nothing wrong with being efficient and consequently more profitable.

By comparison, control of quality at McDonald's is easy. Changes are less frequent and when they occur they are generally modifications of a proven process/product. Here also, the customer is paying a price for quality, but 'economies of scale' ensure that costs of control are spread over a wider range (greater number of consumers).

For all other operations there is generally a compromise. A menu which appears to be constantly changing may be based on a recipe file/manual of several hundred standardized (controlled) dishes, each designed to fit with existing production/service systems.

Error identification (diagnostics)

Errors may be seen to fall into three broad categories:

- random: no pattern, difficult to trace.
- sporadic: pattern may not be immediately apparent, but will become clear in time.
- systematic: easily and immediately identifiable pattern.

Systematized diagnosis is only possible where there is a clearly defined production pattern with standardized processes and procedures for staff, equipment and raw materials (methods/manuals). Product-oriented control procedures cannot compensate for poor service.

Service (assurance)

It may be argued that many services can be controlled in the
same way as manufactured goods. The quality of certain
elements, including facilities, can be assured with some
certainty. However, where there are significant levels of
customer participation, management can face major problems in assuring quality. The source of the problem may not
be the employee. The customer, through interaction with
contact employees, service production processes and other
customers can also have a major impact on the quality of
service. There are three main areas of concern:

- The quality of the interaction between the contact
  employee and the customer.
- The quality of tangible clues such as surroundings and
  facilities.
- The quality of expectation, brand image, mission statement.

Service quality is, to a great degree, dependent on customer/
consumer perceptions, perspectives and participation. Service
activity is both procedural and convivial:

Procedure:	Conviviality:
● flow	● attitude
● timeliness	● body language
● responsiveness	● tone of voice
● anticipation	● tact
● communication	● naming names
● customer feedback	● attentiveness
● supervision	● guidance – suggestive selling
	– problem solving

| Can be set down in manuals and easily trained. | Objectives may be set and good examples recognized, but cannot always be trained. |

Conviviality, the 'human' element, is difficult to control. How do you predict or manage human frailties? How do you cope with those instances where people take an instant dislike to one another? One approach is to develop a system based on procedure without conviviality as evidenced in bank and building society 'hole-in-the-wall' cash machines and, for the hospitality industry, budget hotels. An alternative to avoiding or reducing conviviality is to select staff whose personalities suit your customers, regardless of skill or previous experience. Skills can be developed through training, personality is far more difficult to manage.

The service encounter varies with different sectors; contrast fast food with the five star hotel (Figure 5.4). Each in its own way attempts to assure the whole operation through culture modification.

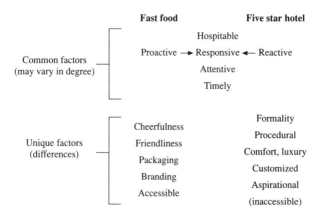

Figure 5.4 The service encounter.

Another problem with service is the nature of the encounter, the number of staff involved and the number of interactions which take place during any given meal experience. While customers find it relatively easy to articulate problems, they are less able to describe what they mean by good service, particularly when their needs change day to day (they may be happy with relaxed service one day, but complaining of staff inattentiveness the next). Even when customers are able to articulate their needs, not all staff will get the message.

These problems may be overcome by introducing an 'internal customer' culture and allowing the development of 'quality circles'.

Assuring quality service

● Define customer requirements	(service characteristics)
● Set standards	(document procedures, define responses and outcomes)
● Provide suitable environment	(internal customers, facilities, products and services)
● Recruit and train the right people	(motivation and morale development)
● Check conformance	(customer feedback, quality audit)
● Problem solving	(immediate response)
● Statistical analysis	(relevant, valid and reliable data)

Checking conformance includes the following aspects:

● customer complaint analysis
● customer feedback (comment cards, surveys)
● quality audit
● observation

- determine cause of problems
- take corrective action

Combining product and service (control and assurance)

The advantages of the traditional (control) approach are:

1 Everyone working to clear guidelines, no confusion over standards.
2 Control systems provide the framework for performance analysis.
3 The same systems can be applied to all units (in a chain).
4 Staff can easily transfer between units.

The advantages of the assurance approach are:

1 Staff sense of pride and personal commitment.
2 Customers receive flexible and responsive treatment.
3 Staff accept responsibility and participate in problem solving (less blame shifting).
4. The operation can respond quickly to change.

Managing products and production quality is technical. Ideas may be adopted and/or adapted from manufacturing. The system is capable of scientific measurement through the identification of physical characteristics. Managing service quality relies on behavioural science. Ideas are adapted from sociological studies. There is little opportunity for scientific management.

Should they, and can they, be separated? Total quality management suggests not. Quality control, quality assurance and total quality management may be seen as different elements of the 'quality pyramid' (see Figure 5.5). Control provides the backbone or framework around which the quality structure is erected; assurance may be seen as a sphere which encompasses most, but not all, of the structure. Total quality can be perceived as the environment which encapsulates the whole structure.

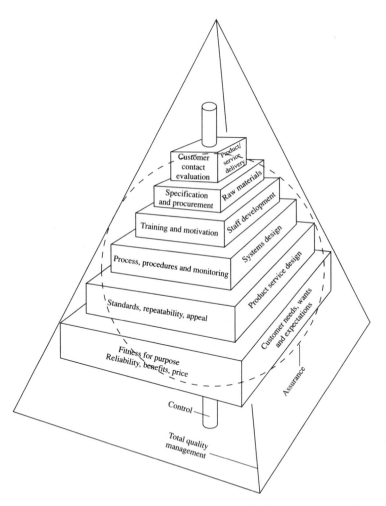

Figure 5.5 The quality pyramid.

Quality tactics

Where can quality be used to gain competitive advantage?

Building on customer perceptions

Our customers are generally provided with a good deal of information – policy, mission statement, marketing and merchandising messages, on which their expectations of quality will be built.

> Peters (1987) suggests that a customer-focused operation will 'under-promise and over-deliver'.

In order to differentiate our products and services from the competition we may well have made a number of 'promises'. In order to fulfil customer expectations it will be necessary to demonstrate our commitment to customers with product and service standards that are backed by guarantees. Staff will be trained to listen and respond to customers and will be invested with the authority to solve problems should the need arise.

Developing the assurance approach means:

- selecting personalities
- training skills
- building quality circles

In some circumstances it may be necessary to control service through the provision of 'scripts', key words and phrases for the staff to work from. In addition to ensuring staff say the right thing a well written script offers increased control over the customer. However, a prescriptive script may give the impression of an unthinking, uncaring automaton. In some circumstances it is easier to change customer expectations of service than change employee performance:

- the hole-in-the-wall bank
- budget hotels
- the mini-bar in the guest's room
- the breakfast buffet

Retention strategy

In order to ensure satisfaction and retain customers in the 'long term', the following areas need consideration:

- Customer relationship: Listen and respond to customers; well-trained staff with the authority to solve problems.

- Customer service standards: Clearly defined procedures governing contact between employees and customers.

- Commitment to customers: Products and services which are backed by guarantees which are made clear to the customer and are upheld 100 per cent.

- Complaint resolution: Employees in contact with customers responding promptly; complaints studied to prevent recurring problems.

- Customer satisfaction data:

  Keep track of how satisfied all types of customers are and use the information to improve the services and customer relations. Compare data over time, trend, reduction in complaints.

- Customer satisfaction: comparison:

  Compare with other companies in this and other industries, especially those that are generally considered to be 'the best'.

(Taken from Randall, L. and Senior, M. (1992) *Managing and Improving Service Quality* (TQM Practitioner Series), Technical Communications (Publishing) Ltd.

Problem solving

Don't just look at the end product, every component and/or step in the process must be examined. Utilize the operational cycle, in particular the principle of HACCP (Hazard Analysis and Critical Control Points). Apply the quality rule of 'fitness for purpose' at each stage: does the raw material, process or equipment contribute effectively to the quality of the end product? If there is a fault does it lie in operational (system) weakness, poor staff performance, working conditions, or defective equipment? If the fault is traced to staff performance, utilize the techniques of job and task analysis to identify the specific weakness. Define needs, plan activities, conduct training and evaluate performance/results. Sometimes the system may appear to be perfect. Problems may result from conflicting objectives, gaps between management and consumer perceptions.

Customers may place emphasis on different factors when identifying poor and good quality. What causes dissatisfaction will not necessarily increase satisfaction when corrected. Some things (e.g. temperature) are either right or wrong, other elements (e.g. recipe) allow for continuing improvement. In particular circumstances customers may be willing to sacrifice good facilities for good service. For example, event catering (a tent in a field) will provide minimal facilities, but high levels of personal service will still be expected.

Generally, hospitality (food and beverage) provision is not either/or (control or assurance); products and service are inextricably entwined and quality management throughout the operation should reflect this. But to begin with, at least, deal with products and services separately.

Quality management is rather like a jig-saw, it looks simple when complete but it is a different story when all the pieces are jumbled, particularly when some of the pieces are viewed from the wrong side. Get all the pieces the right way up find the parameters (corners and edges), build recognizable blocks, connect the blocks, fill the gaps. Avoid external interference (mum wants the table for dinner), but call for help (consultancy) when you need it (you can't tell the difference between sea and sky; it all looks blue to you).

Quality improvement

Apply the rule of continuous improvement, identifying and solving problems at the earliest stage. Quality improvement is more likely to be achieved through assurance but do not neglect controls. The assurance approach gives the caring worker the tools (authority) to deliver:

● customization
● personalization
● empathy

Measuring quality performance

The customer will frequently use the principle of 'benchmarking', comparing your provision to that of another operation, to assess quality. A number of companies recognize the significance of this and use such a system to evaluate their performance in broad terms. This form of measuring tends to be subjective and consequently open to some risk. In particular an operation relying on benchmarking will, by definition, be a follower rather than a market leader. There is a developing trend which tries to overcome this problem by using a benchmark from another industry, rather than a competitor. Such that a hospitality operation might choose a benchmark from the retailing industry (Marks & Spencer) as has, to some degree, already been done in this chapter. Here again there are major risks, particularly in the choice of comparator. The 'benchmark' should be one that offers a similar range of products and services to a market of similar size drawn from a similar population group. Whilst these external comparisons might provide nice icing, the cake needs to be based on a standardized recipe of well specified local (internal) ingredients.

Benchmarking
The process must be continuous, based on specific activities which are valid and reliable, providing a solid, measurable base for comparison. There must be an effective system for the collection, recording and analysis of data (from both institutions).

In regard to the products on offer, and to some degree the service, clearly defined targets can be set and performance measured. However, targets must be constantly re-evaluated against emerging trends. Change is constant yet imperceptible and thus responds to the customer's need for products and services which are responsive yet reliable.

How best to measure the quality of service

Quality should be measured by the systematic evaluation of operational performance, effective implementation of plans, targets and standards being met.

Why?   Efficiency of procedures and processes, system integrity (it actually delivers what it sets out to). Ensuring that everyone follows the plan and that the operation is truly customer responsive.

How?   Audit the system (process), or audit the outcome (performance). Make sure that the difference is understood and the reason for choosing system outcome is valid.

What?   Decide on the objectives (method), plan activity and design analysis (measures). Encourage simplicity and work from a checklist of objectives.

When?   Consider pressure of work; the operation is at its weakest when busy, but this may not be the best time to observe. You may actually be interfering with the system.

Who?   Real customers – difficult to manage, their views may be subject to interpretation.
Internal customers, supervisors/managers – may suffer from the perspective (detail) and bias.
External visitors, head office, consultants – may be considered 'unfair', judge/jury/executioner.
Phantom visitors, mystery guests, quality auditors – simple to design programmes, clear objectives, no bias, visits are repeatable, the system will enable cross-comparison of units.

Phantom customers have the advantage of objectivity,

through their independence, but it is important to ensure that they work from an agreed plan (procedure/standards). Ensure that they are measuring the things that you want measured.

The quality audit may be observation or participative (phantom customers are always participative). Like the phantom customer, a quality audit should be based on well defined methodology and procedure. The benefit of observation is the ability to make notes, its weakness is the reduced ability to empathize with consumers.

There is an inherent weakness in customer surveys/questionnaires (comment by proxy), but they do provide a vehicle for analysis (because data is written down) whereas verbal comments may not be recorded or accurate. Research (Merricks and Jones, 1986) suggests that one in three compliments are expressed in writing as compared with only two in seven complaints (approximately 15 per cent variance), but that many people who are dissatisfied simply do not return. The no-comment non-returners bring into question the value of any (proxy) statistical analysis. Also, human nature being what it is, we tend to complain to friends and relatives about restaurants and poor service far more often than we recommend. Emphasis must be on gathering information while the customer is still on the premises, particularly in regard to their willingness to return.

Install and maintain systems of monitoring which accurately measure real costs and savings of quality management. Seek ways to identify profit improvements that are directly attributable to quality management.

Summary

Designing quality systems

Much has been written of total quality management and in particular of British Standard 5750 (now ISO 9000) which is used as a quality reference. Clearly quality must be related to customer care. However, and BS5750 is a case in point: quality control often relates to processes and procedures. It is possible that although all process and procedures are efficiently audited, the product or service may still fail to perform satisfactorily. Although relatively new to the hospitality industry, several operations have put BS5750 into practice, but despite this there is evidence of at least one such operation going to the wall. The argument about quality and customer care in the hospitality industry relates very much to the service aspect, particularly the convivial versus the procedural nature of service.

There are, within our industry, well-known tensions between systems and functions: the traditional animosity between production and service staff or the feeling that accountants and work study engineers do not understand the real cost or the true implications of service. Incidents far removed from the service contact can result in customer dissatisfaction as a result of the domino effect. An accountant's decision to alter the method of purchasing may, in isolation, be a good one, but the knock-on effect evident in lack of fresh supplies or late deliveries leading to arguments between stores and kitchen staff and chefs and waiters, may all be felt by the customer.

Quality objectives
- clearly define the product/service
- manage the culture
- manage the 'gaps' between expectation and delivery

A positive approach to quality systems should involve:

- market- (not product-) led activities
- people- (community) led organization
- a culture of winning teams

Quality is not a problem, it's a solution!

Properly managed quality programmes will assist in risk identification and error/accident prevention. The development of
quality manuals and quality teams will ensure consistent and
reliable performance. Get it right 'first time every time'.
Developing a quality culture involves a shift of power away
from owners, shareholders and managers towards suppliers,
employees (empowerment) and customers. A change in
management (leadership) style will be required. Managers
will have to learn to listen and recognize that mistakes may be
made. Make it clear to customers how problems will be dealt
with and what outcome they might expect. Encourage staff to
contribute to the solutions.

Investors in People

To be successful quality must be applied throughout the operation; everyone is a customer and our 'internal customers'
have a significant role to play. Investors in People (IIP) is an
alternative quality programme (see Chapter 8, Efficient
staffing, for more details). Investing in people requires quality
management and an empathetic leadership style in order to
encourage the involvement and commitment of all the staff.
Staff are a focal point of effective service operations and to be
successful caterers will have to consider increasing the
empowerment of all staff. Managers will have to learn to
'control' from a distance.

Empowerment	
● the benefits	more customer satisfaction, more customers, better (more committed) staff
● the risks	apparent abdication of management responsibility and loss of control

People-based quality philosophy
- recruit the right people
- employ imaginative ideas and responses to problems, encourage contribution from others
- take a questioning attitude to all aspects of the operation, listen to the views of others
- adopt a total commitment to quality through empowerment
- recognize and reward quality 'heroes'

DO's	and	DON'Ts
Set policy guidelines.		
Define principles in terms of continuous improvement and value to customers.		
Involve everyone.		Impose from the top.
Encourage people to learn through actions and mistakes.		Let people 'go through the motions'.
Ensure that training is focused.		
Encourage collaboration between departments.		Incite unhealthy levels of competition.
Create cross-functional levels of responsibility.		
Encourage teams to tackle the root causes of problems.		Allow solutions which only address the symptoms.
Maintain customer (internal and external) focus.		Become preoccupied with internal issues.

Figure 5.6 Do's and don'ts for managing quality.

Get the mission statement right – deliver what you
promise, not what you would like to achieve.

Suggested additional reading

Coyle, M.P. and Dale, B.G. (1993) *Quality in the Hospitality Industry – A Study. International Journal of Hospitality Management*, **12**, No. 2, 141–53.

HCIMA (1993) *Managing Quality – An Approach for the Hospitality Industry*. The Hotel and Catering International Management Association.

Maslow, A. H. (1987) *Motivation and Personality* (3rd edn). Harper Row.

Merricks, P. and Jones, P. (1986) *The Management of Catering Operations*. Cassell.

Peters, T. (1987) *Thriving on Chaos*. Guild Publishing.

Randall, L. and Senior, M. (1992) *Managing and Improving Service Quality* (TQM Practitioner Series). Technical Communications (Publishers) Ltd.

6
Product and service development

Aims and objectives

The main aim of product/service development is to enable
food and beverage managers to identify the influence of products, services and product/service development on the success
of the operation. Service is an integral part of all hospitality
products, therefore the approach to both product and service
development must be similar. For the purpose of this chapter
at least, the term 'product' may be assumed to include all
aspects of hospitality including service.

The aims of product development are to:
- Improve market share.
- Increase volume.
- Modify customer mix.
- Standardize and replicate existing products, as well as
  to introduce new lines.
- Manage price against current trends in spending and
  competition.
- Identify opportunities to gain advantage through
  product promotion.

The significance of standards and standardization have been
identified and discussed in previous chapters, particularly

Chapter 5, Quality. Clearly an integral part of product development is to arrive at workable definitions and standards. Such definitions and standards must be a direct response to customer need for quality and value (price).

The objectives of product development are to:
- Appraise opportunities for enterprise (product development) to improve trading position.
- Identify a range of strategies for improving the performance of products, services, menus and drinks lists.
- Understand the impact of product development on a range of related activities.
- Review existing products/services in terms of cost, revenue and profit.
- Maximize operational potential by manipulating costs, prices and/or sales mix.
- Justify costing/pricing strategy.
- Focus attention on those areas of the operation (products and services) which yield most effect.

What is product/service development?

Product development may be defined as the examination of products and services in order to identify opportunities for improvement, customer satisfaction and profit. Development may include the modification of existing products in response to identified opportunities and emerging trends. The purpose of product development is to provide popular, high-quality products in an ever changing market, ensuring that such products offer the best value, optimum choice, attract custom and guarantee satisfaction (delight). Effective product development is based on knowledge of current product strengths/weaknesses and customer need (trend), supported by developments in technology and systems.

Product knowledge is based on understanding of:
- product standards, quality
- market position
- location, access, amenities
- price, competition, differentiation
- business patterns together with an appreciation of consumer needs (refer back to marketing):
- product attributes: value and unique selling points
- service characteristics
- staff skills and attributes
- existing customer data
- potential customer research

What is the product?

Before we embark on product development we must have a clear understanding of what products and services are. In the hospitality industry we have a number of layers and inter-relationships within which development can take place: the meal experience, the menu, dishes and drinks, systems of delivery, style of service. For the purposes of development we can identify three specific elements: concept, package, content (CPC). Product development requires the planned, harmonious, integration of each; a weakness in any one might destroy the whole.

- **Concept**   The meal experience, environment, ambience, systems of delivery and service style.
- **Package**   Menus, dishes and drinks, choices and options, providing variety within constraints (limitations based on concept).
- **Content**   Commodity, method and process/procedures, planning and detailed specification.

Different operations may place greater emphasis and focus attention on one particular element, e.g.:

TGI Fridays	the total experience	=	concept
The Savoy Hotel	the menus and drinks lists	=	package
McDonald's	the Quarterpounder	=	content

There are two aspects of product development:

(a) The development of new products/services, either as:
   (i) A response to emerging trends, consumer demand or changes in technology and/or food processing, or
   (ii) Innovation

   For example, the ability of petrol stations to dispense hot meals only became possible as a result of technology (programmable microwaves) and food processing (cook-chill products) and customer acceptance of both.

(b) The modification of existing products/services (quality, efficiency, effectiveness, economy) which, like (a) above must be a response to trend, demand or innovation.
   For example, chocolate sweets do not sell well in hot weather. Many consumers who like chocolate would store it in the fridge. If we recognize this trend/demand obviously it would make sense to display chocolate sweets in chilled cabinets. Add a little innovation supported by food processing technology and we soon have a range of ice creams based on popular sweets (Crunchie, Snickers, Mars, etc.) and we all know how popular they have become.

The main features of product development are concern for:
- quality, raw materials, freshness, temperature, presentation
- health, hygiene, safety
- price, portion size, value

Why is product/service development important?

Product development is visible evidence of our concern for, and response to, customer need and emerging trends. In order to offer good quality and value we must continuously examine issues of economy, efficiency and effectiveness. Keeping ahead of the competition will require innovation – products that are new, different and exciting – refinements to our brand image and reinforcement of product differentiation.

Opportunities and constraints:
- brand image
- nutrition and dietary requirements
- availability of resources (including staff)
- controllability of raw materials (standard yields) through:
  - purchasing (raw material specifications)
  - suppliers
  - perishability (convenience foods)
  - process (testing/tasting)
  - holding (freeze/chill technology)
- style of service
- socio-economic change

The meal experience today is no longer confined to the traditional breakfast, lunch and dinner. Afternoon tea, high tea and supper are already lost as populist eating activities and in their place we have 'all-day breakfasts' and 'grazing'. In the future meals like supper, after the theatre, might reappear but only in response to social and cultural changes. Where opportunities do exist then business is likely to be highly competitive. Increasingly other industries are recognizing the potential offered by the provision of food and drink. They are no longer constrained by the need for production space, equipment and skills. We now find ourselves competing with petrol stations, video rental stores and wine merchants who are trying to develop and sell 'packages' which include food and drink. Some of the best value breakfasts may be found in your local supermarket and this may well be first choice for many people; not only is it convenient but they are familiar with the surroundings. A 'proper' restaurant may appear threatening.

How do we remain competitive and what unique selling points USPs can we identify? We have to be innovative. One approach would be to fight back, for example, by showing videos (as is the case with the increasingly popular 'sports bars'), although we would have to recognize there are some levels, selling petrol for instance, on which we cannot compete.

We may be forced to expand into new areas which may require a unique approach to product development. If we are looking to promote existing products to a new market we will have to maintain standards. In order to deliver the authentic Big Mac to the Russians, McDonald's had to introduce a complete manufacturing system to supply the basic raw materials. This included a brand new bakery to guarantee the specification for their buns. They could not/would not accept a retailing outlet using available, local, produce.

Opportunities and constraints

When considering product development we will be faced with a number of opportunities and constraints. We must consider the 'brand image' that our company is trying to promote. There may be more cost-effective ways of producing our menu items but if these clash with the company image then they will be counter-productive. The manager of a 'healthy eating' restaurant will have to examine carefully the cost of fresh foods and daily deliveries of 'wholesome' items against their generally more cost-effective convenience alternatives. Similarly we must assess the nutritional content of dishes that we produce. It is clear that the general public, our customers, are being educated in health and nutrition both deliberately by the Government, through legislation and public information leaflets, and more randomly by the popularity of cookery programmes on television, cookery books, health and nutrition articles in the media. We should try to be at least as well informed as our customers.

Why bother having a product development plan?

We need an effective plan in order to:

- stay ahead in the market
- streamline activities and costs
- improve quality and profitability

Quality assurance and standardization
- selection (specification) of raw materials
- standardized recipes (recipe manuals)
- standardized methods (task cards)
- standard yields (portion control charts and equipment)

Specification: detail of product in terms of composition, dimension, colour, texture, etc.

Standard: rule, model or criteria against which comparison may be made.

The objective is to match product and service delivery to market expectations by the most advantageous means: to produce saleable and profitable products based on the needs and wants of the customer. The manager's job is to balance innovation and creativity with the needs of efficiency, effectiveness and economy. In order to achieve this successfully we need the following:

● **market research** – in order to determine products and services that the customer requires
● **forecasting** – in order to determine the probable volume of sales

Accurate forecasting ensures availability of raw materials and efficient and effective use of personnel and equipment resulting in a reduction of waste. As was seen in Chapter 3, Marketing, we will require accurate information regarding:

● past activity records (sales history)
● advance bookings
● current events
● current trends
● current promotional activity (merchandising)

On the basis of this information, we can gather a range of dishes and develop menus to meet expected demand. Our forecasting activity should not only predict the number of customers but also their menu choices. This is best achieved through use of a popularity index (see Table 6.1). We should be able to determine the volume production requirements for each dish in advance. Given such information we can now identify raw material requirements. Quantities may then be fixed and the most effective purchase procedure identified.

The popularity index indicates not only the current relationship (sales popularity) of menu items, but also the need to develop new products. We can examine the popularity of menu items (and the need for product development) still further through the use of product life cycle theory.

When examining the popularity of an item we need to put it in perspective with past and expected future sales. All products go through what is called a 'life cycle' (see Figure 6.1). The life cycle may be short or long but the basic pattern of

Table 6.1 Popularity Index

	Number sold	Percentage of total sales
Ham sandwich	20	8.2
Turkey sandwich	15	6.2
Beef sandwich	17	7.0
Ham roll	22	9.0
Turkey roll	10	4.1
Beef roll	21	8.6
Salad roll	35	14.3
Chips	10	4.1
Soup	35	14.3
Ploughman's lunch	41	16.8
Pâté	18	7.4
Total sales (covers)	244	100

rise and fall remains the same. Understanding the position of a product in its life cycle will provide clues as to the most appropriate action to take to improve performance and prolong life. This process of growth, maturity and decline in sales applies equally to menu items, too many items in the decline stage will result in 'menu fatigue', a tired and uninteresting menu. Other industries have recognized the significance of the product life cycle and the pattern of continuous development. Strangely enough, as Figure 6.1 suggests, we should be thinking about new products when we appear to be most successful, such that a new product hits maturity as another reaches the decline stage. The product life cycle may be influenced by management decisions, particularly the way in which the product is promoted: product association, merchandising or by adding value.

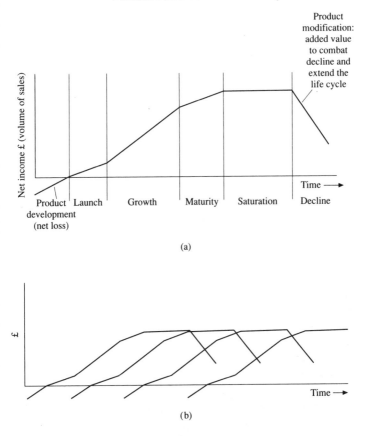

Figure 6.1 (a) Product life cycle. (b) Products should be developed and introduced on a regular basis to ensure continuity. (c) Although the general pattern (sequence of stages) remains the same, the actual shape of each cycle will be determined by the length (time) of the cycle. Consequently, achieving neat sales (as above) is not always possible, but we must at least avoid too many of our products going into decline at the same time; it may be some time before our new product takes hold, indeed, the operation may never survive to see it.

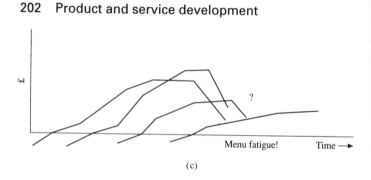

(c)

The purpose of product/service development

Design of products and/or services requires the effective development of an idea that can be sold at a profit. This may include:

- developing new products/services for new markets
- developing existing products/services for existing markets
- developing new products/services for existing markets
- refining existing products/services for existing markets
- developing new applications for existing products and services
- standardizing products and services
- implementing quality improvements
- enhancing customer benefits
- implementing cost efficiencies
- responding to developments in technology
- adapting to new legislation

Development is often concentrated on products and not services. Design of services requires a greater understanding of 'service attributes' which may be physical, sensual (explicit) or psychological (implicit). Consider the opportunities that exist to add value through service, particularly the implied benefits.

Who is responsible for product/service development?

Senior managers

Senior management are not always in the best position to participate directly in product development. A famous story is told of Ray Kroc of McDonald's fame. Allegedly his only attempt at product development, the 'Hula-Burger' (grilled pineapple between two slices of cheese in a bun), was a singular failure. However, senior managers will determine policy and set guidelines for development within an identifiable brand image.

The marketing team will initiate product development based on research evidence. Customers will express needs and expectations. There will also be a response to external influences such as economics and developments in fashion and trend.

Unit managers

Operational managers will primarily be responsible for product design, testing and implementation both of products and of systems of delivery.

Staff

Staff may assist in the initial market research (customer needs/system weaknesses) and product design and testing. Staff, particularly the technical experts will also have an innovative role to play, particularly when it comes to identifying opportunities for the modification of existing products in order to improve processing procedures, quality standards, efficiency and cost-effective processes. Staff will gather data, customer acceptance levels, invent new products, recommend modifications to existing products and processes, and develop service activities.

Customers

Product and service development could not exist in the absence of customers and customer comment. However, more care should be taken to seek customer views. What products and services are missing, which of the existing products/services are superfluous? In particular, how could existing products and services be improved?

Product and service development strategy

How are products and services developed?

We have previously recognized that there are three main elements (CPC) of the hospitality product. Bearing in mind the relationship between concept, package and content it is generally recognized that product development will often be focused on the menu (package). Effective product development will require an operational structure which is adaptable and encourages innovation: a culture which creates the right environment, responsive to customers' needs and encourages staff to generate new ideas.

Concept development

'Shall we eat Italian or Chinese?' is a question commonly asked before an evening out. The meal experience contributes to the evening's entertainment, sometimes as an integral part – cinema then a meal – sometimes as the sole activity. Some elements are beyond the control of the food and beverage manager, choice of friends to dine with and topic of conversation, for example. Customer choice will be influenced by the ambience, decor and style of the operation, and its system (style) of service.

The food and beverage manager must be very clear what constitutes a 'wonderful' meal experience for the customer. On many occasions, ambience and decor will be a significant influence on the meal experience, sometimes more than the products (food and drink) on offer. Superb meals in rural Italy or France bear testimony to the fact that poor facilities and surroundings often have little or no impact on the ultimate customer acceptance and enjoyment. Consider street vendors in the East – Singapore, Thailand, Hong Kong and Japan – attempts to 'clean up' their act would in effect destroy the very experience (concept) and some of the 'adventure' of eating out in an authentic environment. Consider also soldiers assembling on a wind-swept mountain in the Falklands, a desert wadi in the Gulf or the rubble of what was once Bosnia, who appreciate a good plate of 'scoff' and a hot 'brew': simple elements of the meal such as quantity, substance and temperature are far more desirable than ambience or style of service.

Managing resources

A concept will carry with it a number of burdens, features which are all too often forgotten by managers in their efforts to present what they think their customers want. Kitchen, restaurant, and bar areas must be designed to reinforce the concept. Equipment, tables and seating must all conform. Appropriate raw materials must be selected and suitable staff chosen and trained. The concept will influence, or may itself be influenced by, the use and/or availability of space, the style of furnishing, colour and decor. Equipment and furnishings must be set out to meet the demands of the production and service style prompted by the concept. Equipment selection will be influenced, through the menu, by demands associated with methods of cookery, service style and time allowed. The concept will influence staffing arrangements by identifying necessary competences required, assessing skills, training needs, shortcomings and talents. A good manager will take every opportunity to encourage learning, understanding and development among the staff by directly linking skill acquisition to the demands of the concept.

The main components (things that we can change) of product development are:	
Menus and drinks lists • clear, easy to follow • reasonable variety (range of options) • within the constraints of concept • available in different languages	*Systems* • design features • efficiency, effectiveness • quality assurance • internal customers
Raw material input • quality • levels of convenience (pre-processing) • reinforces concept (e.g. healthy eating) • value, benefits, USPs	*Processes* • access, arrival • queuing, free flow • silver service, self service
Price and payment • competitive • clear, unambiguous prices • payment process clear, simple • payment methods, range of options	*Staffing* • technical skills, social skills • customer empathy • problem ownership and empowerment • complaint handling

Characteristics of promptness, responsiveness, safety, service, courtesy, competence and communication will be the measures used by the customer to assess performance of the service provider. By ensuring that the whole 'meal experience' is commensurate with the expectations of the customer we can target effort on sales and promotion where it will yield best effect.

Package development

Development of the 'hospitality' package will primarily be in response to concept needs and is effectively focused on the menu and drinks lists. During discussion reference will frequently be made to 'the menu'. In general, comments will apply equally to drinks lists although more specific reference will be made as and where appropriate.

The function of the menu is to:
- appeal to customers
- inform customers
- direct customers' attention to those items we prefer to sell
- sell food and drink
- enable predictions
- enable planning
- enable costings
- enable records (sales history)
- identify the need for training programmes to be devised

For the customer the menu may represent both physical and psychological aspects of the hospitality package:

Physical	*Psychological*
Information	Experience
Advice	Satisfaction
Choice	Experimentation
Value	Impressions

At best the menu is a physical representation of customer needs and wants, as perceived by the menu planner. At worst a menu can be the embodiment of its writer's ego. Forcing our perceptions onto the customer can only be viewed as a very short-term approach to menu planning. Menu planning is more than putting together a list of our favourite foods.

Menu conventions	**Menu styles**	**Menu attributes**
Balance of colour, texture, flavour	A la carte	Send marketing messages
Nutrition balance	Table d'hôte	Set the theme
Sequence	Carvery	Set the tempo
Language	Grill	Set levels of anticipation
Law	Function	Offer merchandising opportunities

Management activity

Balancing the needs of owners with the expectations of customers (control) and identifying gaps (resource limitations)

Supervision

Skill requirements

Equipment

Figure 6.2 The menu as a focal point.

The menu, especially in banqueting service, generally triggers the planning process, though of course the menu can be derived from that process when it results from careful consideration of the resources available and the specific requirements of customers.

Decisions about what items to include in menus will influence the size and effectiveness of both production and service systems. Unless the intention is to expand the system then it is generally better to increase the variety of choice for the customer whilst maintaining, or even reducing the potential for variety in the system. For example a burger house would need carefully to consider including stews or braises on its menu, since the production and service systems were not established for that purpose; to do so would increase the variety in the system and reduce the potential for control. Variety can be achieved by ensuring products fit the system. Customers can have anything they want, so long as it is a burger: chicken burger, fish burger, vegetarian burger. Variety can be further enhanced by the range of sauces and accompaniments and choice of portion size and/or changes to shape and size of main ingredients, e.g. the long 'double' bun.

Besides communicating with the customer, the menu is a communicator to staff in the kitchen, by way of providing a basis for the production schedule. To restaurant staff, the menu communicates by providing the clues for table lay-up and accompaniments. For bar staff it will provide clues as to likely sales of wines, aperitifs and liqueurs. Staff who are not directly involved in food and beverage production or delivery may be able to make a contribution to sales by actively promoting food and beverage activities.

Menu planning is important because, although the skills that relate directly to it are few, the menu effectively determines the nature of all subsequent activity and thus influences all other requirements.

The menu frequently results from a balancing act between the needs of the customer and the needs of the business. Customers will look for quality and value whilst owners will, in the main, look for a return on investment.

In demonstrating menu planning skills, it is expected that the manager is able to:

- identify a range of suitable dishes and products to meet identifiable customer needs
- inform customers precisely what is on offer
- justify the inclusion, positioning and price of every item on the menu
- identify opportunities which exist for influencing customer choice
- optimize the use of resources in light of the needs of the menu
- assess the individual viability of every item on the menu as well as the efficiency, effectiveness and profitability of the menu as a whole
- make improvements to the menu by modifying items which are not performing to expectations in terms of popularity, sales or profitability
- increase total revenue and gross profit through adjustments to unit margin and average customer spend

Purpose of the menu for the customer

The menu confirms perceptions/understanding of the concept on offer. Whether eating for necessity or pleasure – at work, as part of the daily grind or as part of a unique social occasion – customers will have pre-conceived expectations about the meal experience. In many circumstances the menu will be the basis for choice. At this point it would be appropriate to consider the nature of choice from the customer's point of view. The decision to purchase food and drink results from a range of competing and complementary factors:

- trial and error
- recommendations resulting from other people's experiences
- influence of choice, preference and liking
- whether 'grazing' or more purposeful 'foraging'
- passively participating in other people's decisions

When putting a menu together the food and beverage manager will be aware of all the expectations of customers. The choice of dishes may reflect these expectations but will not, on its own attract desired customers. The menu itself will need to be produced in a way that sends a particular message. The style, colour and layout of the menu will indicate whether the operation is fast service or not, expensive or not, fun or not, the sort of place you may wish to entertain a business or social partner (or someone else's partner!). The menu should be designed to entertain, particularly for groups such as children and especially where menu items themselves may be fairly staid/standard, as in the traditional Christmas menu where turkey and pudding are expected.

Informing the customer (concept reinforcement)

As discussed above, together with the concept, the menu is likely to form the basis of a customer's decision of where to eat. The detailed information will form part of the contract between customer and provider. For this reason, and many others, a menu's meaning must be clearly understood by all who are intended to use it. A menu must describe what is on offer and how much it will cost and it should also suggest how it will be served. If there are to be additional costs, then these must be clearly stated. As well as explicit information, menus contain implicit information. Style and presentation of the menu may suggest how the customer should dress or behave. Menu language, particularly French, is often used to imply 'haute cuisine'. However, menus in French may be infuriating to customers who do not speak the language. The establishment may be out to impress but will fail to do so if the menu is not accompanied by an explanation, especially when service staff are also unsure or ignorant of the content of dishes. Worse still if the staff see this as a failing on the customers' part, censuring the customer with a sigh and smirk for their lack of knowledge.

It could be argued that retailers, like Sainsbury's, are doing more to educate the public about food and good eating than caterers. Customers in the high street or local supermarket are faced with a variety of well-packed, well-presented and prominently merchandised foods and dishes that also, by virtue of current retailing legislation, contain detailed information on nutritional content. However, the caterer must not seek to re-educate the customer, rather they should attempt to widen their experience and expectations.

Appealing to the customer

Not only does the menu provide information to the customer by way of 'explicit' detail of selection on offer and prices, it also informs whether there are cover charges added or whether service is included. A great deal of 'implied' information is also given. If the menu is scruffy and marked or has frequent rubbings out and scribbled alterations to price and content, it will say a lot about the willingness of the management to tolerate and even encourage second best.

Once the decision to eat has been made, the menu then provides the choice of what to eat. Each and every item on the menu should appeal. Prices should be realistic. The popularity of fixed price menus is growing. The public is much more aware of extortionate mark-up on some wines; it is not surprising that these wines do not often sell. Menus that offer value will appeal to customers. That value may be real and/or implied. Real value may be identified in portion size, additional items and linked sales. Implied value may be found in descriptions, presentation and menu design. Caterers should not ignore the fact that customers will be attracted by price and value for money. It would be a mistake to 'hide' additional charges.

The purpose of the menu for the manager

Management activity is primarily that of control, ensuring that what is intended to happen actually happens. The menu is central to control activity (see Figure 6.3).

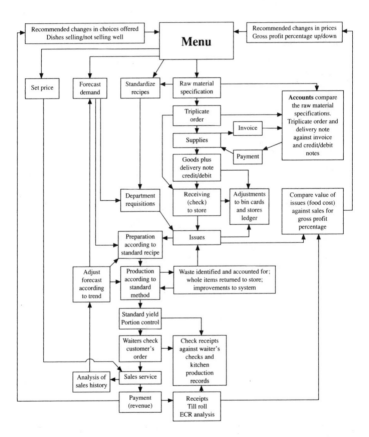

Figure 6.3 The menu and control activity. Source: Fuller and Waller, 1991.

Menu planning

Traditionally, in western society, meals are eaten in a series of courses: a 'starter', a 'main course' and a 'sweet'. A menu may, particularly on special occasions, offer more courses – but often there will be less. Whatever the number of courses there will be a recognizable pattern or sequence to the meal. Additionally there are specific items or methods of cookery and/or presentation that are associated with each of the courses. In addition to accepted sequence and food items there is also an accepted daily pattern and eating at particular times of the day is associated with particular items for those meal times. However it is important to recognize, at this point, that although this accepted procedure remains common there are a growing number of exceptions, particularly in the fast food sector. As society develops, culture changes and adapts. The growth of 'grazing', eating snacks on the run throughout the day (note the growth of the retail sandwich industry) and the increasing popularity of the 'all day' breakfast should not go unnoticed by the menu planner.

The drinks list, with the obvious exception of hot beverages and the cocktail list, differs from the menu in one major respect. Items offered for sale on a drinks list do not require recipes, production or processing procedures. Once cold beverages are delivered to the caterer they generally remain unaltered. Unit pricing, measuring and control are therefore simplified. Like the menu however, there are accepted associations and sequences. For example, aperitif, light wine, heavy wine, liqueur with a meal; fruit juices, tea or coffee with breakfast. Because beverages are less perishable they may be put out on display thus reducing the need for written lists (note the legal requirements for display of prices). This ability to display products may be used to enhance the concept, for instance a Spanish tapas bar may have lots of wine bottles on display. Such displays are not just decoration however, they should be used to enhance sale (see Chapter 4, Merchandising).

The menu as a management tool

If the menu fails to meet the market requirements it will certainly cause a fall in sales and profitability. Therefore develop the menu to suit your market (concept). The menu (sales history) provides a record of popularity for each dish. This enables forecasting and provides basic control data. The menu is, therefore, a means of control; resources should relate to the requirements of the menu (staff, machinery, materials, purchases, usage rates, money, time, space).

Competent menu management

From the manager's point of view the menu provides the principal 'interface' between the product and/or service and the potential customer. Decisions as to whether the customer will patronize the establishment may be taken on the strength of the menu alone. Other decisions are likely to be made on the basis of what the customer sees or does not see on the menu. As we have seen, the menu carries a number of implied messages that may or may not encourage the customer to use the facilities on offer.

The customer is the main focus for all attention to the menu, its design, structure, the items selected and prices should be seen from the customer's perspective. Failure to consider the customer sufficiently may result in technically correct menus that potentially offer profitability but which do not sell food or drink.

As we have seen, as well as explicit and implicit information, the menu can provide a powerful means of communicating a particular theme or concept to customers. Managers must ensure that the message that the customer receives is the same as the one that they intended to send.

Extensive menus carry with them their own problems, not only ensuring availability of all items but also of customers being confused by them. The way in which menus are read will influence the choices that customers make. Eye movement across the card (see Figure 6.4) will mean some items receive more attention than others. The order in which the menu is read – 'primacy and recency', i.e. what was read first and what has been read most recently – will also influence choice. This has clear implications for the designers and compilers of menus, particularly concerning the positioning of profitable or preferred items.

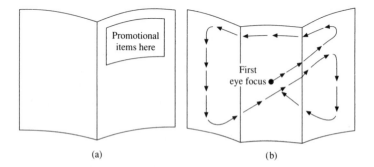

(a)   (b)

Figure 6.4 Menu presentation and eye movement. (a) On an open double page, the eye moves to the top right-hand corner first. (b) The direction of eye movement across a three-fold menu. Source: Fuller and Waller, 1991.

Improving the performance of a menu is dependent on recording its current performance (sales history), setting targets for improvement and monitoring progress. Key points are listed below:

● The menu must reflect what the customer wants, balanced against what can be provided.
● There is little point in developing new menu items simply because the chef or manager thinks it is a good idea.

- Beware of sending the wrong message to customers, because of poorly presented, dirty or unkempt menus.
- Measure and record menu activity, choices and popularity. If you can't measure it you can't improve it.

Content planning

Dish development and commodity planning is an integral part of catering organization. As such it is concerned not just with design and manufacture, but also with setting targets and assessing the relative benefits of alternative strategies. Commodity planning is a continuous process, responding to changes in demand, competition, technology and economics. The manager is principally concerned with controlling performance through the standardization of products and cost-control procedures.

Effective development strategy allows the manager to:
- introduce and develop new recipes
- introduce and develop new recipes for special dietary requirements
- establish and update food production quality control systems and procedures
- maintain food production quality control systems and procedures
- establish and maintain portion control

Products and dishes should be developed according to the needs and wishes as expressed by the customer. Increasingly this seems to reflect the move toward healthy eating. The manager must also consider the suitability and capacity of the production system and the effect that new products may have on purchasing policy and raw material specifications. Above all, dishes, new or old, will have to meet customer's ability/willingness to pay.

Dish development (testing and tasting):
- market potential/demand
- price
- unique selling points (USPs)
- ingredient (availability/cost)
- process, procedures and systems
- equipment
- labour
- food value (nutrition)
- legislation

As noted in Chapter 2, Policy, thought should be given to ethnic and cultural requirements. Merely adding a 'vegetarian alternative' can be counter-productive, especially if this is done with little thought. Consider the number of standard menu items that could be prepared with vegetable stocks and oils and vegetarian cheese (made with synthetic rennet) instead of the more traditional animal derivatives. Restrictive dish naming should also be avoided. Such action would allow a greater number of consumers, not just vegetarians, to select from a wider range of menu items.

Vegan and strict kosher diets, among others, require far greater care in planning which will extend not just to food usage but also to equipment, methods and processes which may be beyond the capacity of the average caterer. Detailed analysis of the various ethnic and cultural requirements is beyond the scope of this book and recommendations for further reading are identified at the end of this chapter.

Commodity planning:
- identifying and listing raw material requirements
- fixing quantities
- purchasing
- storing and issuing

Raw material management

The direct influence the menu has on materials management is great indeed. Food and drink suppliers are selected on the basis of their ability to supply, consistently, those raw materials necessary for items specified on the menu. Consequently food and drink purchasing specifications should be designed around the demands of the menu (see Figure 6.5).

Entrecôte steak

Origin:	From a striploin.
Backstrip gristle:	Leave intact.
Side chain:	Leave intact.
Length of 'tops'	Not to exceed 25 mm (1 in.).
Cutting:	Across/against the grain of the 'eye' muscle so that both cut surfaces will be reasonably parallel to ensure consistent thickness of each portion.
Thickness:	Dependent upon the steak size specified.
Surface fat:	Not to exceed a thickness of 133 mm ($\frac{1}{2}$ in.).
Recommended weights:	115 g (4 oz), 140 g (5 oz), 170 g (6 oz), 200 g (7 oz).

Note: A photograph or clear drawing of the cut specified is a useful accompaniment to the specification.

Tolerances
For a consistent and viable degree of accuracy for both purchaser and portioners, weight tolerances may be applied as follows:

Weight specified	Tolerance
Under 170 g (6 oz)	± 7 g ($\frac{1}{4}$ oz)
170 g (6 oz) but less than 340 g (12 oz)	± 14 g ($\frac{1}{2}$ oz)
340 g (12 oz) but less than 450 g (18 oz)	± 20 g ($\frac{3}{4}$ oz)
565 g (20 oz) plus	± 28 g (1 oz)

Example
If 225 g (8 oz) portions are specified, then individual portions weighing between 215 g–240 g ($7\frac{1}{2}$ oz–$8\frac{1}{2}$ oz) are acceptable.

Source: Sample specification as originally produced by Harrison and King of Kettering, Northants.

(a)

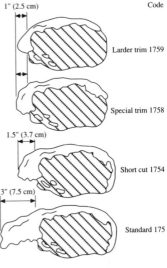

In addition to diagrams, MLC sample specifications also include full descriptions of source joint, depth of external fat and method of cutting.

Source: The Meat Buyers' Guide for Caterers. Moore, Stone and Tattersal, International Thompson Publishing Ltd.

(b)

Figure 6.5 Purchase specifications and the needs of the menu. (a) Specification (description) for sirloin steak. (b) Specification (diagram) for sirloin steak (MLC). Source: Fuller and Waller, 1991.

Food and drink ordering procedures will be based on the need to supply the customer with only those items offered on the menu. Receiving and acceptance is determined by the ability to utilize those items through the menu; food and drink storage space is wasted by goods not utilized through the menu. Delivery and distribution is therefore organized according to a schedule based on menu requirements. Costs and revenue figures should reflect the prices and popularity of menu items. Control of materials is impossible without accurate production and sales records.

The commodity plan must account for the availability of resources. The commodity plan for a city centre restaurant, a country house hotel and a North Sea oil rig will necessarily differ. We cannot assemble a range of classical dishes, with the intention of preparing from fresh ingredients and cooking each dish to order if there is a shortage of labour, or if the labour supply is unskilled. However, we can present such a range of dishes, with limited staff and skills, if we purchase them ready prepared, but this will considerably affect the range, amount and type of equipment that we require. Convenience foods will have an influence on equipment selection such that ultimately, at the highest levels of convenience, only reheating equipment is required. All preparation and cooking equipment becomes obsolete. The need for pan washing facilities is obviated by the use of disposable reheating containers.

In addition to availability of resources, which for raw materials and sometimes labour is often seasonal, caterers will also be concerned with the seasonality of demand: the changing pattern of customer preferences through the year. Many caterers will respond with either seasonal menus, particularly spring and autumn menus, or seasonal specialities.

In examining the range of opportunities that exist, two extremes are clearly identifiable: 'total fresh traditional processing' and 'total convenience assembly serve'. Many options exist between these two extremes and there is no 'least cost' formula that can be applied. A balance will need to be achieved whereby optimum benefit is obtained from each of the main resources. If we choose to increase spending on raw materials then an equivalent decrease must be found in labour and/or equipment spending (see Chapter 7, Systems management, for more details).

Above all the manager will be concerned with a commodity plan that enables control of:
- raw materials
- purchasing
- suppliers
- storage
- perishability
- processes
- holding
- style of service

Production methods

As has already been noted a wide band of production opportunities exists between the two extremes of totally fresh traditional cookery and assembly of convenience products. Of the developing ideas and techniques most attention is focused on the centralization of production, away from the point of delivery and the demands of service. The principal methods involved are cook-freeze, cook-chill and sous-vide.

Products and dishes, customer demand, size and scale of operation together with issues relating to quality, economy and value will influence the choice of production system. While at one time traditional methods, cook-freeze, cook-chill and sous-vide were seen as independent, even incompatible systems, there is a growing trend towards a 'mix'n'match' blend that derives benefits from each without incurring excessive additional costs. It is widely recognized that each system has particular strengths often related to specific raw materials, principles of cookery and groups of menu items. Salads, sandwiches and pastries may be produced on a seven-day 'chill' cycle. Stews, braises, pies and puddings are more suited to a six-month 'freeze' production plan. Roasting and frying may be done daily using traditional techniques. In many situations the precise method of production will be unknown, and of little interest, to the customer.

Effective control requires a production plan that clearly defines processes, procedures and schedules so that monitoring can take place resulting in the generation of production information that is essential to control activity. As a result of management advice, owners will be able to more effectively balance capital and operational investment (systems of production are discussed in detail in Chapter 7).

Recipe development

Recipe development will have to take account of planned production methods and financial constraints. From a business planning point of view the manager will need to be aware of menu fatigue and product life cycle (see Figure 6.1). Examination of sales history should identify those menu items that have been around for a long time and whose popularity is now in decline. These menu items will need to be replaced with new and interesting dishes. Sales history should also be able to demonstrate the direction in which customer tastes are moving. Trends in modern diet and eating habits will have to be accommodated.

Dish development is associated with creativity, new and novel ideas. However we should not ignore the constraints of control. New products will have to encompass the principles of standardization, particularly if, as in the case of restaurant and brewery chains, dishes are to be replicated on a national scale. Whilst a certain amount of experimentation is required, unnecessary waste will be avoided through sound product knowledge and an understanding of the nature of raw materials. For example 'goujon of cod' may sound like a nice idea, but we should not need to prepare and cook the dish to realize that the structure of cod, with its large flakes, will almost certainly result in much of the dish breaking up during cooking. It is no accident that such a dish is primarily limited to softer, finer textured fish such as sole. Dish development should not only involve the cooking and testing/tasting of dishes but also an analysis of the nutritional content and an assessment of food loss during preparation and cooking.

We must be able to produce dishes to a consistent standard. Sometimes it is necessary to modify traditional practice in order to ensure reliability. We need to ensure that if a dish is going to appear on a menu over a given period we have consistent ingredient availability. Take the case of soup; although traditional practice might suggest cooking entirely from fresh ingredients: a tomato soup based on the use of a particular brand of tomato puree from a specified supplier will produce a consistent and reliable product at any time of year and in any part of the country with no adjustments to recipe and very little change, if any, in cost. Because of the inherent variability of fresh produce, the use of fresh tomatoes to produce the same dish would result in either continuous adjustments to the recipe with the associated variation in cost or a variable end product.

Recipe development will involve not just the examination of raw materials and methods of processing but also assessment of cooking and holding procedures and analysis of total cost. Deep fried dishes, for example, must take account of oil absorption and energy costs. For some products oil absorption can be very high. Modifying recipes and or cooking temperatures can considerably affect the life and productivity of frying oils and hence substantially influence costs.

Recipe development should establish the right product to meet customer demands and the correct materials and method in order to be most cost effective. Advantage should be taken of emerging techniques and technology. Above all we must be able to communicate instructions – recipe, method, yield and portion size – to all concerned.

The customer will determine quality based on their perceptions of value (related to price) and fitness for purpose. Much of what was discussed previously, in dish development, will relate to fitness for purpose. Not only must a dish be edible and nutritious, it must also be interesting (colour, texture and flavour) and well presented. Above all, reliability will feature highly in customers' assessment of our product quality. We must plan and organize to minimize defects and ensure consistent results. A quality commodity plan will identify inspection, assessment and evaluation procedures throughout the process. Variances from standard will be identified and causes traced and eliminated.

Quality of end products will be determined primarily by:
- quality of raw materials
- skill of processing
- consistency of methods
- timing of processes and procedures
- consistency in presentation

Planning and standardization procedures

Documentation	Function
● Job descriptions	identify tasks and performance targets
● Personnel specifications	identify skills, knowledge, experience and attitude necessary for effective performance
● Staff training manuals	re-enforce agreed standards

● Equipment design specifications	should be consistent with product (output) specification/standards
● Equipment instructions	(use and cleaning) effective application of process
● Equipment maintenance schedules	ensure consistent performance
● Raw material specifications	ensure consistency with product (output) standards
● Work schedules	determine the allocation of labour resources, time/place

- ● Standard recipes
- ● Standard methods
- ● Portion control
- ● Standard yields

} enable measurable performance and control of waste

(See Chapter 7, Systems management, for more detailed discussion of specifications.)

Standardization:

Advantages:
- ● accurate cost control
- ● consistent purchasing and issuing
- ● predetermined, measurable yield
- ● portion control
- ● consistent quality
- ● accurate sales and profit calculations
- ● streamlined production
- ● efficient, effective, economic

Disadvantages:
- ● customer boredom
- ● loss of staff interest (accidents and mistakes)
- ● lack of staff initiative and involvement in planning
- ● limited skills development

When is product/service development necessary?

Product development should be an ongoing process (see previous comments regarding product life cycle and Figure 6.1). Much of management attention will be focused on maintaining and improving profitability through modifications to the sales mix and adjustments to costing and pricing.

Costing, pricing and control

Product or service development is bound to affect profitability. The food and beverage manager will be concerned to monitor the influence of cost of sales, gross profit and selling price on operational performance. Revenue and ultimately net profit for the unit will be influenced by accurate costings, pricing and control (see Figure 6.6).

Opportunities for cost control
- use cheaper ingredients
- use less of the more expensive ingredients
- reduce labour requirement (skills and/or time), use convenience products
- utilize bulk production methods, economies of scale
- reduce product range
- increase price by a greater proportion than cost

Cost control strategy must take account of the requirements of quality and standardization.

What measures can be taken to improve GP percentage which has fallen below target?

- Check purchases: have all invoices been allocated to the correct period?
- Check wastage.
- Check costings: does the system allow for increases in raw materials?
- Check the stock taking method, ensure consistency.
- Look at pricing policy and menu mix.

To find the GP of a dish:
Selling price – Food cost = Gross profit (SP – FC = GP)
To find the GP percentage:
$$\frac{GP \times 100}{SP} = GP\%$$

Example
The food cost is 48p, the selling price of the dish is £1.20, therefore GP is 72p.
    1.20 – 0.48 = 0.72
and the GP% is 60%.
$$\frac{72 \times 100}{120} = 60$$

To find the cost of goods sold (COGS) for a given trading period:
Opening stock + Purchases – Closing stock = Cost of goods sold (OS + P – CS = COGS)
- Opening stock is the level of stock in store at the last stock take.
- Purchases is the cost of all items (food and drink) bought during that period (not necessarily paid for).
- Closing stock is the value of current stock holdings (at this stock take).

Example

Opening stock (last stock take figure)	= 4000
Purchases	= 6000
Closing stock (this stock take figure)	= 3500
Sales	12000

$$COGS = 4000 + 6000 - 3500 = 6500$$
$$\frac{6500 \times 100}{12000} = 54\% \qquad GP$$

Critical control points (CCPs) form the basis of control. CCPs identify what and where. The simple calculations above defined how.

Figure 6.6 Basic calculations for gross profit and cost of goods sold.

Pricing

The traditional catering concept of pricing is based on raw materials (food cost), to which labour and overheads and net profit (gross profit) are added to arrive at the selling price (before VAT). An alternative view is to divide costs into those which are fixed (e.g. rent and rates), those which are variable (e.g. raw materials) and managed costs (e.g. labour). The use of fixed/variable cost analysis is most useful in break even analysis (see Figure 6.7).

Pricing methods may vary between different operations. However, it is important that individual units are consistent with their approach. Frequent changes in pricing method would make it difficult to monitor performance. The exception to this rule might be an hotel where different methods might be applied to the calculation of restaurant and function prices, where function pricing may well be influenced by incremental price (see below).

Pricing methods include:

- Cost plus percentage (FC + GP).
- Ratio mark up, e.g. 4:1 indicates that price will be four times the cost.
- Fixed sum addition, e.g. £2 per item regardless of basic cost.
- Differential GP, promoting particular products (high volume compensates for low GP).
- Incremental pricing, party bookings, cheaper per head as volume increases.
- Backward pricing, costs are tailored to meet an acceptable price (beware of risk to quality).
- Market pricing, prices determined by customers and competitors.

Predatory pricing, loss leaders (one or more items offered at a low price to attract customers) should be treated with extreme caution. Such activity should only be considered as part of a recognized strategy with clearly defined targets and an identifiable market. If discounts are used then performance should be monitored closely.

Discount strategy should encourage:
- customer loyalty
- increased volume
- repeat business
- off-peak increase in demand
- prompt payment

Pricing objectives:

Long term:
- return on investment
- maintain/improve market position/share
- stabilization
- follow competitors
- differentiation

Short term:
- promotion
- destroyer/predatory
- penetration (to increase volume, regardless of profit)
- skimming (decreasing price to increase volume)

Factors that contribute to determining the price:

- level of profit required
- actual material costs
- associated labour costs
- other costs (fixed/variable) rent, rates, overheads, etc.
- location of the establishment
- amount and type of facilities offered
- nature and size of the competition
- promotion, marketing and merchandising
- company policies

Opportunities for price increase:
- use more expensive, better quality, ingredients
- increase ingredients, portion size
- increase main ingredient
- enhance presentation

At the end of the day it is the total net profit, bottom-line figure that is important. Care should be taken to differentiate between percentage and cash targets/performance, particularly for gross profit.

Costing, pricing and profitability

Although various methods of pricing may exist – cost pricing and market pricing, for example – the costing of a dish must conform to a particular process. Costing necessarily involves the identification of all relevant and contributory expenses, including raw materials, labour and overheads. Costs such as administration, purchasing and development costs should not be neglected. One exception to the rule of including all costs in the calculation, before setting a price, would be the case of marginal costing. The assumption is that where an event has already been costed and all necessary costs (rent, rates, heat, light, labour, etc.) recovered, it would only be necessary to identify the cost of additional raw materials for the additional covers to be catered for. So that whereas the full cost price of a meal was calculated at £10.00 per head (£2000) for a banquet of 200, an additional ten customers could effectively be charged at £2.00 per head (raw material cost) giving a total cost for the banquet of £2020.00 for 210 covers. Such pricing may increase bookings even though apparently reducing profitability. Clearly marginal costing provides the opportunity for promotional pricing and increasing volume.

There should not be too great a difference between the cheapest and most expensive items on the menu. Customers may be discouraged from purchasing what they would really like because it appears too cheap or too expensive.

The effect of sales volume on profitability

Increase in volume does not always increase profit. What revenue does a company require to cover all costs (see Figure 6.7)? As volume increases so too do costs, but in what proportion? There may be a point at which it is too expensive to go on increasing sales! Where/what is the optimum sales level?

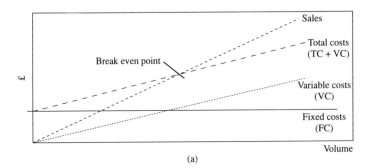

(a)

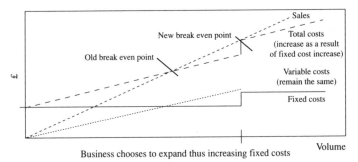

Business chooses to expand thus increasing fixed costs

(b)

Figure 6.7 Break even analysis.

As can be seen in Figure 6.7 (a) above, one of the weaknesses of break even analysis is the assumption that costs are either fixed or variable. Fixed costs will not alter regardless of the level (volume) of business. Variable costs are those which vary in direct relation to the volume of business, typically raw material (food and drink) costs. Uniquely labour cost may be variable, managed or fixed, for example:

Variable: Casual staff employed to cover banquet, ten customers for each member of staff, the cost will vary in direct proportion to the total number of customers served.

Managed: Part-time staff are employed at the weekend to cover an anticipated increase in business, there is not a direct relationship between cost of labour and total number of customers served, but it is monitored and adjusted on a regular basis.

Fixed: Full-time staff who have a contract of employment, specifying rate of pay; regardless of number of customers served this will have to be identified as a fixed cost.

Another weakness in break even analysis, seen in Figure 6.7 (b) above, is the assumption that fixed costs never increase. An expanding restaurant will eventually need to enlarge or move premises, both of which could lead to an increase in fixed cost (rent, rates, etc.). There is a point at which most businesses will have to accept a short-term loss in order to continue expanding. Some will choose not to expand further.

Sales mix analysis

Managers are sometimes reluctant to alter their menus, or they may change the menu religiously every six months, whether it needs changing or not, because that is the way it has always been. Menus contain preferred items. Preferred by whom? More to the point, are these items profitable? Menu analysis provides the means of determining a sales mix which will provide the maximum sales and profitability by optimizing the effect that each dish has on the overall success of the operation. The effectiveness of menu items may be measured by selling capacity, cost price or gross profit contribution.

Sales mix is generally identified as the comparison of performance between products on a menu, but the term may also be used to analyse the performance of departments. The mix between food and drink might differ daily (i.e. more drink sold at the weekend). It is useful to be able to recognize and understand the 'mix' in order to more effectively allocate resources. Knowing the 'mix' is especially important when undertaking promotional activities.

Example
A free glass of wine with the meal? Not at the weekend, it reduces drink sales and consequently revenue. However, during mid-week it may encourage additional and spin-off trade.

Sales mix is a direct result of buyer behaviour and that behaviour can be influenced by selling activity:

- Which items are sold aggressively?
- Which items are de-emphasized?
- What causes staff to influence customer choice?
- Can we identify high activity on low revenue items?

Product and service development tactics

Where can product/service development be used to gain competitive advantage?

While it is easy to identify and blame cost factors for poor performance, we should not underestimate the effect of 'selling' activity. The modern till will effectively identify sales mix and it may be possible to attribute effective selling activity to individual members of staff.

Poor performance may be blamed on:
- poor purchasing
- poor portion control
- waste, loss and fraud
- rising costs
- poor positioning
- poor selling

Menu engineering

The aim of menu engineering is to highlight poor performers and promote good performers. The process of menu engineering begins with a careful analysis of sales. Take a good look at what you sell, determine the menu range and content and calculate costs, based on accurate (current) material costs, recipe, yield and portion size. Ensure that all costs are included in price and insist on accurate detail for number of portions of each item sold. Eliminate or replace those items not 'paying their way'. Increase item prices where viable, decrease price/cost where necessary. Re-position items, increase or decrease their emphasis on the menu and initiate special promotions when necessary (see Table 6.2).

Table 6.2(a) Analysing the menu – finding the achievable gross profit.

	a Cost price	b Selling price	c GP (b−a)	d GP% (c/b ×100)	e Number sold	f Value (e × b)	g % total*	h Weighted average % (g × d)
Ham sandwich	0.25	0.60	0.34	56.6	20	12.00	8.0	452.8
Turkey sandwich	0.25	0.60	0.35	58.3	15	9.00	6.0	349.8
Beef sandwich	0.27	0.60	0.33	55.0	17	10.20	6.8	374.0
Ham roll	0.27	0.65	0.38	58.5	22	14.30	9.6	561.6
Turkey roll	0.26	0.65	0.39	60.0	10	6.50	4.4	264.0
Beef roll	0.28	0.65	0.37	56.9	21	13.65	9.0	512.1
Salad roll	0.18	0.50	0.32	64.0	35	17.50	11.7	748.8
Chips	0.07	0.15	0.08	53.3	10	1.50	1.0	53.3
Soup	0.09	0.10	0.01	10.0	35	3.50	2.3	23.0
Ploughman's	0.30	1.20	0.90	75.0	41	49.20	33.3	2497.5
Pâté	0.65	0.67	0.02	3.0	18	12.06	8.1	24.3
					Total Revenue =	149.41		5861.2

Achievable GP = Total weighted average (5861.2) ÷ 100 = 58.6

*Where column g is derived from the formula: menu item sales value times 100 divided by total revenue

Table 6.2(b) What would be the result of eliminating those items which are not paying their way (soup and pâté)?

	a Cost price	*b* Selling price	*c* GP (b−a)	*d* CP% (c/b ×100)	*e* Number	*f* Value (e × b)	*g* % total	*h* Weighted average % (g × d)
Ham sandwich	0.26	0.60	0.34	56.6	20	12.00	9.0	509.4
Turkey sandwich	0.25	0.60	0.35	58.3	15	9.00	6.7	390.6
Beef roll	0.27	0.60	0.33	55.0	17.	10.20	7.6	418.0
Ham roll	0.27	0.65	0.38	58.5	22	14.30	10.7	626.0
Turkey roll	0.26	0.65	0.39	60.0	10	6.50	4.9	294.0
Beef roll	0.28	0.65	0.37	56.9	21	13.65	10.2	580.4
Salad roll	0.18	0.50	0.32	64.0	35	17.50	13.1	838.4
Chips	0.07	0.15	0.08	53.3	10	1.50	1.1	58.6
Soup	0.09	0.10	0.01	–	–	–	–	–
Ploughman's	0.30	1.20	0.90	75.0	41	49.20	36.8	2760.0
Pâté	0.65	0.67	0.02	–	–	–	–	–
					Total Revenue = 133.85			6475.4

Achievable GP = Total weighted average (6475.4) ÷ 100 = 64.8

Simply removing these two items suggests that GP percentage can be improved by almost six points. But take care when drawing conclusions; the removal of one item will affect other sales, particularly associated items. Pâté, for example, might have been responsible for the popularity of salad, which is a good performer. The best policy would be to promote those items with the largest cash gross profit margin.

How well are menu items performing? We can measure performance on two scales.

- **cash contribution**: GP
- **sales volume (revenue)**: percentage of sales

Cash contribution and sales volume can be plotted on a matrix (see Figure 6.8).

What tactics can be applied to improve performance?

Reducing prices

An increase in volume is required to make up for lost sales.

Example: happy hour (drinks sold at half price)
Under normal pricing strategy.

Selling price   £1.50
Cost price   £0.30
Gross profit   £1.20
GP%   80

At 'happy hour' the new selling price is £0.75, the cost still remains at £0.30.

Selling price   £0.75
Cost price   £0.30
Gross profit   £0.45
GP%   60

	Sandwiches	£GP	% Sales
a	Turkey	0.24	8.0
b	Beef	0.35	6.0
c	Chicken	0.12	16.2
d	Ham	0.40	8.1
e	Ham and cheese	0.38	9.6
f	Cheese	0.50	16.9
g	Prawn	0.09	6.8
h	Tuna	0.17	9.0
i	Salad	0.32	11.7
j	Bacon	0.08	1.0
k	Egg and bacon	0.01	2.3
l	Egg and cress	0.45	4.4

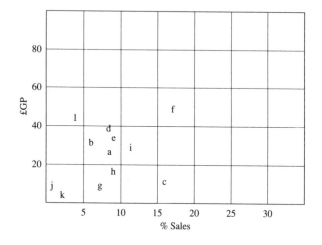

Figure 6.8 Measuring gross profit and sales volume. Items falling outside of preferred limits can be reviewed or withdrawn. For example, if minimum contribution (£GP) was set at 20p and minimum percentage of sales was set at 5%, then items j, k, g, h and c are all falling below GP target and items j, k, and l all fall below the desired sales target. Clearly a case can be made for both c (high sales performer) and l (high contribution earner), items g and h could probably be improved with some modification to either cost or price. But the big problems are j and k (failing both sales and contribution targets), so more serious action is obviously called for.

Increasing sales will not improve the GP percentage, at these prices gross profit will always be 60 per cent because we are measuring it per unit. Simple mathematics shows that no matter how many units we sell the overall GP percentage for the operation will not change, for example:

	Single unit	100 unit	1000 units
Selling price (revenues)	£0.75	£75.00	£750.00
Total cost (at 30p per unit)	£0.30	£30.00	£300.00
Gross profit	£0.45	£45.00	£450.00
GP%	60	60	60

However, total cash revenue is clearly increasing. So what do we need to do to generate the same level of cash gross profit as we were able to achieve at normal selling price. The calculation is:

$$\frac{\text{Old profit level} \times 100}{\text{New profit level}} = \text{required level of sales}$$

So that, in the above example:

$$\frac{1.20 \times 100}{0.45} = 2.66$$

This means that we would have to be sure of selling at least 2.66 times the normal volume in order to make 'happy hour' worthwhile. Contrary to common belief, doubling sales will not recover the effect of halving price. Indeed the lower the initial GP percentage the greater the need to increase sales beyond the assumed double, e.g. if the initial profit had been only 30p (40 per cent GP) we would need to sell four times the original volume to maintain position. GP percentage would have to be at least 80 per cent (unit cost of 15p in the above example) for us to maintain position with only a doubling of sales.

There are clearly implications for staffing and labour costs, which should also be included in the equation. Are we using happy hour to keep existing staff busy, or do we need to take on additional staff to cope with the rush?

Secondary sales

The effect of offering free wine, for instance, may be calculated as follows:

	Food	Wine	Total
Revenue from meals	1100	200	1300
(200 @ £5.50)			
Variable cost	400	80	480
GP contribution	700	120	820
Labour			250
Net			570

$$GP\% = \frac{820}{1300} \times 100 = 63.08\% \quad NP\% = \frac{570}{1300} \times 100 = 43.86\%$$

With a 'free wine' promotion there will be no income from wine, but wine consumed will be 100 per cent. Because of the anticipated increase in volume we will need six additional staff at £20 each. If volume doubles as a result of the promotion, then:

	Food	Wine	Total
Revenue from meals	2200		2200
(400 @ £5.50)			
Variable cost	800	160	960
GP contribution	1400	−160	1240
Labour			370
Net			870

$$GP\% = \frac{1240}{2200} \times 100 = 56.36\% \quad NP\% = \frac{870}{2200} \times 100 = 39.54\%$$

Although the difference in GP percentage and NP percentage is significant (some would say worrying), the improvement in cash GP (income) is more worthwhile. GP percentage could be improved, beyond its original 56.36 per cent, through effective selling by the service staff, e.g. liqueurs and speciality coffees. After all, customers should now have surplus funds and should be 'in the mood' for spending on these little extras.

Two-for-one promotions

A typical 'dinner for two' promotion (the cheapest meal offered free) works in the following manner:

First meal selling price	£19.80
Second meal selling price	£19.30
Wine	£9.95
Coffee (2)	£1.30
Service @ 15%	£7.55
Total	£57.90

As the second meal is the cheaper, this will be deducted (£57.90 – £19.30), leaving the total payable at £38.60.

Why do it?
- to increase volume
- to fill seats
- to cover fixed costs
- to keep staff busy
- to increase awareness

Profit sensitivity

Profit sensitivity analysis is concerned with identifying which elements of revenue have the greatest influence on profit. The emphasis shifts from gross profit to net profit and the examination of those items that respond positively to change.

Price elasticity of demand

A product is 'elastic' when an increase or decrease in its price results in a change in the volume purchased. A product is 'inelastic' if a change in its price results in little or no change in volume (e.g. milk, bread and petrol). Eating out generally is elastic, a 'luxury' which people can choose to take or do without. However, individual items on the menu will be more elastic than others and we need to know which these are. Reducing the price of inelastic items will not increase volume, but increasing price will improve profitability. Increasing the price of elastic items will result in a drop in sales, but reducing the price would lead to an increase in volume which, if managed properly, would result in an improvement to profitability.

It is difficult to predict our customers' responses to price changes. Price changes will need to be monitored carefully to identify trends and determine elasticity.

The profit multiplier

The 'profit multiplier' is a method of identifying those areas where change is likely to have most effect on profit. It assesses the effect of an equal change in a number of factors, each factor being measured independently.

Consider the effect on net profit of a 10 per cent increase in each of the following:

(a) the number of covers served
(b) the price charged
(c) food and beverage costs
(d) fixed labour costs
(e) variable labour costs
(f) other fixed costs

For example if base figures show:

Sales	50 000
Total costs	45 000
Net profit	5 000

Then after a 10 per cent increase in price:

Sales will be	55 000	
Total costs	45 000	(remain the same)
Net profit	10 000	(increase by 5000)

Net profit has increased by 5000 following a 10 per cent increase in price. The profit multiplier is therefore 10, for every 1 per cent increase in price results in a 10 per cent increase in net profit (see Table 6.3 for detailed analysis).

Profit multiplier analysis – process
● identify the key features influencing profit
● assume a small change
● calculate the multiplier
● rank the multipliers (the higher the multiplier, the greater the impact)
● assess the implications

The +/– element is less significant than the size of the profit multiplier (PM); it demonstrates direction rather than impact. It may be assumed that a 10 per cent decrease in food and beverage costs, for instance, would result in a PM of +4.

Table 6.3 Profit multiplier analysis

The effect, on net profit, of a 10% increase in each key factor in this example would be:

Key factors	Base figure	Number of covers	Price per cover	F&B costs	Labour fixed	Labour variable	Other fixed costs
Number of covers	10 000	11 000	10 000	10 000	10 000	10 000	10 000
Price per cover	5.00	5.00	5.50	5.00	5.00	5.00	5.00
Total revenue	50 000	55 000	55 000	50 000	50 000	50 000	50 000
F&B costs	20 000	22 000	20 000	22 000	20 000	20 000	20 000
Labour, fixed	10 000	10 000	10 000	10 000	11 000	10 000	10 000
Labour, variable	2 000	2 200	2 000	2 000	2 000	2 200	2 000
Other costs (fixed)	13 000	13 000	13 000	13 000	13 000	13 000	14 300
Total cost	45 000	47 200	45 000	47 000	46 000	45 200	46 300
Net profit	5 000	7 800	10 000	3 000	4 000	4 800	3 700
Effect on net profit		2 800	5 000	−2 000	−1 000	−200	−1 300
Percentage NP effect		56%	100%	−40%	−20%	−4%	−26%
Profit multiplier		5.6	10.0	−4.0	−2.0	−0.4	−2.6

If the key factors are now ranked by size of profit multiplier then clearly changing price will have most effect and changing variable labour cost will have very little effect.

Price charged	10.0
Number of covers served	5.6
Food and beverage costs	−4.0
Other fixed costs	−2.6
Fixed labour costs	−2.0
Variable labour costs	−0.4

High levels of PM are not necessarily desirable. Because they suggest levels of elasticity they may equally be an indication of stability. A stable business may attempt to manage its product range in such a way as to keep all PM levels relatively low. The basic concept of the profit multiplier may be applied differently in different situations. Different organizations will want to identify different key factors. PM may be calculated for the business as a whole, or for different departments.

Profit maximization

Often popularity and profitability are confused. Menu items can be arranged on a grid – the so-called Boston Matrix (see Figure 6.9) – representing their performance in regard to volume (popularity) and cash contribution (profit).

The cash cow: High sales and high profit contribution make this the ideal product. It can be 'milked' for cash, if cared for and fed regularly.

The plough horse: High sales and low profit contribution. It works hard but the profits are not always immediately apparent; it will take time to reap the full reward from this crop.

The cuddly panda: Low sales but high profit. Loveable but elusive, it will require careful study and special attention.

The dodo: Low sales and low profit. Probably extinct, in which case bury it.

Profit improvement strategy

Profit may be enhanced by manoeuvring 'cash cow' menu items towards the top right of the grid, as shown in Figure 6.10.

Figure 6.9 The Boston Matrix, developed by the Boston Consulting Group. Animal analogies are used to illustrate the effect of popularity and contribution upon performance. Source: Fuller and Waller, 1991.

When considering strategies/tactics be aware of the potential affects and possible consequences.

The plough horse *Tempting, but overpriced* Maintain value, review costs and portion size. Careful price increases through enhanced benefits and added value. Try re-packaging and/or linking.	**The cash cow** *Sought after item, price does not matter* Warrants further promotion and merchandising with prime menu position. Price increases, but with caution.
The dodo *Low price, but uninteresting* Is this an old product in decline, can it be revamped? Is it a new product that needs attention? If both cash contribution and volume remain low it may be wise to eliminate this product.	**The cuddly panda** *Low price, good value* Re-appraise, research (market, raw material, etc.) and try a variety of options. Increase promotions, re-style and/or add value.

Figure 6.10 Boston Matrix Evaluation.

Tactics for 'manoeuvring' menu items (modifying performance)

Wine by the glass

Offering an extended choice of wines by the glass has become common in the USA. Ideally, at least twelve wines should be offered, more if possible. There are problems – keeping quality and pilferage to name the obvious – but technology is now available (vacuum dispensers), so that this is not such a big problem, particularly if good wines are chosen which sell well. The loss of bottle sales is unlikely; it is probably more likely that overall sales will increase. Wines by the glass works better at lunch and quick meals, than it does at dinner, where bottle sales are more appropriate to lengthy (relaxed) dining. It is important to get the price right, identify what wines by the glass are competing with – soft drinks, lager, etc.

– and price accordingly. There is extra potential for sales with dessert – sweet dessert wines, port and Madeira. This type of activity should be supported by merchandising activity and point-of-sale material. In addition it is important to recognize the significance of motivating service (sales) staff.

Real ale and bottle-conditioned ales

Beer, like wine, can be matched with food and because of the wide variety of brews and flavours. 'Beer with food' is fast becoming the popular 'meal experience' choice. There is a recognizably increasing demand for good beers. Real ale, although popular, can be a problem for many caterers; its complex 'technology' means that a degree of skill is required. Bottle-conditioned ales provide caterers with an excellent alternative to real ale, they offer lots of choice and good quality.

Bottle-conditioned ales (BCAs) contain yeast and continue 'working' after bottling; they are alive and require ageing, maturing. Care should be taken when pouring, sediment should be left in the bottle and for this reason BCA bottles normally have high accentuated 'shoulders'.

Potential problems for sales of bottle-conditioned ales
- **customer:** knowledge/understanding – acceptance
- **product:** shelf life and quality*
- **staff:** knowledge and understanding, handling skill, pouring/sediment
- **beer list:** knowledge and understanding required in the writing of a balanced list

*(during ageing there is a marginal increase in alcohol and a decrease in sugar, so the beer becomes drier)

Potential benefits for the caterer selling bottle conditioned ales:
- no capital investment
- purchase amounts can be relatively low, enabling wider choice, variety, frequent change
- experimentation, novelty, USPs
- foreign beers available, particularly Belgian, but also French and German
- added value, high mark-up

Signature dishes

Signature dishes are those items, often having a unique name and/or service style, which are specifically associated with a particular operation. Customers will often seek out such a restaurant because of its association with a speciality dish. Signature dishes normally reinforce the quality image and brand integrity of an operation. They often provide temptation for others to copy.

Signature dish, 'house speciality', needs:
- ingredients which are easily available and of good quality all year (static cost, consistent standard)
- specialist skill, quality standards, standardized recipe/method, specialized equipment
- costing to be profitable, or attract customers who also purchase high profit items

Summary

Effective product/service development

We have seen that, as part of work organization and performance improvement, product development is concerned primarily with productivity, quality and profitability. It might be assumed that an increase in one will lead to a decrease in the other. This is not the case; effective product development can lead to improvements across the board. The philosophy of doing it right, first time, every time ensures that all effort is targeted at producing saleable product not waste.

Measuring performance

It is essential to record sales, profitability and popularity in order to show how menu items are performing. Improvement cannot be shown if the starting point is unknown. Recording and measuring processes allow managers to focus the activities of improvement programmes on specific targets rather than attempting to improve all things all the time.

Beware of fatigue in the menu. A number of indicators suggest that the menu offers items that have seen better days. Menus that are subject to only infrequent or irregular review are most at risk. Customers who ask for additional items or 'something else'; staff who are tired of producing the same old items; sales of once popular items becoming sluggish, may all indicate time for a review of the menu.

Improving profitability

This chapter has identified the means by which the menu can be used to control not only the activities and resources employed but also the elements of the system of provision that result in a return on investment. An alternative to increasing sales would be to consider the relationship between sales, sales mix, costs and achievable gross profit. In any event, the improvement of profitability assumes a sound knowledge of the current state of the operation in profit terms. That is, all items sold, their composition and their contribution. The implications are clear; that the competent manager must be aware of the performance potential of every aspect of the operation's resources. This must include the menu.

Once implemented the effectiveness of any plan must be assessed.

Product development checklist

- Has marketing and forecasting activity accurately predicted the nature and level of demand?
- Has the concept/package/content relationship been clarified?
- Have menus been designed in line with the concept?
- Have dishes been developed according to customer requirements?
- Are dishes and recipes consistent with the limitations of the production system?
- Have dishes been tested and tasted?
- Have raw material specifications, standardized recipes and methods been written?
- Are equipment and staffing allocations consistent with the needs of dishes that have been developed?
- What other quality assurance techniques have been included in the product/service plan?
- Do products and systems comply with current legislation?
- Are accurate and reliable costings available and up to date?
- Have systems been developed for performance monitoring and evaluation?
- Are processes and procedures available for performance improvement?

Legal implications associated with product/service development (menu management)

The menu will form the basis of the relationship between the caterer and the customer. The rights of the customer are protected, by law, in a number of ways:

The Sale of Goods Act 1979: Defines the contractual relationship and in particular specifies fitness for purpose as a prerequisite of a product or service suitability.

Price Marking (Food and Drink on Premises) Order 1979: Specifies rules for the display and content description (prices and portion sizes) of menus. In particular, that accurately priced menus should be displayed at or near the entrance to the restaurant.

The Consumer Protection Act 1989: Reinforces the Price Marking (Food and Drink on Premises) Order, it warns against misleading price information. VAT, service and cover charges must be clearly shown.

Food Safety Act 1990: Concentrates on safety and hygiene, although here too there is reference to the quality and nature of food and particularly descriptive terms. Phrases like 'home-made' and 'fresh' must be accurate and genuine.

Trades Description Act 1968: Defines trading terms, definitions, nature and the sequence of content in dishes (meat and potato pie must contain more meat than potato, otherwise it should be called potato and meat pie). The act also specifies rules regarding quantity, size and method of manufacture. Additionally, it also protects the customer from false or misleading statements.

Fair Trading Act 1973: Also protects the customer from false and misleading statements.

In regard to law and the collection of tax, service is subject to VAT therefore it must be added to the bill first. VAT is payable on products *and* services.

Food production legislation
In addition to commodity planning attempting to achieve optimum levels of efficiency, effectiveness and economy we must also conform to limitations placed on us by the following legislation:

- The Food and Drugs Act 1955
- The Food Hygiene (General) Regulations 1970
- The Food and Drugs (Control of Food Premises) Act 1976
- The Food Act 1984
- The Food Hygiene (Amendment) Regulations 1990
- The Food Safety Act 1990

Suggested further reading

Bareham, J. (1995) *Consumer Behaviour in the Food Industry.* Butterworth–Heinemann.

Fewell, A. and Wills, N. (1995) *Marketing.* Butterworth–Heinemann.

Fuller, J. and Waller, K. (1991) *The Menu, Food and Profit.* Stanley Thornes.

Harris, P. (1992) *Profit Planning.* Butterworth–Heinemann.

Mennell, S. Murcott, A. and van Otterloo, A. (1992) *The Sociology of Food.* Sage Publications.

Miller, J.E. (1987) *Menu Pricing and Strategy*. Van Nostrand Rheinhold.

Tannahill, R. (1988) *Food in History*. Penguin.

7
Systems management

Aims and objectives

The aim of systems management is to enable unit managers to recognize the importance of the inter-relationship between efficiency, effectiveness and economic performance. The choice of systems and the way in which they are integrated and implemented will significantly influence operational outcomes.

The aims of system management are:

- to define the determinants of successful operation
- to identify key systems and sub-systems
- to recognize the influence of management and organizational culture
- to suggest strategies and tactics for successful systems management

It has been suggested (Ritzer, 1993) that Ray Kroc considered many options before deciding on McDonald's as being the ideal 'system' on which to base a franchise business. The key factor was its simplicity. Unlike hot dogs, which he had also considered, there were very few variables. The basic design could be easily replicated and managed to ensure consistency of delivery. It was, in fact, the ideal 'system'.

The purpose of this chapter is to describe the relationship between systems and the necessary operational and control procedures. In addition the impact of consumer behaviour and resource availability on system effectiveness will be evaluated. There is, unfortunately, insufficient space in this text to deal with every element within a catering system (see Figure 7.1 for an indication of the potential detail involved). The intention, therefore, is to concentrate on the main areas of provision, delivery and control.

System management objectives are to:
- Determine operational effectiveness.
- Anticipate likely situations and provide routines for effective/efficient/economic outcomes.
- Apply the principles of the control cycle to set, monitor and maintain standards.
- Provide effective procedures for the collection of systems data (sales history, etc.).
- Develop processes and procedures for the analysis of information collected.
- Identify opportunities for improvement.

What is systems management?

The term 'system' is generally used to define a series of procedures or processes, based on the combination of specific activities and/or specialized techniques and equipment.

Systems management, simply described, is the methodical structuring of operational activities in order that efforts are co-ordinated towards an identifiable goal. Systems exist in a variety of environments – the digestive system in the human body, the sweeper system in a football team, the transport system in a developed culture. It is possible to draw analogies between each of these and industry/business systems, particularly the degree to which a system may be a natural function or an imposition controlled by external forces. Some form of control is necessary in all systems, a system which is out of control will invariably result in disaster. It will be necessary for each operation to decide whether their culture is suited to natural (responsive) systems, team strategy or rigid (bureaucratic) control.

Business systems are concerned with the management of assets and resources in the most effective, efficient and economic manner in order to fulfil company/operational objectives.

The key food and beverage systems are listed below:

- **Communication**   marketing
  - research
  - advertising
  - forecasting
  merchandising
  data management (computing)
- **Provision**   raw materials
  equipment
  staff
  facilities
- **Delivery**   purchasing
  production
  service
- **Control**   quality
  finance (stock and cash)
  risk management (health, safety and hygiene)

Catering systems and sub-systems cannot operate in isolation (see Figure 7.1). Systems management enables planning – the recognition of relationships, goal setting and problem solving – leading to the effective use of resources in combination and the elimination of waste.

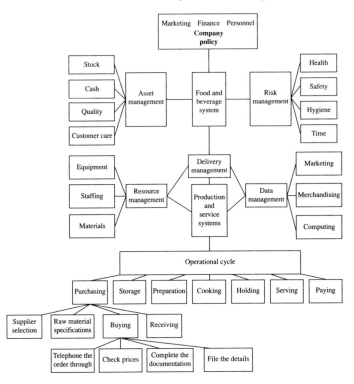

Figure 7.1 The food and beverage system. There would be a similar 'cascading' of further activities for each element of the operational cycle. It is important to understand the inter-relationship that exists at all levels and between systems and sub-systems. For example, purchasing (filing) activities should be related to (invoice) payment systems. Health, safety and hygiene systems feed into the main system and should therefore be reflected in sub-systems. In the example above, purchasing activity should include reference (specification) to product details; size and weight of containers (methods of unloading, lifting and moving), wrapping, packing and temperature of food products (food safety).

Systems management involves:
- identifying and defining activities
- grouping activities to form processes
- linking processes to form sub-systems
- developing 'best' methods and continuous re-examination of effectiveness
- eliminating variety, variance and variables
- resulting in consistent, predictable, reliable performance

The ideal system requires:
- food, drink and services are available on demand
- optimum use of labour/skills, equipment and materials
- quick and simple methods of operational control
- flexible design providing for ease of adaptation

within the constraints of:
- consistent quality
- acceptable costs
- high level of customer appeal/delight

Systems have to be developed within certain constraints which set limits on the opportunities available to us (see Figure 7.2). Because the constraints, patterns and combinations, are unique to individual operations then the resulting systems and method of implementation which develop will also be unique.

Current emphasis recognizes the inefficiencies of traditional (labour-intensive) systems. Future development will concentrate on modifications to the catering cycle (smoothing the peaks and troughs) resulting in more effective time/resource management.

Modern systems will encourage non-time-essential activities to be performed during troughs, e.g. stock management, hygiene, marketing/merchandising activities. Systems will need to be developed to manage the customers during peaks to encourage early/late dining; this may be aided by the trend towards grazing. Managers will adapt systems to be more

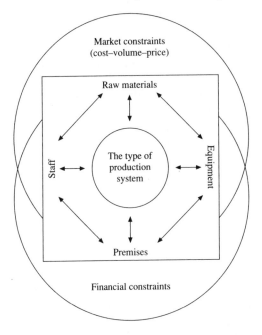

Figure 7.2 The systems approach. System aims are to anticipate operational effectiveness and likely solutions and to provide routines for them. Source: Fuller and Waller, 1991.

responsive at the point of sale. Systems will be service led rather than production led. There is some risk of de-skilling (the dilution of culinary skills, for instance), but this may be overcome by demonstrating the benefits of multi-skilling, further increasing opportunities for system development.

Why is systems management important?

Catering operations are increasingly concerned with efficiency and effectiveness – maximizing output with minimum input whilst at the same time trying to guarantee performance quality. Such objectives can only be achieved if there are effective systems in place, including those systems specifically designed to enable management to monitor and control the operation.

Systems management enables aims and objectives (operational effectiveness, efficiency and economy) to be clarified. Effective delivery requires systematic planning, enabling design of procedures for the implementation of strategy. The implementation of a programme (system) of energy management, for instance, would require a review of all other systems.

Systems cannot be isolated, for example:
An energy management system would involve:
- negotiating terms/tariff
- equipment selection
- equipment management and maintenance
- modification to production/service techniques (systems)
- monitoring energy consumption
- customer comfort: temperature, air conditioning/quality
- staff working conditions: temperature, air conditioning/quality
- cost effectiveness/efficiency, control of waste (heat loss)
  - building, fabric
  - ventilation, windows, extraction
  - equipment, ovens, refrigeration

The potential effects on other systems – customer care, purchasing, production, staffing, etc. – are clear.

Energy management linked to purchasing (energy saving equipment)

- Forced air convection ovens:

  Smaller cabinets, more even distribution of heat, marginally faster, and can additionally be linked to temperature of food rather than oven, switched off immediately cooking is complete.

- High pressure steamers:

  Much quicker than conventional boiling, less energy loss in heating the 'non-essential' water.

- Induction hobs:

  Only working when there are pans in place, very effective heat transfer.

- Hot cupboards:

  Better insulation, less heat loss and better temperature control of food.

- Microwave ovens:

  Heat created within the food, no wasted heat/energy.

- Dish-washing equipment:

  The heat transfer built into modern systems, reduction in humidity and heat in work area may result in savings in ventilation costs.

Many of the above items will require a higher initial investment and choice will be influenced by long-term cost/saving benefits. The use of such equipment may require modification to existing systems of production, service or control. Modifications to purchasing (raw material management) systems may also be necessary.

> **Efficient usage of equipment must be supported by an effective system of equipment maintenance**
> - structured cleaning programmes
> - programmed maintenance schedules
> - specific attention to heating elements and thermostats, doors, seals and safety features
> - clear guidelines on use and cleaning (to all staff)

Energy management linked to production systems

Take the case of cook-chill and cook-freeze systems, not only is such modern equipment (efficient cooking and rapid reduction in temperature) designed to be energy efficient, but the systems themselves enable further efficiencies, particularly in the allocation of labour and the absence of peaks and troughs associated with traditional methods.

Who is involved with systems management?

Clearly systems management is primarily a management responsibility which may be supported by layers of authority identified through recognition of critical control points (CCPs). Supervisors will be responsible for implementing and monitoring system effectiveness. However, the significance of management style and organizational culture (mechanistic/organic) should not be underestimated

> **The influence/significance of management style:**
> - **Crisis management**: ineffective system or no system at all
> - **Management by exception**: a system which highlights but does not necessarily prevent variance
> - **Management by objective**: all systems designed and co-ordinated to the achievement of the prime goals

For systems to be truly effective they must be ~
appropriate management and organizational cu
already been noted systems will be inter-relat
will need to be a culture of shared motiv~
communication.

Staff and managers need to know:
- what is to be achieved
- the current state
- means of improvement: modifications to system
- key result areas: critical control points (CCPs)
- critical success factors: performance measurement
- possible/probable consequences

Communication

The importance of good communication has been discussed in previous chapters, and will be discussed further in Chapter 8, Efficient staffing, suffice to say at this point that to be effective, methods and procedures for communication must not only be appropriate to the needs of the master plan (catering system) but also integrated with other elements (sub-systems). For example, computers may form the basis of the stock management system. They will quickly identify control problems, variances from anticipated outcomes and they may well be suited to the preparation of reports for subsequent management meetings. But they may not be suited to the running of such meetings, strategy discussions, and the development of instructions to staff or the delivery of further training which may result from such meetings.

Communication sub-systems:
- marketing/merchandising (see Chapters 2 and 3)
- staffing (see Chapter 8)
- computing

Systems strategy

How is systems management implemented?

Managers will integrate communication, delivery and control systems. They will then identify and deal with the sub-systems/relationships.

The main elements of the system:
- **input**   customer
  company policy
  resources (including skills, techniques and technology)
- **process** operational cycle
  resource management
  quality standards, methods and procedures
- **output** dishes/meals/services
  volume
  price/value
  satisfied customers

Planning

- **Market need:** type of customer, volume, meal experience, menu and product life cycle (the need for change and/or modification).
- **Operational needs:** space/volume, preparation/convenience/assembly, supplies and storage, services (electricity, gas, water, waste, ventilation), labour/skills availability, finance (capital, debt, cash flow, depreciation).

The main aim of any system must be to provide the desired

product(s), as and when required by the customer, in the most efficient, effective and economic manner. Consequently the choice of system will be determined by the answer to two questions.

1   What is it that my customers want?
2   How can I best provide it (efficiency/effectiveness/ economy)?

Traditionally catering combines manufacturing and retailing under one roof, with production being a direct response to the customer placing an order. The kitchen is a manufacturing unit using highly perishable raw materials – once produced the product must be sold. There are high levels of waste and often long spells of unproductive activity.

The objectives:
- To balance supply and demand more effectively.
- To produce only what is required.
- To increase efficiency (increased output for less input) by:
  - minimizing loss (waste)
  - maximizing potential (profit contribution, volume and margin)
  - reducing costs

  without diminishing customer satisfaction.

Factors affecting the system

- money
- staff availability and skills
- range, quantity and type of equipment
- developments in technology
- trends in production methods

- available production and seating space
- ambience and style of service
- merchandising activity
- meal times and turnover
- total number of meals and range of dishes required
- speed of service and queuing behaviour
- customer control (including payment)
- changes in consumer taste and expectations
- nature, range and availability of raw materials
- frequency of deliveries
- health, safety and hygiene
- cleaning and maintenance

Little can be achieved without the input of some financial resource. The most important thing is to decide, at the onset, the total sum available and how this shall be allocated. In this way budgets – which have been set for capital and operational expenditure – can be divided and responsibility allocated to various cost and profit centres. A balance must then be achieved between staffing, raw material and equipment usage. This balance, normally developed through the commodity plan (Chapter 6) must be achieved in unison with systems of production and service.

Generally, our industry has become very cosmopolitan which means that our customers are becoming used to a wide variety of environments and systems creating a lot of opportunity for new ideas. If we choose a system that involves customers helping themselves to raw ingredients and doing their own cooking, then – so long as the product is packaged, priced and managed correctly – the modern customer is likely to find this quite acceptable.

Some operations will have system decisions forced on them. Catering in the oil fields of the North Sea for instance is limited by the availability of fresh daily deliveries. There is necessarily a high reliance on chilled, frozen and convenience foods. Consideration must be given to the possibility that the rig may be without normal deliveries during bad weather.

Deliveries that are made daily, by helicopter, must be limited to essentials. Allocating production space and time to an 'in-house bakery' may be the only way of obtaining reasonably fresh bread.

Sometimes the choice of system is determined entirely by the size and nature of the occasion. If you are feeding 2000 customers from a tent in an open field, then it makes sense to consider carefully how much work has to be done on site and how much can be done beforehand, away from the point of delivery. Similarly if those 2000 customers are enjoying a fine day of sporting entertainment at the British Open Golf Championship, then speed of service will be critical. Products and services will have to be tailored to very rapid delivery. Customers and customer queues will have to be controlled. Alternatively, if we maintain that we cannot, or will not, compromise on the quality of products and service that we provide then we must ensure that the customer's time inside the tent is made as enjoyable as the sporting activity going on outside. This may mean increasing levels of service, or providing sufficient comfort and televisions such that no customer feels that they are missing out on the main entertainment.

The example of the 2000 golfing customers may also be used to highlight the problems of health, safety and hygiene. Each of these is relatively easy to manage in purpose built, static, kitchens and restaurants. If starting from scratch then systems of risk management – health, safety and hygiene – must be at the top of the planning, architectural and structural considerations. In older buildings some structural alterations may be necessary to comply with the law. For the golfing event none of the basics that we normally rely on may be available and we are faced with new challenges – wind and rain etc. – that we would not normally consider. New EEC legislation relating to health, safety, hygiene and particularly temperature controls may drastically change event catering, systems of production and service in the future.

Delivery systems – the operational (catering) cycle

Systems of production and service

Managers will attempt to find the system that best meets the needs of the customer, as defined from marketing activity, within the constraints of the operation. We have already seen that the main constraints are company policy and the availability of resources with which to accomplish company objectives. Systems of production and service will obviously be related to products (dish development) and services on offer.

History and tradition

Hospitality and catering systems are very much influenced by history and tradition. Auguste Escoffier and Cesar Ritz are generally identified as being responsible for the development of the hospitality (hotel) industry in the early 1900s. Escoffier is credited with the introduction of the 'partie' system to the classical kitchen, although some credit should be given to Alexis Soyer. At the turn of the century many of the gentlemen who served as officers in the British army were in the habit of taking household servants on campaign with them. During the Crimean War, Soyer was forced to use these servants along with soldiers to produce meals in large quantities. It was necessary to develop 'systems' for the delivery of food to the troops. In order to organize and control production he was forced to separate functions and apply a degree of 'regimentation' to the various activities. The lessons learnt in the army were easily transferred to civilian life. Above all it was the abundance of cheap labour that allowed production and service systems to develop as they did. The contrasting trend in labour availability today is the prime motivator leading to changes in systems.

Change might have been more rapid had the industry not

felt constrained by traditional recipes, methods of cookery and service styles. Whilst there still remains a market for traditional hospitality it can only be had at a price. Customers are forcing economies on the industry. Although, as with all things new, there is often resistance to change, customers generally appreciate the improvements to value and reliability that modern changes can bring.

The menu remains the single most important element of constraint on systems development, but now caterers have several options which may result in the delivery of the same menu item (see Figure 7.3).

Method a	Method b	Method c	Method d
Supplier	Supplier	Supplier	Supplier
Ready to serve dish	Fish portion	Fish portion	Whole fish
	+	+	+
	Packet sauce	Fresh sauce ingredients	Fresh sauce ingredients
			Filleting, skinning and portioning
	Poach fish	Poach fish	Poach fish
Reheat dish	Finish sauce	Cook and finish sauce	Cook and finish sauce
Present and serve	Present and serve	Present and serve	Present and serve

Figure 7.3 Options for the provision (delivery) of sole bonne femme. This analysis immediately gives rise to questions about quality. It is not possible to state categorically which method results in the best quality. All of them are capable of producing atrociously poor results. conversely, each system, properly managed, is capable of producing the highest possible standards which, if achieved, make the manner of production irrelevant – to the customer at least.

Systems of delivery

Any system consists of three main activities: input–process–output (see Figure 7.4). The quality of output is determined not only by the processing but also by the input and each must be integrated effectively.

Input	Process	Output

Investment:
   capital
   facilities
 	
 Resources:
   staff (skills)
   equipment
   raw materials
	Purchasing:
	   receipt
	   storage
	   issuing
	
	 Production:
	   prep
	   cooking
	   holding
	
	 Displaying and selling:
	   merchandising
	   special promotions
	
	 Service:
	   billing
	   tilling
	   cashing up
	
	 Control
	
	 Communication
	
	 Training
		Products
		
		 Services
		
		 Evaluation:
		   customer comment
		     compliment
		     complaint
		
		 Delighted customers:
		   reputation
		   brand image
		
		 Revenue:
		   profit
		   re-investment

Figure 7.4 Systems: input–process–output.

Purchasing systems

In the USA, Efficient Consumer Response (ECR) supply systems are becoming common. Such systems are designed to ensure that each sale (at the till) triggers a response throughout the supply chain and shifts the emphasis of stock management from retailer to supplier.

Companies with in-house supply are already using similar stock management processes. The technology (computer/ modem networking) is readily available for independent operators to work more closely with suppliers. The use of such systems will limit choice (the ability to switch between suppliers), but they do allow for tighter control of stock and a consequent reduction in investment.

Increased revenue may be achieved through careful selection of raw materials to attain maximum yield. Additionally revenue may be increased by purchasing materials that are used to produce those products that are most in demand from customers. Although precise policy will vary, the principles of an effective purchasing system (quality, price, continuity of supply) are applicable to all operations.

The aims of purchasing:
- To ensure an adequate supply.
- To minimize investment costs.
- To select and purchase the most appropriate materials – quality and quantity – for a specified purpose at the best price (value).
- To set procedures for documentary control and ensure that all goods are used for the purpose for which they were purchased.
- To enable accurate accounting.

A clear inter-relationship can be identified between the purchase system and other systems, especially the control of costs and quality. Additionally it is important to understand the relationship between purchasing and risk management systems. Hygiene regulations require that caterers demonstrate 'due diligence' in the provision of products for consumption. Having a sound purchasing policy that controls the origin, transportation, delivery and storage (particularly temperatures) of raw materials may be taken as due diligence and may therefore serve as some protection under the law.

Identifying requirement needs

Raw material requirements will primarily be identified as a result of commodity planning and dish development (discussed in Chapter 6). Equipment requirements stem from the commodity plan but are also related to the chosen system of production. Systems development, commodity planning and purchasing must take account of staffing and available skills.

There are two elements to the purchasing system which should, ideally, be kept separate. Firstly there is the selection of suitable materials and suppliers. We will need information on suppliers and our material requirements. Specifications and methods of payment will be agreed and supplier quotations compared. Secondly there is the buying activity, determining the quantity and frequency and placing orders. In some cases, particularly where there is more than one supplier, fruit and vegetables for instance, the buyer may also negotiate 'best price' which is not necessarily the cheapest. A third party should be responsible for receiving, checking and acknowledging receipt of deliveries.

The choice of purchasing system will also be influenced by sources of supply and supply channels. Sources of supply may be divided into:

(a) Primary   growers (fresh produce)
                manufacturers (canned goods, etc.)
                processors (combined preparation)
(b) Secondary   wholesalers
                retailers

An understanding of the supply channel will determine the point at which we obtain our 'raw' materials. With the exception of the small, owner-operator business and those operations large enough to become their own manufacturers/processors/suppliers, there is a growing tendency to purchase later in the supply channel after most processing is complete.

Our purchase policy should aim to minimize costs that may be influenced by the needs of our end product, levels of stock holding, methods of purchasing, type and quality of raw materials, type of supplier, method of payment, bulk purchasing and discounts. We require up-to-date information on prices, availability, demand and trend. Such information may be obtained from supplier, trade press, national press and government statistics.

Purchase contract

Entering into a contract requires knowledge and understanding: ignorance is no excuse in the eyes of the law. The law will not protect a foolish business person, it will uphold the terms and conditions of the contract. Purchasing contracts require both legal and technical knowledge and it is fairly unusual for one individual to have both; teamwork is required. The food and beverage manager will be responsible for the technical detail, most of which will be written into raw material specifications. The legal department, or suitably qualified personnel in the purchasing department, will be responsible for the terms and conditions in the contract.

It is important that both parties have some understanding of the importance and implications of the detail concerned, particularly during negotiations. It would be a mistake for the lawyer to give up the right to refuse delivery if temperature were not within specified limits because it appeared 'just a minor point'.

Product specifications

Specifications for raw materials and equipment have taken on greater importance in recent years. Managers are recognizing the control advantages of tight dish/product specifications, albeit often at the expense of the creative craftsman. Many will see the decline in larder (butchery) and pastry (bakery) activity as sad but inevitable. In particular there is a move towards prepared products with no production waste and no requirements for specialist skilled staff. This is most apparent in the area of meat, poultry and fish supplies although the principle can be equally applied in other areas like vegetable preparation. Potato supplies for instance have shown a marked change in the range and variety of products available – peeled, chipped, diced or turned, fresh, vacuum packed, chilled or frozen.

In the case of meat products many caterers now rely heavily on highly specified prepared cuts allowing in house staff skills to be devoted to cooking and presentation. There are additional cost benefits, skilled teams of butchers can prepare specified cuts much more quickly and therefore more cost effectively than catering staff. Up to 50 per cent of preparation labour costs may be saved in this way. Some savings can be passed on to the caterer; initial purchase (product) cost will be greater (than unprepared alternatives) but total production costs will be reduced. Caterers, working closely with butchers, may prepare their own detailed specifications. Many will rely on standard specifications from the *Meat Buyer's Guide* published by the National Association of Catering Butchers. Many butchers have identified the advantages of dealing exclusively with caterers and many are developing this relationship by producing value-added products like prepared kebabs, pre-marinated meats, seasoned stir fries as well as the more traditional prepared roasts.

The 'due diligence' requirements of the Food Safety Act are encouraging more caterers, not only to tighten their specifications but also to visit their suppliers' premises to reassure themselves of production standards, storage and temperature controls. This should be done at regular intervals. Hygiene standards should be written into the specifications and compliance with standards should be tested.

A purchase specification should include:
- company policy
- menu requirements
- detailed product description: type, grade, size, yield
- allowance for variance (if any)
- production and storage standards, hygiene controls
- transportation and delivery standards
- inspection procedures

Problems may arise with specifications if:

- a standard which is difficult to obtain is specified
- the specification involves a geographical standard (e.g. Jersey tomatoes)
- delivery times are unreasonable
- specification is imprecise, not measurable

Ordering the right quantity

An effective purchasing system should seek to identify economies. Cost-effective stock management relies on efficient purchasing procedures, particularly relating to ensuring purchase of the right quantity at the right time.

The principle of what is known as 'economic order quantity' is relatively easy to understand. The procedure can be somewhat more complex to apply (see Figure 7.5). In principle we need to achieve a balance between frequency of delivery and levels of storage. Allowance must be made for the cost of ordering – the more often we order the greater the cost – and the cost of stock holding (storage).

Unfortunately these costs are not always easy to identify. Storage costs, for instance, should include labour, administration, heat, light and humidity controls. Additionally some account must be taken of the cost of space involved, rent, rates, mortgage interest repayments and the loss of revenue that may have been achieved if that space was used for selling activity rather than storage. Finally we must also make allowance for the loss of investment interest that arises from large stock holding. If stock holding were reduced by £1000 and that sum were invested there would be an additional income of £100 (assuming an annual interest rate of 10 per cent).

Calculation of economic order quantity requires identification of:
- number of units used per year
- order cost per order
- annual storage cost per unit (*approximately 15% of the stock value)

EOQ formula

EOQ (in units) = $(2 \times C \times T) \div S$

where   C = order cost per order
T = total number of units used per year
S = storage costs per year for one unit

* Because of the difficulty of obtaining entirely accurate figures, EOQ calculations are often based on assumed costs. This tends to weaken the value of such activity. The most important thing to appreciate is that cost benefits can be achieved by balancing ordering and storage.

Economic ordering is aided by:
- knowledge of suppliers' delivery schedules
- understanding of 'lead times' (the delay between ordering and receiving)
- minimum, maximum and re-order levels for each stock item

Figure 7.5 Economic order quantity.

Effective purchasing

Purchasing incurs a cost and that cost must be controlled. Control can best be achieved by developing systems of stock control and storage that aid the purchase procedure. Establish stock levels for every item. Make sure every purchase is necessary and timely. Ensure that the materials purchased are required for saleable products. Assess the cost of preparation and decide whether 'in house' preparation is cost effective. Make raw material specifications clear to all and ensure that design standards are adhered to.

Equipment management systems

As we have noted many times throughout this book, there is continuous and increasingly more rapid change in our industry. Change is most apparent in systems of production and the inherent processes and procedures. The effect on equipment selection is dramatic. The traditionally equipped kitchen, containing all manner of pots and pans in an almost infinite range of sizes, is now a thing of historic reference. Specialist items, fish kettles, muslin cloth and jelly bags are museum relics. The most prominent elements of equipment selection are now economy of effort and space, versatility and flexibility and control of process and yield (see Figure 7.6) – all of which should be determined by system (production/ service) requirements, which ideally will be reduced to the minimum.

Choosing equipment – the influence of technology

To consider the influence of technology we must first go back to basics. How is food cooked? Cooking may simply be defined as the application of heat. Why does food

Equipment attributes:	Systems design questions
Ease of use	
Ergonomics	
Free standing	
Modular	
Flexible	Will it do the job?
Fits existing system	
Fit for the purpose (product needs)	Will it fit the system?
Size, capacity and speed	
Fuel and energy saving	
Health and safety	
Durable	
Easily cleaned	

Figure 7.6 Equipment design considerations.

deteriorate? Generally because of the growth of bacteria and/or enzymatic development. Deterioration may be controlled by the removal of moisture and/or air and the control of temperature. How is food delivered to the consumer? A mixture of production and service skills based on technical understanding, product knowledge, human communication and contact.

Traditional cooking (heat transfer) involves conduction, convection and/or radiation as in baking, braising, roasting, grilling, frying, boiling, steaming and poaching. Such processes may now be modified by:

● microwave
● induction
● very high pressure steaming (cabinet construction)
● pressure fryers
● convection (heat distribution/heat exchange)
● combination ovens

Many of the above will rely on the use of 'microchip (computer) control technology' rather than human skill or judgement – particularly in terms of the control of timing, temperature, filtration and self cleaning programmes. The influence of technology may also be seen in the introduction of entire systems: cook-chill, cook-freeze, sous-vide and the related changes in components (convenience), raw materials and staff (de-skilling).

There will always be a need for a traditionally equipped kitchen, in the same way that other crafts (handmade shoes, clothes, furniture and even cars) still exist. Like those other crafts investment in production equipment and labour (per unit output) will be very high. All costs must be passed on to the customer and ever increasing costs will result in a decreasing market. Efficient equipment management can help to limit the effect of increasing production costs and thus help to retain a greater proportion of the market (see Figure 7.7).

System planning (PQRST) from British Gas

Basic components
P.	Product	(materials)
Q.	Quantity	(volume)

Other components
R.	Routing	(process-operation, sequence)	(equipment)
S.	Support Services	(toilets, loading bays, etc.)	
T.	Time	(process method, machinery)	

Product and quantity (PQ)
Menu	(complexity) **(T)**
Food specification	(levels of convenience)
Portioning	(size and control)
Equipment capacity	

Routing (R)
General arrangement of the area	
Flow patterns	(area/activity relationships)
Work study	(including support services) **(S)**
Equipment siting	

Support services (S)
Attitude and performance of staff	**(T)**
Working conditions	(legislation)

Figure 7.7 Efficient use of production and service space.

Production systems

In order to design efficiency/effectiveness/economy into the production system it is important to understand the relationship between production and other systems, particularly purchasing and service.

Input	*Process*	*Output*
Purchasing	**Production**	Service

Production objectives include:

- quality
- yield management: measurement
- standardization: product development
- volume forecasting: product/dish demand/trend
- portion control

Traditional systems
- clear differentiation between front and back of house
- high level of flow and interaction
- customer contact in front
- customer is a passive receiver
- all activities are on the same premises

The production system must be co-ordinated with the service system. This applies even to centralized production units. Where both production and service take place in the same building the closeness of the relationship is clear. Although centralized production units may be far from the service point in distance and times they should not be planned, or managed, in ignorance of the service system. The question of which comes first in the planning process, production or service, is subject to some debate. It is necessary to consider carefully what it is that the customer is looking for and work back from there. In most cases this will mean taking the environment in which the customer need is met, the service system, first. But in many cases the customer will have very specific preferences regarding the product, in which case the production system will come first and the service system will be planned in response to it.

Production planning will need to take account of:
- customer need
- volume (daily and annual turnover)
- scope of menu
- price (production costs and market competitiveness)
- implications of system (operational cycle)
- work flow
- stock holding (raw materials)
- product holding (hot, chilled or frozen)
- equipment (number, range, purpose and versatility)
- staffing requirements
- environmental implications (heat/light/ventilation)
- legislation

Planning of production areas will be influenced or constrained by construction details. However the main aims will be to achieve effectiveness through:

- optimum use of (productive) space
- economy of effort
- maintenance economies
- adaptability (space and equipment capable of more than one use)
- flexibility (power, water and waste points)
- mobile (moveable) equipment

Finally, management of hygiene must be the highest planning priority. Such planning should involve the designation of colour coded equipment and work areas to avoid cross contamination.

Service systems

Like systems of production, effective provision of service systems must be based on the assumption that we are attempting to achieve the highest levels of efficiency, effectiveness and economy whilst maintaining maximum customer satisfaction. For whatever type of operation we are concerned with, our objective is quality service.

Whereas quality will apply throughout the system it is at the point of service that quality is ultimately tested by the customer. The customers' assessment of products is often influenced by their perception of the way in which they are delivered. We have seen, particularly with commodity planning (Chapter 6), how product quality can be maintained. We have discussed (in Chapter 5) the difference between quality control and quality assurance. In the main, discussion has been related to quality of product and it is clear, for products at least, that standards can be set and measured. But the meal experience is concerned with much more than products. It may even be argued that quality of service features more strongly than food or drink in the customer's mind when they measure our performance. This raises the question of whether it is possible to determine, measure or maintain quality service standards.

In order to manage service systems we need to understand how products are delivered, what influences the level of service involved and to what extent that may influence customer assessment of our operation.

How do we deliver?

Menu type/style
- service style
- operating hours
- location
- customer volume

Service method
Waiter
- silver service
- gueridon
- family service
- plate service

Cafeteria
- self service
- free flow/echelon/blister
- food court
- fast food counter

Vending
- merchandisers
- beverage machines

Modern service systems have moved away from traditional skill, hierarchy and authority based methods. There is now more emphasis on social skills. It matters not that the sommelier takes the wine order and pours the wine, the chef du range deals with the customer while the commis does all the fetching and carrying. What does matter is that all employees, regardless of rank or station, are concerned that each and every customer is totally satisfied. While it might be wrong to suggest that the basis for such change was consideration for the customer, it would probably be more accurate to identify financial pressure as the main influence, customer acceptance of change must be recognized. The 'relaxation' of the meal experience has encouraged a much wider proportion of the public to eat out more often without fear of using the wrong cutlery or drinking from the wrong glass.

Influences of changes to production and service systems include:

- economics (increasing costs, reduction in customer spending)
- de-coupling (changes in production systems)
- increasing customer participation

Like other changes in the service system, the move towards increased customer participation may have been forced by the need to economize, particularly on labour costs. As a rule customers have seen the opportunity to participate as a benefit. For the customer, breakfast buffets, carveries and 'do it yourself' barbecues are perceived as added value. However, we should not take this to mean that the customer enjoys being ignored. We should look for opportunities to increase both service and participation wherever the customer identifies the need. Further, we should not assume that 'leaving it up to the customer' absolves us from responsibility. If anything, management problems are increased as a result of customer participation. Such changes carry with them implications for:

- control
- responsibility
- pricing
- commodity management
- facilities management
- customer management

Having examined the general principles of service systems it is necessary to examine those 'sub-systems' on which the service contact relies in order to determine how delivery can be managed.

The general principles will vary according to service environment/opportunities:
- room service
- lounge service
- coffee shop
- wine bar
- carvery
- snack bar
- buffet

Each of the above opportunities may benefit from a variety of strategies or service styles.

A cafeteria for example may offer free flow, carousel or multi-point delivery. We should examine the benefits of each option. The cafeteria may offer flexibility in options of food and dish presentation, merchandising opportunities and greater potential for planning and control of customer flow. Equally, burdens such as clearing must be identified, particularly when costing such exercises.

Some operations may need to rely on highly specialized systems of service. Hospitals, for instance, will have to ensure well-presented meals are delivered to patients on time and at the right temperature. Whilst they could use similar systems of room service provision to hotels, and some in the private sector do, cost-effective provision normally results from introduction of specially designed hospital systems (Ganymede, Finessa, Stellex, Helitherm, etc.). Most involve the plating and traying of individual patient meals in the main kitchen, often on a conveyor belt.

Planning the service system
- market need (type of customer, menu, product)
- operational need (space, volume, production system, staffing/skills)
- customer contact (service activities)
- paying, clearing
- equipment management

Calculation/utilization of space will be based on the style of operation – menu complexity, products and production methods – volume, operating times, structural features, health, safety and hygiene.

Event-specific delivery (service) systems

A function, or event, may mean catering for any number of people from small, one-room events for a party of ten to multiple unit operations catering for thousands. An event may be staffed and managed by a select few of the catering team while the rest of the operation gets on with 'normal' business or it may form the whole basis of company activity. Whether the event is a minor or major occurrence, lasts for a few hours or a few weeks, a few basic, simple rules apply. Many of the competences already identified in previous chapters – customer care, menu planning and merchandising – will also apply to function catering as will all of the rules of good systems management. However, two basic principles stand head and shoulders above the rest when it comes to effective and efficient function administration: planning and communication.

On the one hand it is possible to argue that functions should be no different to other business activity. It is true that total satisfaction of each and every consumer should be the objective of every caterer. However, in most cases a number of characteristics set function catering aside from other business.

Although we are serving many consumers, often we will be dealing with a single customer, 'the organizer', who may be paying a very large bill. Function activity often takes place away from home base, we are left working without a safety net. Even in hotels where banquets take place in the ballroom, or restaurant, seating has to be rearranged. We may find that normal easy access to sideboards, for example, is restricted. We probably work with a greater proportion of part-time or casual staff, some or all of who may need retraining. Functions often provide for us a far larger audience than is usual, every one could be a future customer. The marketing, merchandising, potential is enormous. By the same virtue, however, the risks also are great.

Planning

Functions and events test systems, and systems management, to the limit. Many of the lessons learnt during functions and events can be applied to 'normal' business with few, if any, modifications. As has been previously mentioned, planning, together with good communication, is the key to successful function administration. Such planning is normally influenced by company policy and organizational structure. The structure of a good hospitality company is ideally 'organic' in its nature. Unlike a bureaucracy it does not require forms, procedures and authority to respond to demand. The hospitality industry should look to its customers and gather necessary resources like a plant grows to the sun and sends shoots into the earth in search of nutrients; all energy will be directed to the needs of the customer.

For function administration and planning in particular, a rather more 'mechanistic' structure is required. Bearing in mind that good planning will be supported by good communication, decisions cannot be made 'on the run'. Unless there is clear procedure – steps and stages, authority and delegation, check and control – then mistakes are likely to happen, things will get forgotten. Effective function/event planning requires a structure that identifies authority and a chain of command, for decision making and responsibility. We need to identify the various stages of a function and ensure that each is administered effectively.

Stages in event planning:
- Promotion
- Booking
- Pre-event preparation
- Event activity
- Closing down
- Post-event analysis

Most of the general rules regarding promotion, marketing and merchandising discussed in previous chapters will apply. Additionally, because of the market, competition and potential profit, some companies may use a specialist sales team. The sales team will be responsible for contacting prospective customers, initiating special promotions and possibly negotiating and agreeing price. They are not likely to have any role in the management of the event. Obviously there will be a wide range of differing company strategies in this respect, but the principle of separating sales and promotion from the other function activities is a useful one.

As mentioned above, a sales team may have made the initial contact and may have agreed the price. They may also take details of the booking – such as day, date, time – but this is the most useful point for the food and beverage manager to become involved. The food and beverage manager, in most cases, will be able to make immediate decisions about technical details raised by the customer, thus presenting a more positive, professional image of the company. At this point the food and beverage manager will probably be identified as the main contact for any further enquiries from the customer.

Heads of departments – bars manager, head waiter, head chef – may also be introduced although care in the level of direct customer contact is cautioned. While it may not be a problem for the chef to change the main course from beef to chicken, this may cause confusion when it comes to the wine list, particularly if departmental communication is poor.

Once booking details – nature/style of event, day, date, time, venue, numbers – have all been agreed with the customer then pre-event preparation may begin. This will normally involve:

● identifying resource requirements
● agreeing standards
● identifying responsibility
● setting objectives and deadlines
● arranging meetings

Information is a key business resource. The gathering, collation and dissemination of such information is much assisted by computer systems. Type in the information, customer requirements and, given suitable software (computer programs: word processor, database and spreadsheet), the machine will automatically produce:

● booking form
● letter of confirmation
● function memorandum
● departmental checklists
● menu
● food orders
● recipes
● cellar requisitions
● costings
● diary of events

On this basis customers may quickly be offered a range of options to choose from, all accurately costed and priced.

After the event, further information, revenue and food/drink sales, for example, can be fed in to the computer to initiate the process of analysis.

The use of CAD (computer-aided design) systems will enable the drawing of room plans, designs and layouts. The system relies on a database of basic information such as room sizes, table sizes, number of covers to a table and space allowance between tables. Given additional information about a particular function – type of event, number of covers – it will manage all the calculations and draw a sample plan. Various alternative layouts can be viewed on the monitor before making a printout of the final choice.

Communication and documentation

What provision have we made for post analysis of every event? What systems for reporting, recording and feedback have we installed? What event documentation is used, what happens to it, where is the information stored, who has access to the information, who uses the information and for what purpose?

The customer will communicate their needs and expectations to the manager. It is essential that the manager has an effective system of internal communication that disseminates this information to all who need to know.

There will be four levels of communication:

- **marketing**: the brochure, pictures, plans and video
- **booking**: booking forms, correspondence and confirmation
- **administration**: interdepartmental memos and special requests
- **control**: requisitions, transfers, bills and receipts

Administration of an event generates a wide range of
communication and documentation including:
- notice boards
- table plan
- seating plan
- station plan
- equipment list
- materials requisitions
- staff rotas and instructions
- stations and hotplate queue

Equipment lists are essential to effective preparation and
running of a function. Ensuring sufficient equipment is available at all times as and where it is required. Ingredients lists
should be prepared well in advance although costing of the
event should be based on accurate, up-to-date prices. Staff
instructions should be clear, preferably written, so that no
confusion arises. Such planning and instruction is best based
on the Kipling technique. Make sure that your staff know:

- **What:** has to be done
- **Where:** it has to be done
- **When:** at and/or by what time it must be done
- **How:** by what manner, process or standard it must be
  done
- **Why:** it should be done in that way, policy/speed/
  customer request
- **Who:** is going to do, be responsible for, which job

Are there to be any speeches or toasts? Is the service of a
toastmaster required? Has the organizer stipulated time limits
for his guest speakers? Are they aware of the consequences,
for the food, of any lengthy speeches? Are there to be any
distinguished guests or celebrities? Are staff aware of the
various forms of address for royalty and dignitaries?

Control will include the administration of all documentation, particularly ingredients lists and requisitions, material transfers, waiters' and wine waiters' checks and receipts. Ultimately the control office will be responsible for the preparation of the final account. There is an obvious need for accuracy and thoroughness.

Successful event management

The success of a function is dependent on thorough organization, ensuring that every eventuality is covered. Have in mind the sequence of events and key activities:

- **Arrival**: notice boards
- **Reception**: service style, cash/account
- **Announcements**: speeches/toastmaster
- **Meal**: control/timing
- **Afterwards**: review and test success

For all events, make sure that all information is held for future reference.

Alternative systems of delivery (service)

Vending

Vending is the automated delivery of products to customers. Vending is generally used to extend product availability to a wider audience and/or to minimize labour (delivery) costs. The term 'vending service' is often used, although some would argue that this is a contradiction in terms. Are such things as telephone, TV and shoe cleaning a service? Or, are they in reality short-term product (equipment) loan? No service in its real (human, derived from servant) sense is involved.

Vending machines – definitions:	
Type	*Uses*
Merchandisers	Prepared items, branded snacks, packaged drinks, chilled meals, hot (reheatable) meals.
Beverage machines	Blended, mixed or brewed hot and cold drinks 'to order'. Various methods of blending and brewing may apply.

The customer would perceive the use of the most effective resources in meeting their needs as an efficient service. If we are going to manage a vending service successfully we need to understand what human elements have been taken out of the system: which will the customer miss and what is left in their place? Vending systems (machines) need to be user friendly and responsive. It is not by coincidence that manufacturers lean towards robotics. OK, so the cyborg food dispenser is still some way off, but vending machines with human characteristics, particularly spoken or written (video screen) messages, are not uncommon.

Benefits of vending
- reduction in labour (loading, cleaning, maintenance, cash)
- 24-hour availability
- space utilization
- siting/merchandising opportunities
- standardization and quality control
- stock and cash control – predetermined units
- cost effective
- stand alone facilities, or integral part of overall catering response

As with other systems of delivery, vending systems develop and change in response to product development. Vending has been particularly responsive to innovations in cash handling, and more particularly its substitute, plastic. In terms of stock, unit measurement and mechanised delivery have some control advantages, although it should not be assumed that systems are fraud proof.

Problems
- security controls (vandalism and theft)
- power loss
- customer acceptance
- absence of staff (service) presence

Control systems

The importance of control has been identified many times. An effective/efficient system of control is an absolute necessity for any business that wishes to remain competitive.

The objectives of control are to maintain sales records, sales history (marketing data), compare sales with usage and identify variance. Ensure effective purchasing (quality/price), receiving (quantity/quality), storage (stock management, quality/temperature/humidity) and issues (allocation of costs).

There will be an element of control in all systems, generally associated with finance – cost, sales and stock – and quality. Each system should have clear objectives; control systems should be designed to measure performance and operational effectiveness against these pre-defined targets:

- sales
- covers
- gross margins and profits

- fixed, variable and managed costs
- productivity

thus identifying (highlighting) variance

- purchase costs
- staffing costs
- production costs (waste, portion controls)
- fraud (theft, under-delivery, etc.)

Measuring performance against design

What to measure:
- **quality**: specification
- **quantity**: yield
- **cost**: budget
- **profit**: forecast
- **manpower**: performance/hours
- **equipment**: efficiency/effectiveness (output)
- **customer satisfaction**: trend/competition

Recording and reporting

It is necessary to determine:
- costs
- prices
- revenue
- GP/NP
- waste, loss and/or fraud

In order to reconcile records:
- goods received
- stock held
- sales made

Control documentation

Documents trace the movement of materials and identify changes in value. Requisition and invoices are used as a basis for entry into accounting journals (record books which provide evidence for future inspection). Because most transactions do not take place in the accounts office, there may be a time lag between a transaction and its entry into an account book. A document is the only evidence of that transaction. The auditor will require supportive evidence of all transactions.

Problems of control

The catering industry is relatively unique in that production and retailing take place under one roof. Products are produced from highly perishable stock which requires rapid conversion of raw materials into saleable items. At the service/sales point there is generally a high volume of low value transactions. In addition there is often frequent transfer of materials between departments. All of this results in the potential for human, documentary and physical weaknesses in the system. It is important that systems of control are able to identify any variances which result from such weaknesses.

Managing variance

Variance analysis is used for the identification of errors, waste, loss or fraud by comparing expected and actual results. Variance is the difference between expected and actual.

Variance analysis involves:

- setting standards
- performance evaluation (measurement)
- comparison of budget with actual
- analysis of costs and revenue
- determination of causes
- identification of responsibility
- corrective action

Causes of variance:
- **change in the price of input**: bad estimating or buying
- **change in the quality of input**: poor specification, selection or receiving
- **change in personnel**: inadequate personnel specifications
- **change in methods**: inaccurate job descriptions
- **inefficient usage of materials**: bad workmanship or weak systems
- **theft or fraud**: poor control

Variance may be favourable or unfavourable. These terms are used merely to define the direction of the error. Any variance, favourable or unfavourable, is bad. Variances may be identified as either price or usage variance: we are either paying more/less or using more/less.

Price variance
(Unfavourable)
- paying more
- using more
- neglecting discounts
- incurring interest

Usage variance
(Unfavourable)
- not sticking to standard recipes
- waste
- spoilage (over-production)
- poor portion control
- theft

Price variance	**Usage variance**
(Favourable)	(Favourable)
● paying less	● not sticking to standard recipes
● using less	● poor portion control
● negotiated discounts	● increased efficiency
	● improved kitchen practices

It should be noted that so-called 'favourable' variance is most likely to result in reduced benefit and quality to the customer. Systems of production and service should be designed to reduce variance. Variance can be reduced through stricter operational control throughout the system.

Variance measurement

- **Budget**: the intention stated during the planning stage
- **Potential**: expectations based on current prices
- **Actual**: what actually happens

Variance between budget and potential is a policy problem. Variance between potential and actual is an operational control (system) problem. Food and beverage managers should ensure that potential is clearly identified in order to reduce the confusion of trying to compare actual performance against budget (policy) targets. Variance analysis is a control procedure ensuring that what was expected to happen actually happens. It provides signals for managers to respond to, particularly in identifying system weaknesses that may be highlighted when examining variance between potential and actual performance.

Stock control systems

A stock control system will endeavour to set stock levels, record transfers (use) of stock and carry out stocktaking activity, physical count of stock against documented records. High levels of stock are not only wasteful of cash investment but also likely to result in higher levels of loss through perishable items. Stocktaking is essential to the accurate accounting of performance (profitability) for each trading period.

- physical security of assets
- minimize investment
- documentation of transactions and movement of materials
- accurate costing and pricing

A stock control system needs to be able to show:
- usage rate
- delivery lead times
- stock on hand
- re-order levels and quantities
- buying histories

The purpose of the stocktaking is to establish:

- total purchases of each item
- average price (for the purchase period) of each item
- cost increase/decrease on previous period, for each item
- opening stock, purchases and closing stock per item
- total opening stock, purchases and closing stock
- gross profit performance

Stocktaking effectiveness may be aided by the layout of stores (and design of stocksheets to match) together with logical (tidy) grouping of commodities.

Unsatisfactory results may generally be traced to either poor recording, poor supervision or malpractice. But they may also result from poor menu mix or, in some cases, lack of training.

Liquor stocks are vulnerable because they are:
● a high-value item
● fragile – breakages are costly
● easily consumed on the premises
● relatively simple to adulterate (water down)
● relatively simple to substitute (own stock)
● easily transportable
● broken down into small units for sale

The effects (indications) of fraud include:

● reduction in sales (revenue)
● high consumption
● reduced stock levels
● high sales of minerals (staff selling their own spirits)

When is systems management implemented?

Systems are developed and introduced in order to improve efficiency, the organization of work, and performance measurement. The reason for organizing may seem obvious, to get the work done, but such explanation is too superficial. If we do not analyse 'organizing' more carefully, a number of the benefits that should arise from good organization may be lost. We should be particularly concerned about economy of effort, ensuring that we get maximum output for minimum input. Benefits may also be gained from economic use of space. In some cases thorough organization is an essential requirement, health and safety for instance. Whilst seeking to optimize staffing levels, good organization will also be concerned with generating interest and motivation for staff. Smoothing the flow of work will not only improve efficiency and reduce costs, it should also make it easier for staff to achieve objectives, generating high levels of job satisfaction. Above all system development and implementation is concerned with control of resources; equipment, materials and personnel.

Efficient work organization

Other than strength of personality and leadership, how then does the manager ensure objectives are achieved? The efficient manager will:

- **Plan**: what should be done (planning involves forecasting not coping)
- **Organize**: so that it can be done (defining authority, responsibility for preparing job descriptions and personnel specifications)
- **Staff**: with people who are able to do the job (recruiting, selecting training the right people in the right job, motivation and staff development)
- **Direct**: these people with clear instructions (quality communication and feedback)
- **Control**: in order that the *plan* is achieved (corrective decisions)

Effective organization of work will be achieved as a result of thorough analysis of work activity resulting in the allocation of work to people who are able consistently to achieve desired standards in an environment which extracts maximum benefit from available space, time and energy. Economy of effort is attained through good communication, control and adherence to system design.

A variety of tools are available to assist the manager, these include:

- operational policy — to determine objectives
- organizational chart — to identify roles and channels of communication
- delegation and authority — to identify responsibility
- the menu — to provide the structure for activities
- production plans — based on menu requirements to control output and volume
- operating standards manuals — to ensure consistent quality
- job descriptions — to determine staffing requirements
- work schedules — to clarify tasks and activities
- training programmes — to ensure competence
- performance charts — to evaluate results

Systems tactics

Where can systems management be used to gain competitive advantage?

Competitive advantage may be gained principally by increasing the efficiency, effectiveness and economy of each element of the operation as a result of effective use of control data and performance measurement activities. Access to data (information) is the key to successful systems implementation and speed of access is a significant influence on eventual outcomes. Computers improve speed and accuracy of reporting and, as a result, more timely decisions may be made.

Measuring performance

If we are to improve the system, it will be necessary to determine current levels of performance and measure these against expected targets, e.g. profit. As a result we may be able to highlight variances and shortfalls, ensure conformity and consistency and enable better planning through improved forecasting.

What do we measure?
- People (customers and staff)
- Equipment (capacity, energy usage, output)
- Materials (purchasing, stock control)
- Methods (work study)
- Products (recipes, portion, yield)
- Profits (menu analysis)

Attention will most often focus on profits. Cash flow (liquidity), money coming in and going out and our ability to meet debts will be improved by effective systems of purchasing, stock management, invoicing and payment.

One area of performance measurement which is frequently overlooked is the measurement of mistakes and/or accidents which may suggest system weakness. It is important to identify not only what has happened, where and when, but also frequency and re-occurrence of similar incidents.

Problems with performance measurement include:

- Who is responsible for setting targets?
- Who is responsible for achieving them?
- Who is measuring what and for what reason?
- What action will result from the information gained?
- Does the cost of measuring performance outweigh the benefits?

Performance measurement should result in improved performance but this will only result from clear identification of objectives, authority and responsibility supported by effective communication and systems for recording and reporting.

Computerized control

> **System control problems**
> - time consumed by control activity
> - 'late' information restricting preventative action
> - human error
> - paperwork
> - estimation and accuracy

Computers aid management, system efficiency and performance improvement. Computers will cope with large quantities of figures, store large amounts of information and deal with complex calculations accurately. They will continue to work 24 hours a day for 365 days of the year, dealing with information intelligently and, if told to do so, highlighting variances. Given appropriate instructions they will break down sales (analysis) and indicate the effect of price/sales fluctuations. Whenever required, they will provide up-to-date information in management report style.

There are two basic solutions:

1 a stand-alone computer system
2 linked point-of-sales systems (EPOS)

> **Main applications**
> - point of sale (PLUs (price look-up systems/tills), sales analysis)
> - food and beverage control (stock management, menu explosion, purchasing)
> - accounting (performance ratios and percentages)
> - energy management
> - bookings (guest history, marketing and merchandising)

Opportunities

● Critical path analysis, flow charting, systems planning and analysis.
● 'Check pads' for waiters, food/drink ordering, hand-held terminals
● Forecasting – purchasing, staffing

Cash registers influence speed of service (handling payment) and speed is directly associated with mistakes. Electronic point-of-sale systems (EPOS) offer a solution by providing the opportunity to modify and improve payment systems. Because they work faster they reduce queuing and potentially increase revenue. EPOS systems make use of pre-set keys, some systems have the potential for as many as 100 different keys (separate items). Alternatively we may examine the use of barcodes and barcode readers, many of which are now designed to be hand held. Data can be quickly scanned from menus, wine lists or the products themselves. The information is transferred to a computer which handles both accounting and the printing of customer bills. In addition, food orders can be sent to satellite printers in the kitchen. Each of these systems enables the implementation of simple analysis techniques and report writing as well as stock/sales/cash control. Increasing speed and improving accuracy will enable emerging problems to be spotted early. Additionally, stored data may be used to perform 'what if' analysis (see Figure 7.8). Although it is possible to perform such analysis with pencil and paper, a computer running a spreadsheet program will provide 'instant' response, thus enabling a range of 'troubleshooting' strategies to be compared in a short space of time.

Improving performance implies knowledge of current state (and therefore measurement) and requires effective strategies and tactics (policy development).

Comparing budgeted and actual figures – analysing variance in the net profit

	Budget £	Budget %	Actual £	Actual %	Variance	Variance as % of budget
Sales	75 000	100	75 000	100		
F & b costs	30 000	40	30 600	40.8	0.8	2.0
Labour (f)	15 000	20	15 500	20.7	0.7	3.3
Labour (v)	3 000	4	4 000	5.3	1.3	33.3
Overheads	19 500	26	19 600	26.1	0.1	0.5
Total cost	67 500	90	69 700	92.9	2.9	3.3
Net profit	7 500	10	5 300	7.1	−2.9	−29.3

What would be the result (effect on NP) if each element were corrected separately?

	Budget £	Budget %	Actual £	Actual %	Variance	Variance as % of budget
Sales	75 000	100	75 000	100		
F & b costs	**30 000**	**40**	**30 000**	**40.0**	**0.0**	**0.0**
Labour (f)	15 000	20	15 500	20.7	0.7	3.3
Labour (v)	3 000	4	4 000	5.3	1.3	33.3
Overheads	19 500	26	19 600	26.1	0.1	0.5
Total cost	67 500	90	69 100	92.9	2.1	2.4
Net profit	7 500	10	5 900	⬛ 7.9	−2.1	−21.3

Get the f & b cost right, then NP = 7.9%

	Budget £	Budget %	Actual £	Actual %	Variance	Variance as % of budget
Sales	75 000	100	75 000	100		
F & b costs	30 000	40	30 600	40.8	0.8	2.0
Labour (f)	**15 000**	**20**	**15 000**	**20.0**	**0.0**	**0.0**
Labour (v)	3 000	4	4 000	5.3	1.3	33.3
Overheads	19 500	26	19 600	26.1	0.1	0.5
Total cost	67 500	90	69 200	92.3	2.3	2.5
Net profit	7 500	10	5 800	⬛ 7.7	−2.3	−22.7

Get fixed labour right, then NP = 7.7%

Figure 7.8 continued

	Budget £	Budget %	Actual £	Actual %	Variance	Variance as % of budget
Sales	75 000	100	75 000	100		
F & b costs	30 000	40	30 600	40.8	0.8	2.0
Labour (f)	15 000	20	15 500	20.7	0.7	3.3
Labour (v)	**3 000**	**4**	**3 000**	**4.0**	**0.0**	**0.0**
Overheads	19 500	26	19 600	26.1	0.1	0.5
Total cost	67 500	90	68 700	91.6	1.6	1.8
Net profit	7 500	10	6 300	8.4	−1.6	−16.0

Get variable labour right, then NP = 8.4%

	Budget £	Budget %	Actual £	Actual %	Variance	Variance as % of budget
Sales	75 000	100	75 000	100		
F & b costs	30 000	40	30 600	40.8	0.8	2.0
Labour (f)	15 000	20	15 500	20.7	0.7	3.3
Labour (v)	3 000	4	4 000	5.3	1.3	33.3
Overheads	**19 500**	**26**	**19 500**	**26.0**	**0.0**	**0.0**
Total cost	67 500	90	69 600	92.8	2.8	3.1
Net profit	7 500	10	5 400	7.2	−2.8	−28.0

Get overheads right, then NP = 7.2%

If the results of this activity are then ranked in order of significance:

Labour (variable)	8.4
Food and beverage costs	7.9
Labour (fixed)	7.7
Overheads	7.2

Each cost centre can now be dealt with separately, in order of significance and the causes can be found and remedied.

Figure 7.8 'What if' analysis – troubleshooting the NP.

Summary

The development of effective systems management will enable the successful manager to:

- assess the effectiveness of various operational procedures
- apply the principle of the operational cycle to set and maintain standards
- identify a range of performance measures applicable to food and beverage operations
- measure performance against pre-defined targets
- recognize the effects of undesirable variance on business performance
- implement and monitor cost, quality and personnel control systems
- examine and apply procedures in order to remain competitive.

Questions influencing systems development

Is the system restricted to a single style of service, does it vary with meal times (breakfast, lunch and dinner) or is it completely flexible (responsive to customer needs)? To what degree does the production system influence or determine service style and vice versa? Are we dealing with an existing system or designing from the ground up? Why change?

Tradition would have it that hospitality is all about luxury and extravagance, numerous staff to respond to the customers' every need and a wealth of variety in food and drink available at any time of day of night. Such forms of hospitality exist and will continue to exist, but the cost and consequently the price the customer must pay will continue increasing. For the vast majority of caterers business must be leaner and tighter, using systems which identify and eliminate waste at every opportunity. Change is driven by response to current economics. Customers, although eating out more often, are spending less and demanding more. Caterers are having to cope with changing resource availability, particularly the number of young people coming into the industry. The cost of education and training is reducing the range and depth of skills that people are able to acquire. Chefs are no longer taught how to prepare each of the different dishes in the 'repertoire' and the nuances of classic recipes such as may be found in Escoffier's *Guide to Modern Cookery* may be lost. Trainees and students are taught the 'principles' of cookery, how to braise, stew, roast, etc., and are expected to apply these principles to the operation in which they are employed. Consequently the peripheral skills; those that do not fit easily into principles – stocks, basic and reduction sauces for instance – are rapidly disappearing. Similarly with the restaurant, gueridon work, peeling fruit and making salad dressings at the table, are skills that fewer and fewer people possess. It may be argued that education and training are responding to changing systems of delivery and that as many restaurants no longer utilize classical cookery or silver service skills, such are becoming redundant. As previously mentioned, the need for skills is to some extent offset by the greater variety and improved quality of processed and convenience foods and prepared, ready-to-heat dishes. It is not the remit of this book to say whether such erosion of skills is a good or a bad thing, but it is important to recognize, like it or not, that such change is taking place and it will affect systems development. We must continue to meet specified objectives, the old as well as the new. In order to remain competitive managers must examine all aspects of the system to identify opportunities to economize or improve efficiency. We need to consider carefully the influence of technology and improvements in equipment, particularly the effect on raw material and labour requirements.

Effective systems management

Effective systems management will be based on clear understanding of company policy and market (demand/forecast) from which a commodity plan will be evolved. The commodity plan will influence/determine systems of production, purchasing policy, production and delivery methods and processes and control procedures. Without an effective system plan, which clearly identifies objectives and specifies ways and means of achieving them, it is not possible to perform any analysis. Without analysis it is impossible to accurately identify improvement opportunities.

Suggested additional reading

Cousins, J. Foskett, D. and Short, D. (1995) *Food and Beverage Management*. Longman.

Cracknell, H.L. Kaufmann, R.J. and Nobis, G. (1987) *Practical Professional Catering*. Macmillan.

Croner's Catering. Croner Publications.

Davis, B. and Lockwood, A. (1994) *Food and Beverage Management: A selection of readings*. Butterworth–Heinemann.

Davis, B. and Stone, S. (1991) *Food and Beverage Management* (2nd Edition). Butterworth–Heinemann.

Fuller, J. and Waller, K. (1991) *The Menu, Food and Profit*. Stanley Thornes.

Harris, P. (1992) *Profit Planning*. Butterworth–Heinemann.

Jones, P. and Merricks, P. (1994) *The Management of Food Service Operations*. Cassell.

Ritzer, G. (1993) *The McDonaldisation of Society*. Pine Forge Press.

8
Efficient staffing

There have been many references throughout this text to the significant influence that staff have on successful operations. There has also, necessarily, been some discussion of technology and mechanization. However, despite the increasing importance of non-human factors, there seems little point in considering the development of a service industry without people (staff). Disregarding the social/political significance of increasing unemployment, finding work for people to do in the face of increasing use of technology is a concern for us all. The true strength of a service operation is the opportunity for human interface and the quality of its people. It only remains necessary for us to consider how best to use this valuable resource.

Consider the importance of the role of staff in:

- marketing
- merchandising
- product development
- quality
- systems (efficiency/effectiveness)

All of these have been discussed in earlier chapters. Suffice to conclude at this point with reminders of these activities and identification and assessment of how concentration on personnel management – development of social skills and customer 'caring' attitudes – can enhance total provision.

Aims and objectives

Many businesses have now moved away from the traditional personnel department, relying instead on the ability of the unit manager to provide for effective staffing. This has meant that many managers have taken on new areas of responsibility. In some respects, particularly in regard to responsibilities enshrined in current legislation, it would be wrong to attempt to review these responsibilities in a single chapter. Consequently this chapter deals with the more pragmatic issues of operational effectiveness. It is left to the reader to examine other texts for more detailed advice in regard to legal obligations and responsibilities.

The purpose then of this chapter is to identify best practice in regard to efficient staffing. Theories of human behaviour will be briefly examined in order to provide basis for some of the proposals offered.

What is efficient staffing?

Efficient staffing may be defined as the ability of management to optimize the potential of human resources through effective planning, scheduling and instruction.

Cost-effective provision

A prime objective will be to obtain maximum benefit for minimum cost. However, in a service industry, cost reduction (the absence of staff) may have a negative effect. We will need to ensure that adequate provision (service quality) is maintained without excessive waste.

Effectiveness, optimizing provision, will depend on organizational structure/culture and staffing levels/availability. The most critical factor, however, is forecasting. We will be unable to provide effective staff cover if we have no clear picture of need. While we may accept that the hospitality industry is, by nature, responsive to demand and therefore difficult to forecast, this should not prevent us from using available data to obtain the most accurate picture possible. In particular we need to know volume of demand and precise product/service needs (skill requirements). In addition to forecasting it may be necessary to manage demand, such that we encourage an increase in custom to ensure that staff are always busy and/or discourage custom when staff are stretched. Additionally we may manage demand for 'skills' by identifying alternative opportunities for our customers. This may require modification to systems and/or products. For example, if the kitchen/restaurant team are working to capacity then there may be opportunities to meet customer needs in the bar using self service techniques and/or pre-prepared (reheatable) dishes.

Typically the hospitality industry requires a staffing strategy which is able effectively to provide for 'additional' business, special functions, etc., over and above the normal. Traditionally we have relied on casual and/or part-time staff, many of whom are loyal and hard working. However, the economics of such provision must be questioned, particularly the way in which it is managed. Frequently the cost of managing such provision is ignored, thus giving the impression of cost effectiveness. If all the costs – management time, administration, phone calls, etc. – were identified, a different picture might emerge. One alternative is to rely on an agency or contractor to provide teams of staff as and when required. In this way, management costs may be reduced. However, standards may conflict: the agency staff are no better or worse than our own, they are merely different.

Another alternative to the casual/part-time/sub-contract argument is to employ more full-time staff and to equip them with a wider range of skills in order that they are more able to respond to demand in different areas of the operation.

Whether staff are full-time, part-time or casual there must

be an effective system of rostering to allocate staff to activities. The normal process is to use daily, weekly or monthly charts. Many designs are available and choice may be dependent on personal/style preference. Computer models are available or may be written to suit a need. Critical to the success of any rostering system will be the ability to see easily, at a glance, the following details:

Demand	*Cover*
Customer volume	Staff numbers (names)
Service area needs	Bar, restaurant, kitchen
Products	Skills
Day/date	Duty days (absence, holidays, etc.)
Time	Hours

Appropriate 'fail safe' features (cover for sickness) should also be identified, including increase/decrease in customer volume and staff flexibility/mobility (telephone numbers).

Getting the right number of staff in the right place at the right time is only half the battle. Ensuring that they are provided with appropriate instructions and have the necessary skills to provide the required service is the other prime objective. Effective staffing will be supported by appropriate documentation and communication.

Staffing documentation and communication
- policy documents
- staff handbook
- training manuals
- function memoranda
- job descriptions
- task cards
- product/service quality standards

As an alternative to reducing staffing costs, managers should identify opportunities for increasing productivity and improving quality. Staff can be encouraged to assist in this regard through increasing their sales activity/potential. The benefits of an organizational culture based on 'internal customers' should not be ignored, particularly the opportunity which such a culture provides for quality improvements. Such quality improvements should be apparent to customers, hence increasing demand, productivity and quality has a cyclical effect.

Cost-effective provision
- rostering
- instructing
- increasing productivity
- guaranteeing quality

In addition to providing appropriate numbers of staff, we will also need to ensure that staff are provided with the appropriate skills. In particular we should aim to ensure that skills and knowledge are used to greatest effect.

Managing staff may mean modifying the system to suit availability of staff/skills. One method of coping with the staffing problem is to eliminate the need for staff and/or their skills. Many see skill reduction as a threat. The de-skilling argument should be examined in relation to kitchen activity, however. The so-called 'experts' of today would be seen as nothing more than a 'jack of all trades' by the chefs of the 1920s. Over time we have lost many chefs de partie – the bouchier, charcutier, volailleur, rôtisseur, poissonier, etc. – roles which have commonly been absorbed by the garde manger and saucier. Chefs of today could never claim to offer the combined skills of chefs of the past. Modern moves toward further de-skilling may be criticized but they should be seen as a return to past levels of expertise, albeit contracted out. Preparation skills are transferred to the suppliers (under the guidance of strict raw material specifications). The use of prepared meats, poultry and fish should provide the chef with more time to concentrate on the skill of cookery itself. It is possible in this way to reduce costs and improve efficiency.

The cost effectiveness of transferring preparation skills to the supplier

The following figures were taken from an article in the *Caterer and Hotelkeeper*, 'Gleneagles Fuels De-skilling Debate', December 1995.

	1993	1994	1995 (est.)	1996 (est.)
Bed nights	93 800	90 117	82 785	90 696
Food and beverage revenue	£4.6m	£5.2m	£4.8m	£5.5m
Food costs	32.8%	31.2%	31%	30.7%
Kitchen numbers (staff)	76	72	55	55

Food costs are clearly reduced, preparation skills are transferred to the suppliers and cookery skills are more focused. It may well be argued that quality as well as efficiency have been improved.

Appropriate skills and training

The importance of recruiting, training and motivating the right people should not be underestimated. The provision of appropriate attitude, skills and qualifications supported by up-to-date technical and product knowledge is a desirable asset for any operation. Choosing people and monitoring results is a key function of management. The effectiveness of staff selection, performance and the monitoring of results will be influenced to some extent by organizational culture and management (leadership) style.

Commitment and job satisfaction

To be successful, organizations will need to encourage involvement and initiative from staff and managers will need to be willing to 'let go' of the reins. Operations must be driven by results and managers' prime objective must be enabling achievement. Managers and staff will gain job satisfaction from continuing team development/achievement.

The manager's role in team achievement requires:

● Sharing	open communication	involved in problem solving
● Coaching	tailored	practical tasks and interpersonal skills
● Encouraging	team members	sharing skills
● Motivating	identify benefits	rewards (not just the financial)
● Empowering	delegating	clarifying responsibilities (and limits)
● Staff ownership	quality	products, service, problems (and shares)

The supermarket chain Asda may be highlighted as a good example in this context. It is not so many years ago that they were struggling to compete. They have had the benefit of dynamic management, but that management also recognized the importance of team effort and commitment. They are very customer focused and managers are expected to spend a good deal of their time talking to staff and customers.

Why is efficient staffing important?

Staffing is often the single largest cost for a catering operation. Efficient staffing is important because it provides practical evidence of optimizing potential, which may be defined as maximum output for minimum input. This often causes attention to be focused on the minimization of input (staffing costs). We need to switch concentration to maximizing output, not necessarily volume and/or profit, but certainly quality and customer care.

Continuing concern with staffing problems

There is continuing concern within the industry about the lack of high calibre recruits. For many caterers this is the cause of increasing spend on training. There is nothing wrong with increased training costs if it can be seen to be moving the business forward, but if costs are increasing just to keep the business where it is then something must be wrong.

For most of the catering industry there will be constant fluctuations in demand and, as with any service industry, the demand for labour is direct. We are additionally faced with the problem that because our customers may have differing expectations, standards will be measured with a degree of subjectivity. One advantage that we do have over other industries is the innate transferability of many of our skills.

The 'demand' problem

● If labour exceeds demand then ...	there will be too many staff, labour costs will increase comparatively, as a result (margin) profit will decrease.
● If demand exceeds labour then ...	there will be too few staff, it is likely that custom will be lost, as a result revenue/profit decreases

Responding to the 'demand' problem requires accurate forecasting plus clearly defined and measurable productivity standards. Matching performance to objectives will be a key human resource aim. Managers will be concerned about the apparently uncontrollable problem of absenteeism and sickness. Naturally instances such as this can not be 'planned' for on a rota basis. However, in addition to having a contingency plan, we might examine the potential for reducing the problem, in particular we should try to identify cause and

Absenteeism	Causal relationships
Accident at work	
● Equipment	Poor maintenance
● Operator	Poor training (don't know how to use it)
	Poor procedure (short cuts) 'too busy'
	Poor (careless) attitude
Minor (self certified) sickness	
● Job related	
Headache, asthma, etc. (role avoidance)	Work environment, atmosphere, noise associated with particular days/nights or specific shifts
● Poor health (poor nutrition)	Overwork, irregular or missed days off, inappropriate meals/food eating habits or lack of proper meal breaks
Stress-related illness (undervalued) (poor communication) (difficult customers)	Overwork, short-staffed and/or unpaid or inappropriate levels of overtime insufficient management recognition, pressure, confusion, panic and anxiety, poor management, quality, complaint

frequency. While sickness may result from unavoidable accidents or 'uncontrollable' viruses, other illnesses might be related to work. A good deal of absenteeism might be directly attributable to the work environment and this should be within the manager's control.

Contributing to productivity and profit

Staff are a key element of performance improvement. It is the manager's responsibility to ensure that staff are used effectively. This may primarily be achieved through the development of positive attitudes toward operational effectiveness. Key areas of effective (profitable) performance include 'selling' and 'quality'.

Selling involves:
- merchandising
- temporal sales promotion
- product promotion
- public relations

Quality involves:
- quality circles
- people to people
- control versus empowerment
- investors in people

It will also be the manager's responsibility to ensure effective performance in the more practical areas of production and service, not just the provision of staff with appropriate skills, but also the support of necessary resources, equipment and materials.

Effective performance	The manager's role
● knowledge	
● understanding	providing objectives,
● skills	standards, instructions,
● resources	feedback
● time	

Who is responsible for efficient staffing?

Managers and supervisors

Managers define and implement policy and set budgets. Supervisors (shift and team leaders) provide the link and, importantly, maintain communication. Indeed the supervisor may be seen as the 'linchpin' of efficient staffing having, as they generally do, a key role in training, scheduling and monitoring performance.

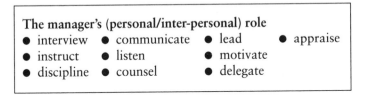

The manager's (personal/inter-personal) role
- interview   ● communicate   ● lead   ● appraise
- instruct   ● listen   ● motivate
- discipline   ● counsel   ● delegate

The supervisor's role in the system
- control of the operational cycle
- administration
- minimization of waste (management of equipment, materials and staff)
- maintenance of health, safety, hygiene and security
- record keeping

It is important that managers and supervisors apply the principles of MBWA (management by wandering about) effectively. Wandering about, not aimlessly of course, but with a purpose. Looking at what is going on. But not just looking: looking and seeing, understanding and where appropriate asking questions.

The supervisor's role in the organization will be influenced by size, objectives, tradition and finance. The supervisor will ensure that the unit is organized to meet objectives – profit/quality/service – and to keep within budget. In doing so each supervisor will liaise with other supervisors/departments.

The supervisor's role in communication
- to pass information to staff
  - policies
  - objectives (motivation)
  - production demands
  - discipline (conformity)
- to pass information to the management
  - monitoring standards
  - monitoring performance
  - problems and grievances

Supervisors will play an important role in planning, organizing and communicating. They will be involved in seeking and providing advice and consultation. In particular they will normally be the source of expert technical knowledge and skills. In terms of the direct management of staff, supervisors will allocate work (roles, responsibilities and authority), provide resources and assess work. Ideally they will be qualified to assess NVQ competences, thus enabling the development of staff. The function of assessor is often related to their role as a trainer.

The supervisor's role in training
- determining the need
- task analysis
- on the job training
- assessing performance and achievement
- development and re-training
- replacement and induction

Assessing work requirements

Our marketing, merchandising and customer care activities will have determined the nature and quality of products and services that we offer. To some extent marketing will have identified the volume required and forecasting will provide a more accurate picture of demand, particularly labour/staffing requirement. On the basis of the assessment of work required, provision will have to be made for the supply of resources. Making sure that there is sufficient, not excessive, supply – of staff, raw materials and equipment – in the right place at the right time, is a critical element of organization. There is always a temptation to over supply, particularly staff and raw materials, at great cost.

Allocating work

As previously mentioned there is much to be gained from choosing the right people to do specific jobs. Balancing work load, reward and motivation is another key factor. Work will be allocated on the basis of recognized work schedules, attempting to match supply (of labour) to demand (for products and services) from the customer. The peaks and troughs of meal times have always been a problem for the catering industries. Traditionally the split shift system was imposed in response to the demand for labour at the two peak meal times. The modern manager is more likely to rely on good forecasting to accurately predict requirements. Lines of demarcation will be reduced by the employment and training of 'multi-skilled' staff, allowing for greater flexibility of response and more acceptable shift patterns for employees.

Determining training requirements

If things are not going according to plan, we must first try to ascertain the cause of the problem. Faults may be traced to machinery, materials or people. In the case of machinery and materials, re-examine purchasing, specification, maintenance and monitoring programmes. In the case of personnel, problems may arise for two main reasons: the person is either unwilling or unable to perform the tasks involved. Assuming, for the moment, that the person involved is a committed, well-motivated member of staff and that their unwillingness is not due to weaknesses in our selection procedure or job descriptions, then the most likely reason is either fear of getting the job wrong or lack of the necessary knowledge, technical or procedural detail. Where staff are unable to perform a particular task successfully it may be because that person does not have the skills required, or the job itself has changed (new skills or new technology) since that person was originally employed. In all the above cases there is a clear need for training.

Before such training takes place we need to closely examine the activities that make up a particular role or job. To do this each job must be broken into its component tasks and each task analysed separately. Such task analysis, together with the opportunities to restructure activities that often arise from it, can have a profound influence on work organization, improving efficiency and effectiveness. This is seen more and more as we continue to break away from traditional concepts of catering operation/activity.

The key factors in the staffing element of work organization are:
- task cards
- job descriptions
- personnel specifications
- motivation (reward/achievement)
- performance measurement

Dealing with staff

Committed and enthusiastic staff are essential to the smooth running of any operation. Such commitment and enthusiasm needs nurturing and it cannot be abused. Care and concern for staff welfare must be a high priority for managers. Preparing a staff rota means more than just putting names in boxes. We should be concerned about staff development, providing them with the right opportunities to succeed. Delegation should provide an element of challenge, not risk. On the one hand there should be few rules, providing sufficient opportunity for every member of staff to achieve at their own pace and in the direction that they choose. However, at the end of the day, the law imposes on us certain regulations, conditions of employment. In particular we need to recognize the need for formal disciplinary and grievance procedures. In good organizations these procedures are little used, but if the need does arise then they should be administered openly and sympathetically.

The supervisor's role with staff
- being aware of disciplinary procedures
- being aware of grievance procedures
- ability to delegate
- ability to lead by example
- to respect and be respected

Dealing with customers

In Chapter 2 we examined customer care and the point was made that care activities should be planned into the operation. Work organization and target setting must have customer care as a key factor. The manager will be aware of customer needs and expectations, and will utilize social skills and integrity to deal effectively with customers.

The supervisor's role with customers
- social skills
- awareness of consumer needs and expectations
- ability to deal with complaints and problems
- integrity

Undoubtedly individual, personal qualities are a significant influence on the quality of work organization, supervision and management.

What are the qualities of a good supervisor?
- honesty
- reliability
- fairness
- empathy
- technical competence

Doing the right thing – doing the thing right

Argument may arise in regard to the respective power of technical authority versus bureaucratic authority. Appropriateness will be dependent on organizational culture. In an 'organic' organization where individuals are responsive to consumer need/demand then technical authority is likely to hold greater sway. Bureaucratic authority usually only exists in mechanistic organizations where power is based on 'office' and individuals are instructed to respond to the demands of the system. The concept of power is worthy of some mention at this time. There are various sources (interpretations) of power. The difference/relationship between authority and power may be defined as:

- authority, the right to decide what will happen, and
- power, the ability to make it happen, through physical force, bargaining, rules, knowledge, and/or personality.

A link may be drawn between communication and authority. Regular clear communication results in:

- Employees understanding what you want and why you want it.
- Employees realizing that you know what you want.
- Employees seeing continuity in your instructions.
- Employees understanding your logic, and being more comfortable with your authority, because there are no surprises.
- Employees understanding what you stand for.

Staff

Staff may be considered as both individuals and teams. Both are complex and management strategies may differ in each case.

Whilst individual traits are too numerous to deal with here, there are group/team attributes and distinguishing factors that are worthy of brief discussion. Groups may be divided into two specific categories, technical and social. Technical groups are generally initiated and controlled by management.

Individuals – group identity (individual/group perfor-mance)

Individual work	*Group work*
● totally autonomous	interdependent tasks
● independently resourced	shared resources (competition for scarce resources)
● only vertical communication required	horizontal and vertical communication
● self-motivating	group 'norms'
● independent standards required and set	uniform standards required and set

---

Conversely social groups are formed by staff. Management, however, should not ignore the power and importance of such groups.

● Technical groups   earnings related
                      performance related
● Social groups   group (social/informal) norms

The power of social groups should not be underestimated. Individuals who are quite capable of improving individual performance may consistently under-achieve so as not to be out of step with the group 'norm'. There is much to be gained from encouraging 'informal' groups to set themselves higher goals.

Culture modification, team building (creating a sense of belonging) is an important concern for management as it can be a major influence on performance.

Both individuals and teams can be encouraged to take responsibility. This is particularly important in the hospitality industry where the dynamic nature of the service transaction determines that almost every customer encounter will be unique.

Attributes of a team
- identity   consensus with group (not company)
- behaviour   conformance to group norms
- purpose   shared aims and objectives
- hierarchy   determined by the group
- exclusivity   membership selection
- solidarity   loyalty (to each other)
- capacity for change   ability to form and reform (without direction from management)

Empowerment (taking control/responsibility at the point of sale)

Needs:
- strong management support
- training and communication
- limitation guidelines
- clear outcomes (objectives) direction

Results in:
- fewer complaints
- fewer 'adjustments' to bills
- fewer interruptions
- less blame shifting – increased co-operation
- staff personal/professional development
- increased customer satisfaction, delight guaranteed

Employing the customer

Customer participation in production and service is an increasing phenomenon and, interestingly, one that seems to be welcomed by customers. Just as the 'hole in the wall' was considered to be the only 'rational' option for banks who wished to offer services outside of normal banking hours, then hospitality operations may be rationalized and service improved by removing layers of traditional staff-intensive service. It is worth noting that, given the choice, many bank customers prefer to queue for the 'wall' rather than the cashier.

Customer participation (rationalization) in production and service
- **Self-service:** increasing productivity
- **Service to others:** creating the right environment, carrying and clearing
- **Service to the organization:** market analyst, quality manager, performance appraisal

---

If our customer becomes an unpaid employee then, to some degree, personnel management activities must be employed in the customer relationship. This may mean managing the customer selection, supervision, training, dismissal, discipline and grievance procedures, as well as dealing with unruly customers. The benefits of customer employment must be enhanced and the rewards – added value, USPs (unique selling points), etc. – must be emphasized.

Customers must be made to conform to service standards and quality in much the same way that we manage staff. Training and the provision and use of information and instructions – manuals, task cards, etc – will inevitably be more subtle as will the use of roles and scripts (discussed in Chapter 5, Quality).

Staffing strategy

How is efficient staffing implemented?

In order to consider the implementation of efficient staffing strategies it is necessary to recognize the influence of organizational structures, systems of production and service, the influence of technology and the associated costs of over/under staffing.

Determinants of staffing levels
- size of operation
- layout and design of building
- range and type of facilities, products and services
- delivery – production and service methods/style
- quality of staff, skills, etc.
- organizational culture
- levels of demand/competition for labour

Structures and systems will determine the need for skills: de-skilling, multi-skilling, mobility, job sharing and flexible working. The introduction of technology and prepared foods will enable convenience assembly and increased customer participation. Staffing strategy will also be influenced, if not determined by wider socio-economic issues, particularly demographics (human resource availability). Issues such as the employment of the 'older' worker will have to be addressed. Efficiency will be dependent on effective management of labour demand and supply.

Managers will need to differentiate between employment of skilled and unskilled staff. Skilled staff are inclined to be expensive, but have the benefit of previous knowledge and experience which should enable relatively high levels of productivity. However, in a changing environment skilled staff may be less responsive; adapting to new systems and new technology may be a problem. The immediate benefit of unskilled staff (lower wages) must be measured against hidden costs. Unskilled staff may be less productive, particularly in the initial stages. There will be a training need, even where tasks are relatively simple, and the need for supervision may be greater.

Staffing strategy
- Type of customer
- Type of product   } **Demand**
- Pattern of demand

- Labour source
- Type (availability) of skills
- Type of resources (raw materials)   } **Supply**
- Access to technology

- Staffing budget   } **Control**

It is important that performance targets, volume and standards, are both specific and realistic. Target performance and productivity levels must be agreed and measurable. Performance targets will be set as a result of human resource planning; measurement methods and activity will be incorporated into the supervisory role.

Planning selection and supervision (PSS)

Staffing strategy may be divided into three main elements: planning, selection and supervision. Whilst each may be managed separately it is clear that objectives and relationships will need to be determined at the outset.

Planning
- **considerations:** the amount and type of work
- **tradition versus convenience:** levels of skill
- **the operational cycle:** staffing requirement at each stage of the cycle
- **organizing work/work study:** job/task analysis
- **productivity calculations:** numbers and types of staff
- **optimum efficiency/effectiveness:** doing it right, economy of effort
- **job descriptions**
- **personnel specifications**
- **rostering**

The key factor in planning is to ensure that the staffing needs of the operation are clearly understood. The system of delivery (operational cycle) will be examined and specific skill requirements identified. In particular the emphasis will be on clear and precise job descriptions: what is required, based on detailed task analysis. Job descriptions should not be confused with personnel specifications which are an attempt to define the personal traits most suited to the performance of tasks specified in the job description.

Selection
- sources of information
- sources of staff
- types of work people are good at
- attributes of a good employee
- cost of a new employee (cost of high staff turnover)
- recruitment and selection methods
- induction programme – ability to earn revenue (return on investment, ROI)

It will be important to ensure that all available information is to hand before embarking on the selection process. Obviously the job description and personnel specification are critical but careful consideration should also be given to the sources of staff and the type of work people are good at. The selection procedure should be well planned and carefully managed. In particular the effectiveness of the traditional interview should be re-evaluated. For the hospitality industry in particular it may be more appropriate to see prospective employees in a work environment. The so-called 'trade test' – asking staff to demonstrate their skills in a realistic work environment – may provide a much more reliable basis for selection. This is not to say that 'standard procedures' – the viewing of CVs and the following up of references – should not be adhered to. Effective selection is not cheap; all costs, management time, administration, advertising, correspondence, phone calls, interviewees' expenses, etc. should be properly accounted for. Managers should examine whether selection costs, particularly where there is high turnover, would not be better invested in retaining staff and/or improving the selection procedure so that the right people are selected in the first place. Additional costs arise out of introducing new staff to the workplace. The cost of 'induction training' should be added to selection (recruitment) costs and in the same way that selection must be made more cost effective so too should induction. In particular we need to ensure that the new member of staff becomes productive as quickly as possible, thus providing an earlier return on investment (ROI).

Interviewing (selection)

- past behaviour/future performance: read the CV
- evaluate skills rather than personality: customer skill?
- prepare questions: maintain control and listen to the answers
- check supporting evidence: ask questions about previous experiences
- follow through: response to candidate, tracing references

For further information on recruitment interview techniques, see Riley, 1995.

Supervision.
The following should be provided in order to obtain optimum staff performance:
- objectives, reward and motivation (Maslow and Herzberg)
- positive re-enforcement
- leadership
  - effective directing
  - quality decisions (predictable, reliable, firm and fair)
- good supervision
  - encouraging teamwork, initiative and pride
  - communication, informative and consultative
- job satisfaction
  - security
  - income
  - benefits
  - accommodation
  - status (responsibility – authority)
  - promotion (development)

Once staff are in place we will need to ensure maximum efficiency. A number of opportunities are available to us, including effective job design, work study and effective communication (motivation).

Job design

Job design is critical to efficient staffing; it almost goes without saying that staff can never be completely efficient if their work is poorly managed. The purpose of job design is to ensure that input (effort) is converted into maximum output (performance). In order for job design to be effective we must examine the job content: the variety of skills, the number of tasks performed and task significance. Examination of the job should be kept in context with the working environment and conditions including contact with customers and colleagues and levels of control, authority, responsibility and autonomy.

Job design involves the following elements:

- **job analysis**: manpower planning, scheduling work
- **task analysis**: activity planning, resource management
- **recruitment**: selection and training the right people
- **job evaluation**: conditions of employment, staff welfare

This initial element of job design will remain under management control. However, staff involvement and participation will be encouraged in relation to further development.

- **job enlargement**: horizontal, add related tasks
- **job rotation**: variety, challenge
- **job enrichment**: vertical, add different types of task

Work study

It is possible to achieve more efficient staffing and improve productivity, products and service, through:

- improvements to system design
- more effective layout of facilities
- optimum use of resources
- improvements to working conditions (ergonomics)
- optimum skill usage and development
- economy of effort/energy

Efficiency (economy of effort) may be achieved
the simplest forms of work study, such as basic ob
individuals and/or team members. Observers shou
specific tasks or activities and through careful obser
to separate productive effort from non-productive ....ies
such as lifting, carrying and delays (waiting for more ingredients or for a cooking process to be completed). Attempts
should then be made to redesign the job to eliminate the non-
productive activities through the use of technology
(time/temperature controlled equipment), mechanics (mobile,
modular equipment) or system redesign (changes to stock
management procedure to ensure ingredients are always
available when required).

Special attention should be paid to ergonomic design, the
structure of work areas and equipment to suit physical ability.
To what extent is effort expended unnecessarily because
shelves are too high or too low, chopping boards are too large
or too small, the phone is in the wrong place, etc.

Work study – job design opportunities
- modify system design
- re-design facilities layout
- reduce effort/energy requirement
- understand ergonomics
- optimize existing skills
- develop/train new skills
- manage the environment: temperature, humidity and noise

Communication

Managers and particularly supervisors are an important
point of contact for staff. Although the informal 'grapevine'
may be recognized as still being very significant, surprisingly

most employees it is not the preferred method of communication. Staff would rather hear from the 'horse's mouth'.

Success is frequently determined by a sense of belonging and pride. Successful companies keep staff informed about activities and provide clear direction supported by a wealth of feedback. Poor communication usually results in poor motivation which inevitably causes poor performance.

Motivation

It would be a mistake to think that if staff are underpaid they will work harder for overtime or tips. It may be possible to identify some increase in productivity, but only in the short term. Ultimately staff will become more concerned with providing for their daily necessities and not with the improvement of business performance. For example, staff may 'honestly' put a lot of effort into earning tips in a way which may not be to our advantage, e.g. helping customers choose cheaper items on the menu, recommending that they don't purchase an additional salad 'because you get plenty of garnish anyway', or giving larger than specified portions. Given sufficient 'incentive' (hardship) they may be tempted to dishonesty – helping themselves to food so that they do not have to spend too much of their hard earned wages on food – or dishonestly handling drinks, in exchange for money, to buy the basics.

Maslow's theory of human need (see Figure 8.1) is reasonably well known and it can be used to develop positive attitudes (behaviour) through the identification of attainable goals, published achievements and support and encouragement for low achievers.

Managers should be aware of the implications of positive and negative re-enforcement. Whilst negative re-enforcement – punishment for inappropriate behaviour – can have immediate effect, the response to positive re-enforcement is

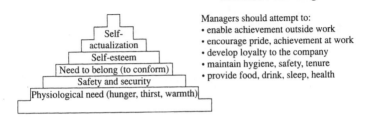

Managers should attempt to:
• enable achievement outside work
• encourage pride, achievement at work
• develop loyalty to the company
• maintain hygiene, safety, tenure
• provide food, drink, sleep, health

Figure 8.1 Maslow's pyramid of human needs. Get the best out of staff by enabling attainment at higher levels, ensuring basic needs are met so that staff concern for the lower levels becomes superfluous.

generally more permanent. Positive re-enforcement (reward) need not entail cost; the simplest form is to recognize contribution and effort (easier said than done). All too often the effort of individuals goes unrecognized, if not unnoticed. The words 'Thank you' used honestly and appropriately can be one of management's most effective tools.

Staff will generally be well motivated if their basic personal needs are satisfied and their contribution is valued. Performance may be enhanced if additional needs (benefits) can be identified. As these needs may differ for each member of staff, benefits (incentives) may need to be individualized. Money is often identified as a panacea for all. However, it is the benefits which money can buy, not the money itself which is the motivator. The hospitality industry is in a unique position to be able to provide many of the benefits that staff crave – holidays, accommodation, dining out, food and drink – on a much more cost-effective basis. Further advantage may be gained by providing benefits, such as dining out, at cost. A meal out provides not just a motivational opportunity, but additionally staff development and competitive intelligence.

> **The operational benefits of staff eating out**
> - In the best places   learning about products and services that we aspire to, assessing the competition, observing and comparing pricing strategy.
> - In our place   understanding the customer perspective reaction to selling and merchandising activity appreciation of product/service value.

Staff incentives can and should be related to individual performance. Technology provides us with the opportunity to identify and measure performance accurately. Profits in hospitality can be related directly to staff performance through the use of modern 'EPOS' (electronic point-of-sale) systems and computerized tills. Whatever the form or method of incentive 'payment', care should be taken to ensure that incentives are available to all and that all can achieve some benefit (see Figure 8.2).

Effective motivation encourages pride in work at all levels, it creates a sense of belonging and achievement and enables job building (enrichment). Staff become used to taking responsibility, they will acknowledge problems and, what is more, they are likely to do something about it.

Counselling

At times it will be necessary to communicate with staff on an individual basis. Typically, topics may include:

- appraisal
- promotion
- counselling
- discipline
- grievance
- retirement
- termination

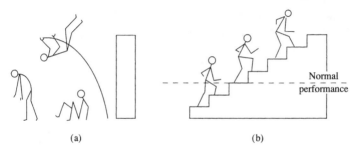

(a)   (b)

Figure 8.2 Achievable incentive schemes – step bonuses. (a) One-step bonuses are only achievable by the 'high flyers'. Most of the staff will be disenchanted. (b) With step bonus schemes everyone can achieve something. All staff are committed and high flyers are not held back. Step bonuses may be more complex to operate, but should be worthwhile. It is normal to set the first step(s) below standard performance in order to encourage commitment. Everyone is capable of earning some level of bonus.

Staff appraisal – management action	
● organize meeting	time, place, comfort, disturbance free
● set the scene	agree the rules
● let the appraisee lead	summarize, do not impose
● listen	ask questions (open questions)
● concentrate on performance	not personality
● be specific	identify success/failure
● be constructive	agree objectives
● monitor progress	follow through

The outcome of an appraisal interview should be an assessment of current and past performance, clarification of priorities and the identification of potential barriers to performance. The end result should be an agreed plan of action for the future with staff being fully committed and involved in shaping the future.

Grievance and disputes

There will inevitably be times when things do not go entirely to plan. Discipline and grievance procedures should be detailed in writing and displayed for all to see. Ensure that any action which may be taken is clear to all. Identify all those concerned and chains of communication (authority) where appropriate. It is important that all formal grievance/disciplinary procedure follows a set, identifiable pattern, with appropriate levels of authority at each stage. Make sure that the appeals procedure is clear. In the case of grievance or disciplinary procedure arising, first carry out a detailed investigation to ensure, as far as is possible, the accuracy of all the facts. Inform all concerned and act speedily but with due caution.

There may be times when speed seems appropriate, particularly if there is conflict between co-workers. Justice takes time; advise participants that a quick solution is only an interim measure, effective solutions (justice) will take longer.

Policies and procedures
- consistent approach
- clear objectives/purpose
- valid and reliable
- documented
- confirm previous agreement

There are several ways in which adherence to a procedure may help to resolve grievances (Riley, 1995):

- It helps to identify those to whom a grievance should be put and those who may be approached for assistance.
- It may help to clarify the issue if the grievant has to write it down or explain it to a representative.
- It may help to obtain appropriate information.
- It may speed up resolution in so far as it specifies time limits and ensures only those with appropriate authority are involved.
- By requiring that records be kept it lessens the chances of ambiguous customs and practices becoming involved.
- It reduces the level of emotion involved.

While it may appear tempting to offer 'on-the-spot' resolutions, informal procedures, by definition, contain none of the above safeguards.

Generally accepted disciplinary procedure/process
- informal oral warning
- formal oral warning (witnessed)
- formal written warning (advising of consequences) – obtain signature of receipt
- action (as promised)

Exit interview

An exit interview is a fact finding exercise and should not be used to change anyone's mind, but rather to find out why the decision to leave has been made. Leavers present an 'image' of the firm to future employees. Gather the facts: was the decision to leave avoidable (wages, etc.) or unavoidable (retirement). Even in the case of retirement the exit interview is still worth while as the retiring employee may be prepared to be more open in their criticism, thus providing us with the opportunity to correct matters for those that remain. It is advisable in these sessions to work from a list of prepared questions.

When is efficient staffing implemented?

In order to be effective, unit managers should develop a greater understanding of the personnel function. Changes in staffing policy are often introduced because of external pressure – following competitors, changes in society/culture, changes in legislation (we should note in particular the demands of the EU). But staffing policy should not be a reactive response to pressure. Changes and developments to staffing policy should result from a recognition of the opportunities that arise from more effective use of human resources. Many would view developments in European employment legislation as threatening. What is currently seen by many in our industry as 'traditional' flexibility is seen by some of our law makers as an abuse of human rights. Managers will increasingly be required to find new approaches to flexibility. Clearly developments in organizational culture are required.

Organizational culture

There are many facets to organizational culture and flexible employment. It would seem apparent that, although staff might view de-skilling as a threat, the management (removal) of traditional skills does provide opportunities for greater flexibility without reliance on unsociable working conditions. Similarly the separation of production and service can create more socially acceptable conditions, at least for the production staff. However, many staff (not to mention customers) would not welcome such changes. Perhaps the best opportunities are to be found in multi-skilling and job enlargement. It is only possible to make general comments here; each operation will be able to find strengths in different aspects of employment. Suffice to say the most effective method of employment will be that which provides for greatest efficiency based on the demands of society at large, the needs of the consumers and the current organizational culture.

Organizational culture – employment flexibility (Jones and Lockwood, 1990)	

Functional
    multi-skilling
    job enlargement
    job enrichment
    job rotation
    career development
    re-training
	Numerical
	    Part-time
	    temporary
	    job sharing
	    overtime
	    sabbaticals
	    flexi-time
	    annual hours
	    shift work
	    short-term contracts

Distancing
    agency staff
    subcontracting
    home working
    computer terminal
      systems
    government subsidized
      trainees
	Pay
	    incentive schemes
	    rare skills payment
	    multi-skill payment
	    performance related pay

An organization's culture is often self-evident in its 'organization chart', a diagrammatic representation of linear communication. Many organizations have turned the traditional 'pyramid' shaped chart on its head, thus 'demonstrating' that the front line staff are the most important. Others have attempted different 'flatter' diagrams which attempt to show that everyone in the organization is of equal importance. Unfortunately it is impossible to represent true organizational culture on paper, much as it is impossible to represent a person's soul in a picture. Culture is a living form, what is actually happening on a daily basis. The organizational culture will evolve, not so much from an organizational chart as from the way in which unit managers implement staffing policy. This will involve planning work, monitoring performance and demonstrating concern for staff.

Work planning should be based on:
- **customer demand**: volume
- **productivity**: standards, quality/quantity
- **job design**: task analysis
- **staffing structure**: hierarchy and rotas

Managers will develop and refine work (job) schedules, allocating tasks to people, managing timing, and sequential activities. The management of work schedules will be heavily influenced by the degree of flexibility and multi-skilling of the staff concerned. Managers and supervisors will remain responsible for the co-ordination and control of activities, which may be achieved either through direct supervision or the provision of work manuals and or job/task cards.

Co-ordination and control – job cards:
- name of job/task
- equipment/materials required (recipe)
- method (detailed)
- standard required
- safety/hygiene notes

Monitoring performance

A good deal has already been said about the empowerment of staff. Empowerment does not mean the abdication of responsibility by line managers. Managers will still need to know what is going on at all times. There will inevitably need to be some form of performance monitoring, be it discrete or otherwise. Much has been made in the past of McGregor's theories about the average working person, particularly the 'theory X' element. If such circumstances did exist then performance monitoring would require a high degree of 'physical' presence from unit managers. Ideally a 'culture' will have been developed by management which makes continuous direct observation superfluous.

McGregor's Theory X and Y		
Type of worker	*Work style*	*Management style*
● Theory X man	is lazy, needs bossing	authoritarian
● Theory Y man	likes work, is self motivated	democratic

Labour costs are high and we must therefore monitor and measure performance. Such monitoring and measurement needs clearly defined procedures and standards supported by effective communication of objectives, processes, and suitable feedback. Effective maintenance of standards will require a suitable system of training. In terms of increasing skills development, multi-skilling and efficient flexible staffing, training takes on even greater significance.

Training

Unit managers will be responsible for developing and implementing training policy in line with operational objectives and organizational culture. Such policy should include a clear statement of intent (objectives), commitment and purpose. Managers will identify training need, develop a training plan and design training programmes. Whilst they may not always be directly involved in the delivery of training, managers should participate in a review progress.

Training	
● need	appraisal, accidents, mistakes, new systems/procedures/methods
● plans	prioritize needs, identify funds
● programme	time, availability
● delivery	task analysis, standards, assessment
● resources	money, facilities, equipment, people (skills)
● requirements	based on needs, identified above
● training method	based on who needs training, who and where training will be delivered
● benefits	to the operation, its customers and the staff involved

Training may take place on or off the job and it is important to differentiate between the needs and benefits of both. The distinction between in-house trainers and external trainers is becoming less apparent. The advent of the NVQ programme has placed greater emphasis on the 'real work environment'. Although many colleges are able to provide realistic working kitchens and restaurants, there is an increasing recognition that industry provides the most realistic environment. Consequently there is a growing tendency for part-time students in particular to be assessed and/or trained in their own place of work by qualified staff and/or visiting lecturers/assessors. Although most would agree that the workplace is the best place for the acquisition and development of practical skills, there are good reasons for taking staff out of the work environment. When considering the acquisition of knowledge and understanding – the development of theory rather than practice – a fresh environment is desirable. This is also particularly true when a change or development in attitude is felt necessary and clearly this has some relevance in regard to the organizational culture.

The organization of training

In-house:

- improve employee skills
- increase output/sales
- increase (reinforce) loyalty – job satisfaction
- development/promotion of brand image

External:

- improve employee knowledge and understanding
- develop (modify) employee attitudes

When organizing training programmes managers will be concerned with the catering/operational cycle, identifying the needs (skill/staffing requirements) of systems and procedures. Training programmes may be influenced by trends in both consumer/product demand and styles of delivery. In particular managers should be concerned with:

- Health and safety
- Hygiene
- Safety, security
- Marketing, merchandising
- Computers, control
- Technology, efficiency, de-skilling/multi-skilling, increasing output

> **Objectives of training**
> - reduce accidents, mistakes, waste, breakages, equipment breakdown
> - reduce absenteeism
> - reduce labour turnover
> - reduce stress (staff/customers/management)

Training may be seen as one of the more visible aspects of an organization's culture – its employment policy, investment in human resources and commitment to staff.

Investors in People

The 'Investors in People (IIP)' award may simply be defined as a public recognition of commitment to staff. But to be truly effective it must be more than just 'apparent' window dressing. Staff have to believe and that belief only arises from true management commitment, throughout the company, which must be almost religious in its fervour.

> **Investors in People: a national standard which embraces four key principles**
> 1. An Investor in People makes a public commitment from the top to develop all employees to achieve its business objectives.
> 2. An Investor in People regularly reviews the training and development needs of all employees.
> 3. An Investor in People takes action to train and develop individuals on recruitment and throughout their employment.
> 4. An Investor in People evaluates the investment in training and development to assess achievement and improve future effectiveness.

An Investor in People programme should include:

- induction, training
- communication
- agreeing targets, setting standards
- developing skills and knowledge, qualifications and career progression
- management development

The Investors in People award is made for three years, subject to the approval of a qualified assessor nominated or employed by the Training and Enterprise Council.

Every operation is unique and the way people work will influence success/failure. People are a valuable asset. Adaptability, flexibility and enthusiasm should be valued and willingness to learn should be encouraged. Financial performance can be improved as a direct result of managing the workforce more effectively. In today's competitive environment there are fewer opportunities for product-based advantage, hence reliance on the workforce. Organizational culture is likely to be the most obvious of our unique selling points (USPs).

Developing an IIP culture
- value employees as a resource
- avoid preoccupation with cost
- apply consistent employment policies
- enhance training and development
- measure the right things
- rationalize change

Investing in People is concerned with setting and communicating business goals and developing people to meet these goals, so that what people can do, and what they are are motivated to do, matches what the business needs them to do. A company's involvement will only be effective if supported, through belief and commitment, from the very top.

Planning and implementation of IIP
- audit current situation/attitudes
- identify what needs to done/changed
- develop an action plan (commitment of all)
- involve everyone

IIP management commitment and responsibility
- commitment
- planning
- action
- evaluation

The operational benefits of IIP include:
- improved performance
- increased commitment, motivation, loyalty
- higher standards, quality
- increased customer satisfaction
- improved brand image

Some companies will go beyond the basic requirements of an IIP programme and examine the needs of employees outside of the workplace. Such companies recognize that employee performance is often influenced by things not strictly within the realms of management control.

EAP – Employee Assistance Programmes
An investment which pays off:
- recruitment and training costs down
- loyalty and commitment up
- higher productivity (ownership and enthusiasm)

An EAP programme is based on the recognition that personal problems will encroach on work. In an attempt to support staff in solving their problems, a company may employ in-house counselling staff, although this can cause problems of confidentiality. An alternative procedure would be to offer support 'at arms length'; counselling would be contracted out, companies may provide a free phone for employees, their spouses and immediate family. Such provision may involve company commitment to pay for the first three counselling sessions, it is rare that more are needed. Problems may often be resolved with one 'phone call. Unit managers may advise, but should not instruct, staff to use the service and the use of such a facility must remain voluntary; management may only enquire whether staff have taken the initiative. Counselling services such as these are not and must not be a substitute for grievance or disciplinary procedure, but they may work alongside more formal procedures and may prevent more drastic action in the future.

The benefits of EAP programmes

A decrease in:
- grievances
- absenteeism
- accidents
- health care costs
- staff turnover

An increase in:
- customer care
- quality
- morale
- efficiency

Staffing tactics

Where can efficient staffing be used to gain competitive advantage?

Primarily through both quality improvement and increased productivity.

Increasing productivity
- modify production/service systems, work organization
- modify production/service methods, work study
- encourage and reward multi-skilling
- increase the emphasis on promotion and merchandising activity
- modify the trading period, respond to changes in customer demand (grazing), open all hours
- manage customers, bookings – two sittings per meal
- encourage customers to queue (in the bar) rather than book in advance
- increase staff involvement, consider incentives, encourage commitment

Staff do not always appreciate your costs, generally they don't have to, they have no 'real' interest. Improve productivity by providing the interest. Staff may become keener to get involved (in improving profitability) if they benefit directly. This may well mean sharing 'sensitive' information as well as profits.

Help staff to identify responsibility (ownership) through:
- more effective communication
- recognition and reliance on shopfloor expertise
- team building
- increased understanding of company needs

Help staff to identify costs, particularly wastage; they will deal with it if they 'own' the problem. Get staff involved in work study/workplace design and the reduction of costs. Highlight the benefits of cost reduction to both the operation and employees. A reduction in accidents would be a particular benefit to them, but would also reduce operational costs.

Employee involvement
- team briefings
- company newsletter
- attitude surveys
- quality circles
- staff appraisals
- profit sharing (ownership)

Demonstrate the importance of staff participation in equipment care and maintenance, storage and stock control, and observation/control over swill/waste disposal. Use cost savings to improve staff facilities – the operation will eventually benefit when sales start to improve as a result.

Managing productivity
- job design: efficiency/effectiveness/economy of effort
- rostering: supply and demand
- forecasting
- technology: raw materials, convenience products
- methods: task analysis
- procedures: standards, monitoring, control

Other opportunities available to the manager include outsourcing – what the Americans call 'the contingent worker' – that is to say the increasing use of short-term contracts. Such strategy may carry a high risk; loyalty and confidentiality may be placed in some doubt. But such methods can be effective in the right circumstances and some short-term contract employees can be highly motivated and responsive to 'frequent' change. Part-time and casual staff often carry hidden costs. Training, control and maintenance of data (files, etc.) may all incur relatively high costs. There may not be a pro-rata increase in productivity. Commitment and reliability may be questionable. The effective use of such a strategy would be dependent on the area and local labour source/demand.

More effective use may be made of full-time staff by encouraging flexible working. This may be achieved in a variety of ways: hours per week, short and long days as required, or annual targets which allow for seasonal adjustments to the working week. Multi-skilling brought about through 'cross-training' (staff training one another) provides positive activity during slack periods (out of season), which may bear fruit during busier periods when staff are more adaptable, mobile and flexible.

It will be essential for managers to manage other resources – equipment, materials, time – in order to get the best out of staff whatever the employment strategy used.

Do not look for immediate benefit – invest in the future.

Summary

Managers frequently 'over-manage'; it may be more efficient to release the talent and creativity of staff. Develop attitudes that create an environment of maximum involvement and contribution to the satisfaction of all concerned.

Use management and motivational skills to achieve improved performance through goal setting, skills development and training. Enable staff to achieve at the highest level through multi-skilling, flexibility and empowerment. Total quality needs 'valued' employees who are made to feel involved and important.

Examine staffing strategy, identify the real costs of staff turnover, invest in keeping, improving and developing staff. Encourage staff to develop outside interests; the qualities required of community service (scout master, lay preacher, support for the disabled, music) are often of benefit to the operation and its customers (care for others, entertaining).

Riley (1995) suggests that seven factors might constitute 'good housekeeping':

- clearly communicate – objectives, rewards, performance
- use 'teaching' to motivate
- recognize achievement
- offer 'valued' rewards
- ensure that rewards are equitable
- ensure all aspects of employment tell a coherent story
- do not 'over' control

If the industry is to respond to the increasing use of technology/mechanization then it should encourage development that moves people from the back of house to the front (customer contact), serving (talking to) customers and adding value (service benefits). There will be a need to develop social skills, body language, attitude, 'performance' ability and confidence as both a host and entertainer. This cannot be achieved against a background of pressure and low pay. Recognizing the importance of staff sharing in the benefits of their labour is not a political statement but a matter of common sense. Against a background of increasing rationalization, a friendly face may be the only unique selling point that is left to us. If you want your staff to care for customers then you must care for the staff. If you seek to turn customer satisfaction to delight, then seek to delight the staff. Develop and improve conditions of service, add value to employment (job satisfaction) through added employment benefits.

Suggested additional reading

Gale, G. (1985) *Behavioural and Supervisory Studies*. Gale and Odgers.

Jones, P. and Lockwood, A. (1990) *The Management of Hotel Operations*. Cassell.

Riley, M. (1995) *Managing People*. Butterworth–Heinemann.

Venison, P. (1990) *Managing Hotels*. Butterworth–Heinemann.

9
Summary

This book set out to help food and beverage managers to identify and respond to opportunities for performance improvement, improved quality and profitability, by assessing the potential for operational efficiencies.

Aim

- The development of a programme of 'health care' for food and beverage operations.

We have argued that good management is based on the effective use of objectives in order to develop suitable strategy and tactics by which to achieve this aim.

Objectives

- Improved performance, productivity, quality, value and service.
- Added benefits for customers, owners, managers and staff.
- Total customer satisfaction.
- Increased profits.

Objectives, strategy and tactics will need to be reviewed constantly. However effective we become there will always be more room for improvement. Successful strategy development must be based on continuing concern for customer care. The only enduring way to improve profit performance is by continuously seeking to meet customer needs more effectively.

The effective food and beverage manager needs to clearly understand the operating environment: the market, customer needs, wants and expectations. Thorough knowledge of resource availability, technology and system design will enable effective and economic plans to be produced.

We should be 'listening' more effectively and 'selling' ourselves and our products more efficiently. Performance improvement is based on careful customer observation and examination of point-of-sale activity. Keeping existing customers can be seen to be more profitable than chasing new ones. A customer's decision to return is assisted by the quality and perceived value of our products and services.

The competent manager must be aware of the performance potential of every aspect of the operation's resources. Performance measurement is essential in all areas of the operation. Improvement, focusing activities on specific targets, will be impossible if the starting point is unknown. Without careful analysis of accurate data it will be impossible to sensibly identify improvement opportunities.

Staff are the focal point of effective service operations. To be successful we must invest more in people. To encourage the involvement and commitment of all the staff, managers will have to consider increasing use of empowerment. The challenge for management is to learn to manage from a distance while not distancing themselves from staff or customers.

We began by proposing the following questions:

- What business am I in?
- Why am I in business?
- Who are my customers?
- How can I remain successful?

- When should I be reviewing operational performance?
- Where can I look for further advice?

Hopefully we now know the answers. Discussion should have caused closer examination of current activity – a questioning of why and how we currently operate, what modifications can be made, where can performance be improved and who shall be involved.

One question only remains. When shall we start to take action ...

The answer: ... immediately, and on a regular, continuous, basis.

Bibliography

Bareham, J. (1995) *Consumer Behaviour in the Food Industry*. Butterworth–Heinemann.

Cousins, J., Foskett, D. and Short, D. (1995) *Food and Beverage Management*. Longman.

Cracknell, H.L., Kaufmann, R.J. and Nobis, G. (1987) *Practical Professional Catering*. Macmillan.

Croner's Catering. Croner Publications.

Dale, B.G. and Plukett, J.J. (1990) *Managing Quality*. Philip Allen.

Davis, B. and Lockwood, A. (1994) *Food and Beverage Management: A selection of readings*. Butterworth–Heinemann.

Davis, B. and Stone, S. (1991) *Food and Beverage Management* (2nd edition). Butterworth–Heinemann.

Fearn, D.A. (1985) *Food and Beverage Management*. Butterworth–Heinemann.

Fewell, A. and Wills, N. (1995) *Marketing*. Butterworth–Heinemann.

Fuller, J. and Kirk, D. (1990) *Kitchen Planning and Management*. Hutchinson.

Fuller, J. and Waller, K. (1991) *The Menu, Food and Profit*. Stanley Thornes.

Gale, K. (1985) *Behavioural and Supervisory Studies*. Gale and Odgers.

Harris, P. (1992) *Profit Planning*. Butterworth–Heinemann.

HCIMA (1993) Managing Quality – An Approach for the Hospitality Industry. The Hotel and Catering International Management Association.

Jones, P. (1983) *Food Service Operations*. Cassell.

Jones, P. (ed.) (1989) *Management in the Service Industries*. Pitman.

Jones, P. (ed.) (1996) *Introduction to Hospitality Operations*. Cassell.

Jones, P. and Lockwood, A. (1990) *The Management of Hotel Operations*. Cassell.

Jones, P. and Merricks, P. (1994) *The Management of Food Service Operations*. Cassell.

Maslow, A.H. (1987) *Motivation and Personality* (3rd edition). Harper Row.

Medlik, S. (1990) *The Business of Hotels* (2nd edition). Butterworth–Heinemann.

Mennell, S., Murcott, A. and van Otterloo (1992) *The Sociology of Food*. Sage Publications.

Merricks, P. and Jones, P. (1986) *The Management of Catering Operations*. Holt, Rinehart & Winston.

Miller, J.E. (1987) *Menu Pricing and Strategy*. Van Nostrand Rheinhold.

Peters, T. (1987) *Thriving on Chaos*. Guild Publishing.

Riley, M. (1995) *Managing People*. Butterworth–Heinemann.

Ritzer, G. (1993) *The McDonaldisation of Society*. Pine Forge Press

Seaberg, A.G. (1991) *Menu Design, Merchandising and Marketing*. Van Nostrand Rheinhold.

Shepherd, W.J. (1985) *Marketing Practice in the Hotel and Catering Industry*. Batsford.

Sprenger, R.A. (1988) *Hygiene for Management*. Highfield Publications.

Tannahill, R. (1988) *Food in History*. Penguin.

Venison, P. (1990) *Managing Hotels*. Butterworth–Heinemann.

Journals

Caterer and Hotelkeeper
Hospitality
Management Today
Professional Manager

Index

Absenteeism, 321
Accessibility, 133
Achievable GP, 235
ACORN (A Classification Of Residential Neighbourhoods), 95, 96
Actual (performance variance), 300
Added value, 100, 143, 200
Advertising, 73, 76, 123
AIDA (Attention Interest Desire Action), 100, 101
Allocating work, 325
Alternative systems of delivery, 294
American Deep Pan Pizza, 56
Analysis (market, competition, customer), 94
Analysis of sales, 235
Appraisal (staff), 343
Appraisal costs (quality), 162
Asda, 319
ASP (average spend), 44, 47, 83, 91, 122
Assessing work requirements, 325
Assurance, quality, 28, 172, 176, 179
Attributes (quality), 167
Attributes of a team, 330

Bar codes, 307
Barriers to satisfaction, 62
BCA (bottle conditioned ales), 249
Beecham, Sinclair, 56
Behaviour, customer, 116
Benchmarking, 185
Benefits (product/service), 100, 135, 170
Benefits of quality, 162

Benihana, 156
Body language, 132
Boston Matrix, 246, 247
Brands, 81, 100
Brand image, 15, 29, 44, 57, 115, 119, 125, 130, 159, 165, 176, 196, 197
Brand integrity, 250
Break even analysis, 4, 232
Brewer's Fayre, 116, 165
British Gas, 164
British Telecom, 164
Browsing, 131
BS5750 (ISO 9000), 187
BSI (British Standards Institute), 152, 172
Budget, x, 3, 43, 300
Burger King, 115, 168
Business environment, 5, 6
Business patterns, charting, 83
Buyer behaviour, 113, 114, 233
Buying up, 136

CAD (Computer Aided Design), 292
Calendar, marketing, 97, 98
CAMRA (Campaign for Real Ale), 159
Care, customer, 35
Career development, 45
Carrington Arms, 99
Cash contribution, 237
Cash GP, 239
Catering (operational) policy, 43, 45
Catering cycle, 30, 56, 173, 260
Catering systems, 259

Causal (forecasting model), 107, 108
Cautious customers, 134
CCCCP (Customer centred critical control points), 35, 36, 37
CCPI (Customer-centred performance improvement), xvi
CCPs (Critical control points), 173, 264, 265
Centralized Production, 161
Centres, profit/cost, 4
Change, 28–32
Channels (supply), 274
Characteristics (customer profile), 116
Characteristics (operational style), ix, 45
Characteristics (quality), 153
Charting business patterns, 83
Charts, organizational, 56
Chicago Rib Shack, 56
Choice, 128
Choice (customer), 210
Choice (preference), 113
Choosing, 130
Classical conditioning, 128
Classification, market, 95
Coca-Cola, 100, 159
Cold spot, 139
Commercial sector, ix, 2, 3
Commitment (job satisfaction), 319
Commodity planning, 217, 218
Communication, the supervisor's role, 324
Communication, 265, 292, 339
Communication (employees), 329
Communication systems, 265
Communications (impact, marketing), 79
Company policy, 164
Competition, xvi, 18, 89
Competition (analysis), 94
Competitive tendering (market testing), 3
Complaints, handling, 64
Computerized control, 306–9
Concept (CPC), 115, 194, 205, 21
Concept development, 204
Concept reinforcement, 211

Conditioning (classical, Pavlovian), 127, 128
Conditions of employment, 327
Conformance, 178
Constraints (on food and beverage management), 35
Consumer expectations, 164
Consumer preference, 61
Consumer/customer (definition), 70
Content (CPC), 194
Content development, 217
Content planning, 217
Contingent worker, 357
Control, 46
Control (cost), 226
Control, computerized, 306
Control documentation, 298
Control, quality, 172, 179
Control questions, 98
Control systems, 34, 296–302
Convenience assembly, 220, 333
Convenience foods/products, 156, 220
Convivial quality, 155
Conviviality (service quality), 176
Cook-chill, 32, 158, 161, 221
Cook-freeze, 32, 158, 161, 221
Core Periphery Split, 33
Corporate culture (marketing), 84
Cost, opportunity, 167
Cost (fixed, variable, managed), 232
Cost centre, 4, 163
Cost control, x, 226
Cost dumping, 163
Cost effective staffing, 314
Cost of quality, 162
Cost/profit strategy, 4
Counselling staff, 342
CPC (Concept, Package, Content), 194, 204
Crisis management, 264
Critical path analysis, 307
Cross selling, 124
Cross training, 358
Culture, organizational (mechanistic/organic), 61, 62, 264, 329, 346

Culture, IIP (Investors In People), developing and implementing, 353
Customer, dealing with the, 328
Customer analysis, 1, 94
Customer behaviour, 114, 116
Customer care, 35, 64, 188
Customer care legislation, 50
Customer care philosophy, 68–70
Customer care policy, 67
Customer care programme, 67, 150
Customer characteristics (profile), 116
Customer choice, 22–4
Customer complaints analysis, 178
Customer constructs, 129
Customer flow, 146
Customer loyalty, 18, 163
Customer mix, 70, 192
Customer needs, wants and expectations, 1, 21–2, 32, 74, 82, 93, 120, 152, 164, 170, 196
Customer observation, 146
Customer participation, 156, 176, 331
Customer perceptions (quality), 181
Customer preference, 115
Customer profile, 44, 89
Customer satisfaction, xi, 21, 28, 46, 65, 97, 123, 147, 170, 193
Customer survey questionnaires, 187
Customer/causal relationships, 110
Customer/consumer (definition), 70, 170, 171
Customers, internal, 37
Customers, one stop/cautious/impulse, 134
Customers, 19–21
Customize, 115, 184
Cycle, catering/operational, 29, 30, 173

Data, historical (forecasting), 109
Dealing with the customer, 328
Decision to purchase (influencing), 111
Delegation, 27, 327

Delight, 153
Delivery, systems of, 270
Delivery systems (event specific), 288
Demand, predicting, 104
Demand and supply matrix, 112
Demand for labour, 320
Demand management, 111
Descartes, René, 127
Desk research, 91
De-skilling, 261, 317, 333
Detection of errors, 172
Determining staffing levels, 333
Determining training requirements, 326
Development, product/service, 28, 98
Development, policy, 53
Diagnostics (error identification), 175
Differentiation, 154
Differentiation (market), 118
Differentiation (product), 159
Differentiation (product/service), 115
Direct mail, 101, 102
Disciplinary procedure, 327
Discount strategy, 229
Dish development, 217, 218
Display, product, 138
Display counters, 138
Display promotion, 125
Disposable income, 19, 20
Documentation, 292
Drinks list (menu), 29, 136
Due diligence, 273, 276

EAP (Employee Assistance Programmes), 354, 355
Economies of scale, 175
Economy, 37, 256, 261
ECR (Efficient consumer response), 272
Effective forecasting, 111, 279
Effectiveness, 37, 256, 261
Efficiency, 37, 256, 261
Efficient staffing, 320
Efficient work organization, 303
Elements, hard/soft (quality), 172

Elements (systems), 266
Employee involvement, 357
Employing the customer (customer participation), 331
Employment strategy, 32
Empowered staff, 164
Empowerment, 27, 49, 57, 59, 166, 169, 189, 319, 331, 349, 358
Energy management, 262
Environment, business, 5
Environment, hospitality, 2
EOQ (Economic order quantity), 277
EPOS (Electronic point of sale) systems, 306, 307
Equipment management, 279
Error detection, 172
Error identification (diagnostics), 175
Error prevention, 172
Errors, random/sporadic/systematic, 175
Escoffier, August, 270
Escoffier's *Guide to Modern Cookery*, 311
ESP (Environment, Systems, People), marketing, 85
Evaluation, post purchase, 113
Event specific delivery systems, 288
Exit interview, 345
Extrapolative (forecasting), 107
Eye movement, 216

Failure costs (quality), 162
Field research, 91
Finance policy, 40, 43
Financial strategy, 6
Financial structure, 4
Fitness for purpose, 147, 152, 159, 160, 183, 224
Fixed cost, 4, 232
Flexibility, 348
Flexible working, 358
Flow (customer), 146
Flow charting, 307
Food and beverage manager, 24–7, 53
Food and beverage systems, 157, 259

Food guides, 104
Foraging, 21, 210
Forecasting, 57, 105–12, 199, 215
Forecasting effectiveness, 111
Four Ps (marketing mix), 84
Fraud, effect/indication of, 302
Function planning, 288

Gaps in the market, 90
Gardner Merchant, 142
GP (gross profit), 3, 47
GP, achievable, 235
GP (gross profit) calculation, 227
GP (gross profit) improvement, 226
GP cash, 239
GP, measuring, 238
GP percentage, 6, 239, 241, 242
Grazing, 21, 196, 210, 214
Grievance procedure, 327, 344
Grouping (meal/product), 139
Groups (and individuals), 329, 330
Guaranteed standards of performance, 164
Guest questionnaires, 98

HACCP (Hazard analysis and critical control points), 155, 183
Happy Eater, 165
Happy Hour, 237
Hard elements (quality), 155, 172
Harvester, 116
Henry J. Bean's, 56
Herzberg, 337
Historical data (forecasting), 99, 109
History and tradition (systems), 270
Hobbes, Thomas, 127
Hospitality environment, 2
Hot spot, 139
Hula Burger, 203

IIP (Investors In People), 189, 352, 353
IIP culture, developing an, 352, 353
Image, 115
Implied value, 143
Improving profitability, 251
Impulse, 60

Impulse customers, 134
Income, disposable, 19, 20
In house marketing/selling, 124
Incentive schemes, step bonuses, 343
Incentives (staff), 340
Increasing productivity, 356
Individuals (and groups), 329
Induction training, 336
Industrial knowledge, 74
Influence, the purchase decision, 111
Input-process-output, 158, 266, 272
Instrumental learning, 128
Internal customers, 37, 166, 169, 178, 186, 189
Interviewing (staff selection), 336

Job descriptions, 45, 56, 225, 327, 335, 336
Job design, 337
Job enlargement, 347
Job enrichment, 347
Job evaluation, 347
Job rotation, 347
Job satisfaction, 319, 337, 338
Job/task analysis, 183, 338
Judgemental (forecasting), 107, 108

Kipling, Rudyard, vii
Kipling, questions/technique, x, xv, xvi, 38, 69, 96, 293
Kipling's marketing calendar, 98
Knowledge (technical/industrial), 74
Kroc, Ray, 203, 256

Labour, demand for, 320
Labour availability, 33
Learning, 127
Learning, instrumental, 128
Legislation, customer care, 50
Legislation, merchandising, 148
Legislation, product development, 253
Life cycle, 83, 199, 222, 226
Liking (preference and choice), 22, 128

Liking, psychological aspects of, 127
Linking, 140
Little Chef, 165
Locke, John, 127
LOOK, 146
Lyons Tea Houses, 161

Managed cost, 232
Management by exception, 264
Management by objective, 264
Management style, 264
Management Wheel, 27
Manager's role (staffing), 323
Managing productivity, 357
Managing variance, 298
Manoeuvring (modifying profit/product performance), 248
Manuals (handbooks), 42, 166
Marginal costing, 230
Market, eating out, 8 - 14
Market, gaps, 90
Market analysis, 94, 164
Market classification, standard, 95
Market data, 87
Market differentiation, 118
Market function/purpose, 73, 75
Market information, sources, 18, 91
Market intelligence, 83
Market mix, 44
Market orientation (product), 77
Market promotion, 28
Market research, primary/ secondary, field/desk, 91
Market research, 28, 73, 75, 76, 88, 92, 163, 199, 203
Market segmentation, 74, 115, 116
Market share, 44, 159, 192
Market strategy, 75, 88, 120
Market study, 89
Market testing (competitive tendering), 3
Marketing, 123
Marketing, in house, 124
Marketing, measuring performance, 98

Marketing, staff involvement, 80
Marketing activity, 82
Marketing calendar, 97
Marketing department, 85, 86
Marketing Mix (the 4Ps), 84
Marketing plans, 97
Marketing policy, 40, 43, 44
Marks and Spencers, 160, 185
Maslow, 337
Maslow (theory of human need),
    341
Material management, 219
Maximizing profit potential
    (merchandising), 142
MBWA (Management By Walking
    About), 324
McDonald's, 142, 168, 175, 195,
    197, 203
McGregor (theory X and theory Y)
    (staffing), 349
Meal Experience, 21, 47, 59, 60–1,
    64, 65, 66, 77, 155, 204, 207,
    249
Meal grouping, 139
Measuring GP, 238
Measuring performance, 251, 297,
    304
Measuring performance
    (marketing), 98
Measuring success, 37
Mechanistic (organizational
    culture), 173, 264, 329
Mechanistic systems, 289
Media, 100, 101
Menu (drinks list), 29, 136
Menu, function, 207
Menu, focal point, 208
Menu, purpose, 210, 213
Menu analysis, 233
Menu engineering, 234
Menu fatigue, 200
Menu objectives, 31
Menu planning, 208, 209, 214
Menu presentation, 212
Merchandising, 28, 101, 122
Merchandising aims, 122
Merchandising legislation, 148
Merchandising objectives, 122
Message (marketing), 100

Metcalfe, Julian, 56
Miller's Kitchen, 116
Mission statement, 42, 153, 165,
    169, 176, 181
Mix, market, 44
Mix, sales, 43
Mongolian Barbecue, 156
Motivation, 327, 340
Multi-skilling, 33, 49, 261, 333,
    326, 347, 348, 349, 358
Mystery guests, 186

Negative reinforcement, 130
Net profit, 3, 47
NP percentage, 241, 242
NVQ (National Vocational
    Qualifications), 324, 350

Objectives, merchandising,
    122
Observation, (customers), 146
Occupancy, 44
One stop customers, 134
Operational cycle, 29, 335
Operational (catering) policy, 41,
    43, 153
Operational style, 45
Opportunity cost, 167, 168
Organic (organizational culture),
    173, 264, 329
Organic systems, 289
Organization of training, 351
Organizational charts, 56
Organizational culture, 264, 328,
    346, 353
Organizational structure
    (mechanistic/organic), 289
Organoleptics, 127
Outcome (market research), 96

Package (CPC), 194
Package development, 207
Participation, customer, 156
Partie system, 270
Pavlov, Ivan, 128
Pavlovian conditioning, 128
Payton, Bob, 56
Performance, guaranteed standards
    of, 164

Performance, variance (budget/potential/actual), 300
Performance improvement, x, 147
Performance measurement, 304
Performance measurement (staff), 327
Personnel policy, 40, 43, 44
Personnel procedures, 44
Personnel specification, 45, 166, 225, 327, 335, 336
Phantom customers, 186
Phantom visitors, 186
Philosophy, customer care, 68–70
Physical characteristics, 179
Physical quality, 155
Place (the 4Ps), 84
Planning (staff), 335
Plans, marketing, 97
PLU (Price Look Up) systems, 306
PO box reference, 92
Point of sale activity, 132
Point of sale promotion, 124, 145
Poka-Yoke, 155
Polarizing Markets, 15
Policy, 42
Policy, catering, 45
Policy, company, 164
Policy, finance/marketing/personnel, 40, 43
Policy, operational, 40
Policy development, 41, 53, 54, 55
Policy manuals (handbooks), 42
Popularity index, 199, 200
Portions, single, 140
Positioning (brand), 115
Positive reinforcement, 130, 337
Post code, 92
Post purchase evaluation, 113
Postal data, 92
Potential (performance variance), 300
Predicting demand, 104
Preference, 10–14, 61, 128, 113
Preferred items, 138, 142
Press, advertising, 103
Prêt à Manger, 56
Prevention of errors, 172
Price (the 4Ps), 84
Price elasticity, 242

Price factors, 229
Price increase (opportunities), 230
Pricing, 228, 229
Primacy, 216
Primary (supply channel), 274
Primary, market research, 91
Principles of cookery, 311
Procedure, 42
Procedure (service quality), 176
Procedure, sales development, 145
Procedures, standardization, 224
Product (the 4Ps), 84
Product benefits, 100
Product development, 28, 56, 98
Product development check-list, 252
Product development legislation, 253
Product differentiation, 154, 159, 196
Product display, 138
Product grouping, 139
Product knowledge, 131, 194, 223
Product life cycle, 83, 199, 222, 226
Product orientation (market), 77
Product promotion, 124
Product quality, 63
Product specifications, 275, 276
Product/Service differentiation, 115
Production methods, 220
Production objectives, 282
Production planning, 283
Production systems, 46, 282
Productivity, increasing, 356
Productivity and profit (staffing), 322
Profile (customer characteristics), 44, 89, 116
Profit, gross/net, 3
Profit, maximizing potential (merchandising), 142
Profit (and volume), 231
Profit and cost centres, 58
Profit and productivity (staffing), 322
Profit centred orientation, 4
Profit improvement strategy, 245
Profit maximization, 246

Profit multiplier, 242, 243
Profit sensitivity, 242
Programme, customer care, 67
Promotion, market, 28
Promotion, temporal/product/display, 124
Promotion (the 4PS), 84
Promotional activity, 125
Promotional materials, 132
PSS (Planning, Selection and Supervision) of staff, 334
Psychological aspects of liking, 127
Psychology of choice, 22
Public relations, 101, 102
Purchase behaviour, 89
Purchase contract, 275
Purchase decision, 111, 126, 135
Purchase evaluation, 113
Purchase specifications, 219
Purchasing, the aims of, 273
Purchasing systems, 272–81

Qualities of a good supervisor, 328
Quality, cost/benefit, 162
Quality (control/assurance), 172, 179
Quality (hard/soft), 155
Quality (physical/convivial), 155
Quality, product/service, 63
Quality assurance, 28, 198
Quality attributes, 167
Quality audit, 178, 186
Quality chains, 166
Quality characteristics, 153
Quality circles, 87, 166, 167, 169, 178
Quality culture, 169
Quality management aims, 150
Quality management objectives, 151
Quality management/assurance/control, 154
Quality manuals, 189
Quality objectives, 188
Quality philosophy, 190
Quality programmes, 188
Quality pyramid, 179
Quality systems, 187

Quality teams, 189
Questionnaires (guest), 98
Questions (research/control), 98

Radio (advertising), 103
Random errors, 175
Range, size, 140
Ratios, 47
Ratners, 160
Real value, 143
Recency, 216
Recipe development, 222, 223
Recruitment, 44
Regimentation, 270
Reinforcement (positive/negative), 130
Reliability, 160
Reputation, 160
Research, 28, 88
Research (primary/secondary), 91
Research data, 119
Research questions, 98
Retention strategy, 182
Revlon, Charles, 78
Risk management, 269, 273
Ritz, Cesar, 270
Role, Food and Beverage Manager, 53
Role Set, 26
Roles and scripts, 78
Rostering, 316
RRT (Rate of restaurant turnaround), 44
RWE (Realistic work environment), 336

Sainsbury's, 212
Sales department, 86
Sales development, 125
Sales development procedure, 145
Sales history, 199, 216, 222
Sales mix, 43, 105, 226, 233, 235
Sales popularity, 199
Sales records, 87
Sales targets, 44
Sales team, 85
Sales technique, 131
Sales volume, 237
Satisfaction, customer, 28, 65, 153

Satisfaction, barriers to, 62
Savoy Hotel, 195
Scheduling,
Scientific measurement, 179
Scripts, 78, 181
Secondary research, 91
Secondary sales, 240
Secondary (supply channels), 274
Sectors of the hospitality industry, ix, 2
Segmentation (market), 116, 118
Selection (staff), 335
Selling, 73, 76, 101
Selling (in house/cross), 124
Selling effort, 144
Sensory domination, 133
Sensory perception, 127
Service assurance, 176
Service attributes, 202
Service benefits, 100
Service chains, 83
Service contact, 123
Service development, 28, 98
Service encounter, 125, 133
Service marketing (problems), 79
Service planning, 288, 289
Service quality, 63
Service quality, procedure, 176
Service quality, conviviality, 176
Service quality measurement, 186
Service systems, 46, 284
Sight sales, 141
Signature dish, 115, 250
Signposts, 104
Single portions, 140
Sizes, range of, 140
Skills and training, 34, 79, 318, 353
Socio-economic grouping, 89, 117
Soft, elements of quality, 155, 172
SOP, Standard Operating Procedures (manuals), 42
Sources, market information, 91
Sources of supply, 274
Sous-vide, 32, 158, 161
Specification, 174, 198, 219, 225
Specification, personnel, 166
Specifications (product/raw material), 166, 275
Spending power, 20, 74, 76, 167

Sporadic errors, 175
Staff appraisal, 343
Staff development, 44, 327
Staff incentives, 340
Staff skills, 317
Staff training manuals, 225
Staffing, cost effective provision, 314
Staffing, documentation/communication, 316
Staffing, the manager's role, 323
Staffing levels, 333
Staffing strategy, 315, 334
Standard(s), 2, 34, 151, 165, 192, 198
Standard market classification, 95
Standardization, x, 151, 156, 192, 198, 217, 222, 225
Standardization procedures, 224
Standardized method, 198, 225
Standardized recipes, 166, 198, 225
Standardized yield, 225
Statement of intent, 41
Strategy, financial, 6
Strategy, cost/profit, 4
Statistics, 109, 110
Stock control, 300
Stocktaking, purpose of, 301
Strategy, xii–xv
Strategy, market, 120
Strategy, retention, 182
Structure, organizational (mechanistic/organic), 289
Style, operational, 45
Supervision (staff), 337
Supervisor, qualities of, 328
Supervisor's role (communication), 323
Supervisor's role (training), 325
Supply, sources of, 5, 274
Supply and demand, 267
Supply channels, 274
Supply management, 111
SWOT (Strengths, Weaknesses, Opportunities and Threats), 53, 88, 120
System factors, 267
Systematic errors, 175
Systemize, 115

Systems, food and beverage, 157, 259

Systems, main elements, 266

Systems (operational cycle), 29, 30

Systems management, 225, 256, 260

Systems management tools, 303

Systems of communication, 265

Systems of control, 34, 296

Systems of delivery, 75, 270

Systems of delivery (alternative), 294

Systems of production and service, 46, 270

Tactics, xii–xv

Target groups, 74

Targets and objectives, 34

Task analysis, 183, 326, 338

Task cards, 335, 336

Team, attributes, 330

Technical knowledge, 74

Technology, the influence of, 279

Television (advertising), 103

Temporal promotion, 124

Tendering, competitive, 3

TGI-Friday, 142, 195

Theory X and theory Y, McGregor (staffing), 349

Thompson's Directory, 104

Toby Restaurants, 116

Tour Guides, 104

TQM (Total Quality Management), 154, 179, 187

Trade test, 336

Trading opportunities, 15

Training, 45, 350

Training (skills), 318

Training, determining requirements, 326

Training, induction, 45, 336

Training, organization of, 351

Training, the supervisor's role, 325

Trend, 77

Troubleshooting the net profit, 307

Two for one promotions, 241

USPs (Unique Selling Points), 57, 88, 100, 197, 250, 332, 353

Value, 136, 153, 154, 212

Value, added, 100

Value, added (real/implied), 143, 212

Value added products, 276

Variable cost, 4, 232

Variance, 224

Variance analysis, 299

Variance favourable/unfavourable, 299

Variance measurement, 300

Variance price/usage, 299

Variance, management, 298

Variance, performance (budget/potential/actual), 300

Vending, 294

Visual overload, 139

Volume (and profit), 231

Welfare sector, ix, 2

What If analysis, 307

Word of mouth, 81, 123

Work planning, 348

Work study, 337, 339, 356

Workplace design, 356

Yellow Pages, 104

Yield management, 282

Zero defects, 155